AMERICAN
GANGSTER

MARC JACOBSON is the author of *12,000 Miles in the Nick of Time: A Semi-Dysfunctional Family Circumnavigates the Globe*, *Teenage Hipster in the Modern World*, and the novels *Gojiro* and *Everyone and No One*. He has been a contributing editor to *Rolling Stone*, *Esquire*, *Village Voice* and *New York Magazine*.

Also by Mark Jacobson

Novels

Gojiro

Everyone and No One

Non-fiction

Teenage Hipster in the Modern World: From the Birth of Punk
to the Land of Bush, Thirty Years of Apocalyptic Journalism

12,000 Miles in the Nick of Time:
A Semi-Dysfunctional Family Circumnavigates the Globe

The KGB Bar Non-fiction Reader (edited)

American Monsters (edited, with Jack Newfield)

AMERICAN GANGSTER

and Other Tales of New York

MARK JACOBSON
Foreword by Richard Price

Atlantic Books
London

First published in the United States of America in 2007 by Grove/Atlantic Inc.

First published in paperback in Great Britain in 2007 by Atlantic Books,
an imprint of Grove/Atlantic Ltd.

Copyright © Mark Jacobson 2007

Foreword copyright © Richard Price 2007

The moral right of Mark Jacobson to be identified as the author of this work
has been asserted in accordance with the Copyright, Designs and Patents Acts of 1988.

All rights reserved. No part of this publication may be reproduced, stored in a
retrieval system, or transmitted in any form or by any means, electronic,
mechanical, photocopying, recording, or otherwise, without the prior permission
of both the copyright owner and the above publisher of this book.

Every effort has been made to trace or contact all copyright-holders.
The Publishers will be pleased to make good any omissions or rectify
any mistakes brought to their attention at the earliest opportunity.

2 3 4 5 6 7 8 9

A CIP catalogue record for this book is available from the British Library.

ISBN: 978 1 84354 730 3

Printed in Great Britain by
Clays Ltd, St Ives plc

Atlantic Books
An imprint of Grove Atlantic Ltd
Ormond House
26–27 Boswell Street
London WC1N 3JZ

Contents

Foreword

I've always felt that the only subjects worth writing about were those that intimidated me, and the only writers worth emulating were those who left me feeling the same way. I've felt intimidated by Mark Jacobson since 1977 when I first read "Ghost Shadows on Chinatown Streets," his portrait of gang leader Nicky Lui, in the *Village Voice*. I remember being overwhelmed by both Jacobson's reporting skill and his intrepidness, empathizing with his attraction to the subject; could see myself attempting something like that if I had both the writing chops and the nerve. It was one of the most humbling and enticing reading experiences of my life, and in many ways set me on the path to at least three novels.

Jacobson belongs to that great bloodline of New York street writers from Stephen Crane to Hutchins Hapgood to Joseph Mitchell, John McNulty, and A. J. Liebling, through Jimmy Breslin and Pete Hamill, and now to himself and very few others (his friend and peer Michael Daly comes to mind). Jacobson is drawn to these streets and to those who rose from them: the outlaws, the visionaries, the hustlers, and the oddballs. His voice is often sardonic, bemused, and a little in awe of the man before him. Like a judo master, he knows how to step off and let the force of these personalities hoist their own banners or dig their own graves. But even in the case of the most heinous of men, Jacobson's ability to unearth some saving grace, some charm, or simply a shred of sympathetic humanity in the bastard is unfailing.

From heroin kingpin Frank Lucas to the Dalai Lama, Jacobson's fact-gathering is impeccable, his presentation of the Big Picture plain as day, the conversations (you can't really call them "interviews") often hilarious. Most important, though, his love for this world, these people, is apparent in every nuance, every finely observed detail. His is the song of the workingman, the immigrant, the street cat, the cryptician with more crazy-eights than aces up his sleeve, and Jacobson knows that the bottom line for this kind of profiling is self-recognition; each character, each sharply etched detail in some way bringing home not only the subject, but the reader and author, too.

—Richard Price

Never Bored: The American Gangster, the Big City, and Me

I was born in New York City in the baby boom year of 1948 and lived here most of my life. I started my journalism career back in the middle 1970s, writing more often than not about New York. There have been ups and downs over the past thirty years, but I can't say I have ever been bored. After all, the Naked City is supposed to have eight million stories and, as a magazine writer, I only need about ten good ones a year. So I can afford to be picky. Whether I've been picky enough—or managed to tell those stories well enough—you can decide for yourself by thumbing through this book. That said, some stories are just winners, fresh-out-of-the-blocks winners. The saga of Frank Lucas, Harlem drug dealer, reputed killer, and general all-around enemy of the people, was one of those stories.

An odd thing about the genesis of my involvement with Lucas is that I'd always been under the impression he was something of an urban myth. That was my opinion when Lucas's name came up in a conversation I was having half a dozen years ago with my good friend, the late Jack Newfield. Newfield said he'd seen Nick Pileggi, the classic pre-Internet New York City magazine writer who had been smart enough to get out at the right time, making untold fortunes writing movies like *Goodfellas*. Nick had mentioned to Jack that Lucas was alive and living in New Jersey.

"You mean, Frank Lucas, the guy with the body bags?" I asked Newfield, who said, yeah, one and the same. This was a surprise. Anyone who had their ear to the ground during the fiscal crisis years of the 1970s, those Fear City times when New York appeared to be falling apart at the seams, remembered the ghoulish story of thousands of pounds of uncut heroin being smuggled from Southeast Asia in the body bags of American soldiers killed in the Vietnam War. The doomsday metaphor—death arriving wrapped inside of death—was hard to beat, but this couldn't really be true, could it?

This was one of the first things I asked Lucas when, after much hunting, I located him in downtown Newark. "Did you really smuggle dope in the body bags?" I asked Frank, then in his late sixties, living in a beat-up project apartment and driving an even more beat-up 1979 Caddy with a bad transmission.

"Fuck no," responded Lucas, taking great offense. He never put any heroin into the body bag of a GI. Nor did he ever stuff kilos of dope into the body cavities of the dead soldiers, as some law enforcement officials had contended. These were disgusting, slanderous stories, Lucas protested.

"We smuggled the dope in the soldiers' coffins," Lucas roared, setting the record straight. "*Coffins*, not bags!"

This was a large distinction, Frank contended. He and his fellow "Country Boys" (he only hired family members or residents of his backwoods North Carolina hometown) would never be so sloppy as to toss good dope into a dead guy's body bag. They took the trouble to contact highly skilled carpenters to construct false bottoms for soldiers' coffins. It was inside these secret compartments that Lucas shipped the heroin that would addict who knows how many poor suckers. "Who the hell is gonna look in a soldier's coffin," Lucas chortled rhetorically, maintaining that his insistence on careful workmanship showed proper deference to those who had given their life for their country.

"I would never dishonor an American soldier," Frank said, swearing on his beloved mother's head as to his "100 percent true red, white, and blue" patriotism.

Frank and I spent a lot of time together back in the late winter and spring of 2001 as he told me the story of his life. It took a lot to make him the biggest single Harlem heroin dealer in the 1970s, and Lucas was determined that I know it all, from the first time he robbed a drunk by hitting him over the head with a tobacco rake outside a black-town Carolina whorehouse, to his journey north where he would become the right-hand man of Bumpy Johnson, Harlem's most famous gangster, to the heroin kingpin days, when he claimed to clear up to a million dollars a day.

Declaring he had "nothing but my word," Frank said every little bit of what he said was true. This I doubted, even if some of his most outrageous statements seemed to bear out. Most of the tale, however, was hard to pin down. When it comes to black crime, organized or not, there are very few traditional sources. I mean, forty years after the alleged fact, how do you check whether Frank really killed the giant Tango, "a big silverback gorilla of a Negro," on 116th Street? Some remembered Lucas being with Bumpy the day the gangster keeled over in Wells' Restaurant. Some didn't. The fact that Frank can't read (he always pretended to have forgotten his glasses when we went out to his favorite, TGI Friday's) didn't matter. We were in the realm of oral history narrated by some of the twentieth century's most flamboyant bullshitters and Frank Lucas, with "a PhD in street," can talk as well as anyone.

Even though I often employed the phrases "Frank claims" and "according to Lucas" when writing the piece, the tale's potential sketchiness did little to undercut what I always took to be its cockeyed verisimilitude. The enduring importance of Lucas's story can be found in the indisputable fact that very few people on earth could reasonably invent such a compelling lie about this kind of material. If nothing else, Lucas is a knowing witness to a time and place inaccessible to almost everyone else, and that goes double for white people. The verve with which he recounts his no doubt self-aggrandizing story is an urban historian's boon, a particular kind of American epic. I considered myself lucky to write it down.

Now, Frank's life, or at least some highly reconfigured version of it, will be on display in the big-budget Hollywood picture *American Gangster*, with Denzel Washington, no less, playing the Frank part. By the time they get done advertising the film, which also features Russell Crowe and was directed by Ridley Scott, something like $200 million will have been spent to bring Frank's story to the silver screen, which might even be as much money as Lucas made pushing drugs all those years. By the time you read this Frank Lucas will be perhaps the best-known drug dealer ever.

There is a bit of irony in this, since back in The Day, Lucas's claim to fame was that he had no fame. While rivals like Nicky Barnes were allowing themselves to be photographed on the cover of the *New York Times Magazine* section and claiming to be "Mr. Untouchable," Frank kept studiously below the radar. He trusted no one, and almost always appeared on 116th Street, his primary stomping ground, in disguise. With the release of the film, however, Frank, now in his seventies and confined to a wheel-chair, will have his picture taken by hundreds of Hollywood photographers. Knowing him, he'll go with the flow, laughing his blood-curdling laugh and gloating about how great it is "to be on top again."

To have shared this Hollywood business with Frank has been a whole other trip. After Imagine Pictures optioned the story and Frank's "life rights," we were flown out to Los Angeles. How marvelous it was to sit with Frank and Richie Roberts, the man who prosecuted Lucas in the Essex County courts (Russell Crowe plays him in *American Gangster*) in a big-time meeting with the brass from Imagine and Universal Pictures. Seated around a long conference table, Lucas leaned over to me and asked, "Who's the guy in the room with the juice?" I told him it was "the one with wacked-off hair and the skinny tie," that is, überproducer Brian Grazer.

"That guy? No way," scoffed Frank. "What about him?" Lucas asked, pointing to a dark-haired thirty-year-old wearing an expensive Rolex. "He's just a studio flunky who is going to be fired next week," I informed Lucas, again telling him Grazer was the guy.

An hour later, when the meeting was over, Lucas, nothing if not a quick study when it comes to power relationships, came over to me and said, "You know something, Mark? I thought I was in a rough business, but these people are off-the-hook sharks."

Richie Roberts, now an attorney handling criminal cases in North Jersey's Soprano belt (he was once the star running back at Newark's Weequachic High School, where he passed, and ignored, Philip Roth in the hallways) has known the old drug dealer for more than thirty years.

The producers of *American Gangster* have hung much of their film on the relationship between the two men.

"Frank, Frank and me . . . that is a long story," says Roberts, who has decidedly mixed feelings about his relationship with Lucas. "I know who he is, the horrible things he'd done. Don't forget, I put him in jail. And if there's anyone who deserved to got to jail it was Frank Lucas. I was proud to get him. I'm still proud of it. . . . As for us being such good friends, I don't know if I'd call it that. He has a young kid, Ray. When he was little I paid for his school tuition. I really love that kid. As for Frank, let's say he's a charming con man. But even knowing everything I know, God help me, sometimes I just can't help liking the guy."

As you will see from reading the piece, Lucas has always relied on his ability to make people like him. "People like me, they like the fuck out of me," he says, cackling. I had to agree. There I was, sitting and listening to him talk about all the people he had murdered, how his brother, Shorty, used to delight in holding enemies by their ankles over the railing of the George Washington Bridge. He said they better talk or he'd drop them. They'd talk and Shorty would drop them anyway. Of course, Lucas was a miserable human being. On the other hand, he was giving me a heck of a story. And, to be honest, I liked the guy. I liked the fuck out of him.

The movie business cut into this. From the get-go, I told my agent that if a deal was to be made, my interests had to be separate from Frank's. "I don't want to be in business with him," I said. Yet, somehow, this never got done. Now the money was on the table, waiting to be split up by me and my new partner, Frank Lucas.

When Frank called me one morning and said to come on over so "we can talk this thing out like men," my wife, who upon hearing the tapes of our interviews had asked "Who you doing a story on, Satan?" told me not to go. She didn't think I should talk about money with Frank. That was what lawyers were for, she said. I told her not to worry. Frank and I were friends. Buddies. I'd been over to see him in Newark a dozen times. Why should this be different?

I began to notice something might be amiss when I entered the restaurant and was told Frank was waiting for me in the back room. Lucas was sitting at a table off to the side. Against the wall were a few guys, big guys. I'd seen them before, on and off. One, Lucas's nephew Al, about six-foot-seven, 240 pounds, had played football in the arena league. Al and I were friendly. I'd given him rides to the City a couple times. We'd smoked weed together, had some laughs. Now, dressed in black leather, Al stood impassively behind Frank. When I said hello, instead of his usual ghetto bear hug, there was only a curt nod.

"What's this about, Frank?" I asked.

"It's about I got to have all the money," Frank said, smiling.

"All of it?" I'd already decided to give Frank a larger share. It was his life they were buying after all. But all?

"You can't have it all," I said. "That wouldn't be fair."

"Don't care if it's fair. I got to have it all," Frank repeated, leaning forward. Once, when Lucas and I were riding around in Newark, he told me to drive over near a nasty-looking bunch of guys hanging out on a street corner. "Open the window and shout, hey you," Lucas demanded. When I protested, he screamed, "Just do it." I did. The guys froze. "Tell them to come over," said Lucas, now crouching under the dashboard. When I didn't he yelled, "Get your black asses over here." The bad guys complied, nervously. When they got close Lucas sprang out and screamed, "Boo!"

"Uncle Frank!" the guys screamed, cracking up. Being as I was white, there was no reason for me to be in that neighborhood unless I was a cop. Scaring the guys was Frank's idea of a joke.

This money demand could be one more laugh, but I didn't think so. This was another kind of Frank Lucas, not the semi-lovable historical figure for whom I'd bought all those pitchers of Sam Adams. It occurred to me that long after my story about him was written and published, I'd missed a good portion of what I'd set out to find. It wasn't until that very moment that I saw the real Frank Lucas, or at least the part of him that enabled all those nefarious deeds I'd been so enthralled to hear about. Eyes set, mouth motionless, for the first time he looked like the stone killer I knew him to be.

Frank had a piece of paper the agent had sent over. We were supposed to fill in what percentage of the option money each of us would get. Frank suggested I write "zero" next to my name.

At this point, I suppose, I could have told Frank Lucas that if it wasn't for me, he wouldn't be on the road to having Denzel Washington be him on the silver screen. If it wasn't for me, he'd still be up there in his rat hole project apartment, where the only place to sit was on those five-foot-high red vinyl bar stools he'd obviously got off a truck somewhere. But I didn't.

"Look, Frank," I said. "I'm gonna get up and go back to my car. Then I'm going to drive back to the City. We can work this out later, okay, on the telephone."

So maybe Frank had lost a step or two, or maybe he wasn't as hard as he made himself out to be, because no one jumped me. I didn't take a shiv in the back. Probably the wily old operator realized that wouldn't have served any purpose, since the paper required both of our signatures. If I was dead, I wouldn't be able to sign. Then Frank would get nothing.

This became the strategy: I wouldn't sign. I figured I could live without the money longer than Frank could. One day I told him he could have one more percent than me, and he agreed. All of a sudden, we were cool again, just like before. I heard Frank bought himself a brand-new SUV with some of his take and smashed it up the very next week. That was too bad, I thought. Because when it comes down to it, I like Frank. I like the fuck out of him.

All in all, *American Gangster* has been a winning experience for me. Better than the usual dealings I've had with Hollywood. The producers bought my story. I got paid. I didn't have to do anything but cash the check. This is good. Most times when Hollywood guys buy the rights to these journalism stories—as they often do—things don't go so smoothly. Years ago some guys took an option on a piece I wrote about the New York City high school basketball championship, Canarsie High School vs. Lafayette, both of them from Brooklyn, and hard-nose. The story, written in 1976, took a while to "set up." In 1992, the buyers said it finally looked like a go, except now the story had been changed some. Now it was about two girls softball teams in Compton, California. They hoped I didn't mind. Why should I mind? As a big NWA fan, Compton softball sounded great to me. Needless to say, nothing ever happened.

This said, the specter of Frank Lucas, icon of a New York City that no longer exists, hangs over this entire collection of stories. It is like Frank says about how he feels going into a giant Home Depot. In his gangster days whenever he walked into any bank or store—anyplace where they had money—he'd reflexively figure what he'd do if he wanted to rob the place. But at Home Depot, he was stumped. The place was so big, so decentralized, confusing.

"You don't know where to stick the knife in," Frank allowed dejectedly, as if the changing times had just passed him by.

Reading over many of the pieces in this book, I wonder if that is true for me as well. After all, much of the stuff I write about here either no longer exists, or has changed irrevocably. Little of this change is to my liking. Not that it hurts the work since in New York, the journalist accepts that what he writes about today may not be there tomorrow. All you can do is try to capture what's put in front of you, on the day you're looking at it. Once the parade passes by, the work becomes part of urban history. Besides, there's plenty new around that isn't owned by some tinhorn condomeister. Those supposed eight million stories have become twelve million, maybe even fourteen if you count all those Mexican soccer fans out in Queens. That should be enough to keep anyone busy.

No introduction is complete without the usual-suspect acknowledgments. For the most part the pieces in this book are different from the ones that appeared in the first collection of my journalism, *The Teenage Hipster in the Modern World*, but most of the thank-yous remain the same. Special shout-outs to Morgan Entrekin, the publisher of this book, John Homans, editor of many of these pieces, Caroline Miller, and Adam Moss, boss of *New York* magazine, who continues to enable my health plan. Ditto the wife and kids. But tell me, how mauldin is it to thank the City itself: always my inspiration, mentor, and antagonist.

Mark Jacobson, 2007

UPTOWN

1

The American Gangster, a.k.a. The Haint of Harlem, the Frank Lucas Story

Face-to-face with the charming killer. If Frank wasn't born black and poor, he could have been a really rich, corrupt politician. Instead, he became a really rich drug dealer. But he did call his mom every day. An epic tale of the vagaries of race, class, and money in the U.S. of A, this is the basis for the Ridley Scott film, American Gangster, *with Denzel Washington in the Frank role. As Frank says, "I always knew my life was a movie," even if he saw himself as more of the Morgan Freeman type. "Denzel, however, will do." From* New York *magazine, 2000.*

During the 1970s, when for a graffiti-splashed, early disco instant of urban time he was, according to then-U.S. District Attorney Rudolph Giuliani, "the biggest drug dealer" in Harlem, Frank Lucas would sit at the corner of 116th Street and Eighth Avenue in a beat-up Chevy he called Nellybelle. Then residing in a swank apartment in Riverdale down the hall from Yvonne De Carlo and running his heroin business out of a suite at the Regency Hotel on Park Avenue, Lucas owned several cars. He had a Rolls, a Mercedes, a Stingray, and a 427 four-on-the-floor muscle job he'd once topped out at 160 miles per hour near Exit 16E of the Jersey Turnpike, scaring himself so silly that he gave the car to his brother's wife just to get it out of his sight.

But for "spying," Nellybelle worked best.

"Who'd ever think I'd be in a shit three-hundred-dollar car like that?" asks Lucas, who claims that, on a good day, he would clear up to a million dollars selling dope on 116th Street. "I'd sit there, cap pulled down, with a fake beard, dark glasses, maybe some army fatigues and broken-down boots, longhair wig . . . I used to be right up beside the people dealing my stuff, watching the whole show, and no one knew who I was. . . ."

It was a matter of control, and trust. As the leader of the "Country Boys" dope ring, Frank, older brother to Ezell, Vernon Lee, John Paul, Larry, and Lee Lucas, was known for restricting his operation to blood relatives and others from the rural North Carolina backwoods area where he grew up. This was because, Lucas says in his downhome creak of a voice, "A country boy, he ain't hip . . . he's not used to big cars, fancy ladies, and diamond rings, so he'll be loyal to you. A country boy, you can give him a million dollars, five million, and tell him to hide it in his old shack. His wife and kids might be hungry, starving, and he'll never touch your money until he checks with you. City boy ain't like that. A city boy will take your last dime and look you straight in the face and swear he ain't got it. . . . A city boy'll steal from you in a New York minute and you've got to be able to deal with it in a New York second. . . . You don't want a city boy, the sonofabitch is just no good."

But trust has its limits, even among country boys, Frank says. "A hundred sixteenth between Seventh and Eighth Avenue was mine. It belonged to me. . . . I bought it. I ran it. I owned it. And when something is yours, you've got to be Johnny on the Spot, ready to take it to the top. So I'd sit in front of the Roman Garden Restaurant, or around the corner by the Royal Flush Bar, just watching."

There wouldn't be much to see until four in the afternoon, which was when Frank's brand of heroin, Blue Magic, hit the street. During the early seventies there were many "brands" of dope in Harlem. Tru Blu, Mean Machine, Could Be Fatal, Dick Down, Boody, Cooley High, Capone, Ding Dong, Fuck Me, Fuck You, Nice, Nice to Be Nice, Oh—Can't Get Enough of that Funky Stuff, Tragic Magic, Gerber, The Judge, 32, 32-20, O.D., Correct, Official Correct, Past Due, Payback, Revenge, Green Tape, Red Tape, Rush, Swear To God, PraisePraisePraise, KillKillKill, Killer 1, Killer 2, KKK, Good Pussy, Taster's Choice, Harlem Hijack, Joint, Insured for Life, and Insured for Death are only a few of the brand names rubber-stamped onto the cellophane bags.

But none sold like Blue Magic.

"That's because with Blue Magic you could get ten percent purity," Frank Lucas asserts. "With any other if you got five percent you were doing good. Mostly it was three. We put it out there at four in the afternoon, when the cops changed shifts. That gave you a couple of hours to work, before those lazy bastards got down there. My buyers, though, you could set your watch by them. Those junkies crawling out. By four o'clock we had enough niggers in the street to make a Tarzan movie. They had to reroute the bus coming down Eighth Avenue to 116th, it couldn't get through. Call the Transit Department to see if it's not so. On a usual day we'd put out maybe twenty-five thousand quarters (quarter "spoons," fifty dollars' worth, enough to get high for the rest of the day). By nine o'clock I ain't got a fucking gram. Everything is gone. Sold . . . and I got myself a million dollars."

"I'd just sit there in Nellybelle and watch the money roll in," says Frank Lucas of those not-so-distant but near-forgotten days, when Abe Beame would lay his pint-sized head upon the pillow at Gracie Mansion and the cop cars were still green and black. "And no one even knew it was me. I was a shadow. A ghost . . . what we call downhome a haint . . . That was me, the *Haint of Harlem*."

Twenty-five years after the end of his uptown rule, Frank Lucas, now sixty-nine, has returned to Harlem for a whirlwind retrospective of his life and times. Sitting in a blue Toyota at the corner of 116th Street and what is now called Adam Clayton Powell Boulevard ("What was wrong with just plain Eighth Avenue?" Lucas grouses), Frank, once by his own description "six-feet two-inches tall, a handsome fashion plate, rough and ready, slick and something to see" but now teetering around "like a fucking one-legged tripod" due to a cartilage-less, arthritic knee, is no more noticeable than he was all those years ago, when he peered through Nellybelle's window.

Indeed, just from looking, few passersby might guess that Frank, according to his own exceedingly ad hoc records, once had "at least fifty-six million dollars," most of it kept in Cayman Island banks. Added to this is "maybe a thousand keys of dope" with an easily realized retail profit of no less than three hundred thousand dollars per kilo. His real estate holdings included "two twenty-plus-story buildings in Detroit, garden apartments in Los Angeles and Miami, another apartment house in Chicago, and a mess of Puerto Rico." This is not to mention "Frank Lucas's Paradise Valley," eight hundred acres back in North Carolina on which ranged three hundred head of Black Angus cows, "the blue ribbon kind," including several "big balled" breeding bulls worth twenty-five thousand dollars each.

Nor would most imagine that the old man in the fake Timberland jacket once held at least twenty forged passports and was a prime mover in what Federal Judge Sterling Johnson, who in the 1970s served as New York's special narcotics prosecutor, calls "one of the most outrageous international dope smugglers ever . . . an innovative guy who broke new ground by getting his own connection outside the U.S. and then selling the stuff himself in the street . . . a real womb to tomb operation."

Johnson's funerary image fits well, especially in light of Lucas's most audacious, culturally pungent claim to fame, the so-called cadaver connection. Woodstockers may remember being urged by Country Joe and the Fish to sing along on the "Fixin' to Die Rag," about being the first one on your block to have your boy come home in a box. But even the most apocalyptic-minded sixties freak couldn't have guessed that the box also contained half a dozen keys of 98 percent pure heroin. Of all the dreadful iconography of Vietnam—the napalmed girl running down the road, Lieutenant Calley at My Lai, the helicopter on the embassy roof, and more—the memory of dope in the body bag, death begetting death, most hideously conveys Nam's still-spreading pestilence. The metaphor is almost too rich. In fact, to someone who got his 1-A in the mail the same day the NVA raised the Red Star over Hue, the story has always seemed a tad apocryphal.

But it is not. "We did it all right . . . ha, ha, ha . . ." Frank chortles in his mocking, dying crapshooter's scrape of a voice, recalling how he and fellow Country Boy Ike Atkinson arranged for the shipment. "Who the hell is gonna look in a dead soldier's coffin? Ha, ha, ha."

"I had so much fucking money, you have no idea," Lucas says now, his heavy-lidded light brown eyes turned to the sky in mock expectation that his vanished wealth will rain back down from the heavens. "The forfeits took it all," Frank says mournfully, referring to the forfeiture laws designed by the government under sundry RICO and "continuing criminal enterprise" acts to seize allegedly ill-gotten gains amassed by gangsters like Frank Lucas.

Some think Lucas still has a couple of million stashed somewhere, perhaps buried in the red dirt down in North Carolina. Hearing this only makes the old dealer grimace. "If they find it, I sure hope they send me some, a mil or two. Shit, I'd take a hundred dollars, 'cause right now I'm on my ass," Frank says, driving downtown on Lenox Avenue behind the wheel of my decidedly un-Superfly powder blue Toyota station wagon, the one with Milky Way wrappers and basketball trading cards on the floor. We were going to go in Frank's car, a decade-old Sedan de Ville, but it was unavailable, the transmission having blown out a few days earlier. "Motherfucker won't pull, gonna cost twelve hundred bucks, that a bitch or what?" Lucas had moaned into his cell phone, calling from the rainy roadside where a tow truck was in the process of jacking up his bestilled Caddy.

An informative if wary guide, Lucas, who said he hadn't been to Harlem in "five, six years," found the place totally changed. Aside from the hulking, cavernous 1365th Infantry Armory, where Lucas and his Country Boys used to unload furs and foodstuffs from the trucks they'd hijack out on Route 9, nothing looked the same. Still, almost nearly every block, every corner, summoned a memory. Over on Eighth Avenue and 127th Street, up above the rim and tire place, used to be Spanish Raymond Marquez's number bank, the biggest in town. On one Lenox Avenue corner is where "Preacher got killed," on the next is where Black Joe bought it. Some deserved killing, some maybe not, but they were all dead just the same.

In front of a ramshackle blue frame house on West 123rd Street, right next to where the two-eight precinct used to be, Lucas stops and gets nostalgic. "I had my best cutters in there," he says, describing how his "table workers," ten to twelve women wearing surgical masks, would "whack up" the dope, cutting it with "60 percent mannite." The ruby-haired Red Top was in charge. "I'd bring in three, four keys, open it up on the table, let Red go do her thing. She'd mix up that dope like a rabbit in a hat, never drop a speck, get it out on the street in time. . . . Red . . . I wonder if she's still living. . . ."

At 135th Street and Seventh Avenue, Lucas stops again. Small's Paradise used to be there. Back in the Day, there were plenty of places, Mr. B's, Willie Abraham's Gold Lounge, the Shalimar if you were hungry, the Lenox Lounge, a nice place to take your girl. But Small's, then run by Frank's friend, Pete McDougal, was the coolest. "Everyone came by Small's . . . the jazz guys, politicians. Ray Robinson. Wilt Chamberlain when he bought a piece of the place and called it Big Wilt's Small's Paradise . . . At Small's, Frank often met up with his great friend, the heavyweight champ Joe Louis, who would later appear nearly every day at Lucas's various trials, expressing outrage that the State was harassing "this beautiful man." When Louis died, Lucas, who says he once paid off a fifty-thousand-dollar tax lien for the champ, was heard weeping into a telephone, "My Daddy . . . he's dead." It was also at Small's, on a cold winter's night in the late 1950s, that Frank Lucas, haint of Harlem, would encounter Howard Hughes. "He was right there, at the bar, with Ava Gardner . . . Howard Hughes, richest mother fucker in the world, the original ghost—that impressed me."

In the end, the little tour comes back to 116th Street. When he "owned" this street, Frank says, "you'd see a hundred junkies, lined up, sitting there, sucking their own dicks. . . . That's what you called it, sucking their own dicks . . . their heads on their laps, down in the crotch, like they was dead. People saw that, then everyone knew that shit was good."

Now, like everywhere else, 116th Street is another place. Only a few days before, the *New York Times* had a piece saying that Frank's old turf was a key cog in the current real estate boom characterized as "a new Harlem renaissance." An Australian graphic designer just purchased a steal of a brownstone for $237,000, the *Times* reported, cheering that whole area "once destroyed by drugs, crime, and debilitation . . . [an area which is] on the way up." This news does not please Lucas. He and his Country Brother Shorty used to own property in the area, so that's just more millions out the window.

"Uh oh, here come the gangstas," Lucas shouts in mock fright, as he regards a trio of youths, blue kerchiefs knotted around their heads, standing by a car, blaring rap music. Partial to James Brown, and "soulmen I knew like Chuck Jackson and Dennis Edwards," Frank says he is no fan of "any Wu-Tang this and Tu Pac that." One of his sons tried rapping, made a couple of records, but it was "that same ba-ba-ba . . . it don't do nothing for me." Once the possessor of a closetful of tailor-made Hong Kong suits, seventy-five pairs of shoes, and underwear from Sulka, Frank doesn't care much for the current O. G. styles, either. "Baggy pants prison bullshit," is his blanket comment on the Tommy Hilfiger thuglife knockoffs currently in homeboy favor.

"Well, I guess every idiot gets to be young once," Lucas snaps as he starts the car, driving half a block before slamming on the brakes.

"Here's something you ought to see," the old gangster says, pointing toward the curbside between the Canaan Baptist Church and the House of Fish. "There's where I killed that boy . . . Tango," Frank shouts, his large, squarish jaw lanterning forward, eyes slitting. "I told you about that, didn't I? . . ."

Of course he had, only days before, in distressing specific, hair-raising detail.

For Frank, the incident, which occurred "at four o'clock in the afternoon" sometime in "the summer of 1965 or '66," was strategy. Strictly business. Because, as Lucas recalls, "When you're in the kind of work I was in, you've got to be for real. When you say something, you've got to make sure people listen. You've got to show what exactly you're willing to do to get what you want.

"Everyone, Goldfinger Terrell, Hollywood Harold, Robert Paul, J.C., Willie Abraham, they was talking about this big guy, this Tango. About six-foot-five, 270 pounds, quick as a cat on his feet. . . . He killed two or three guys with his hands. Nasty, dangerous mother. Had this big bald head, like Mr. Clean. Wore those Mafia undershirts. Everyone was scared of him. So I figured, Tango, you're my man.

"I went up to him, just talking, I asked him if he wanted to do some business. He said yes. I gave him five thousand dollars, some shit money like that. . . . Because I know he was gonna fuck up. I knew he wouldn't do what he said he would and he was never, ever, going to give me my money back. That's the kind of guy he was. Two weeks later I'm on the block, and I go talk to him. 'Look man,' I say, 'you didn't do that thing, so where's my money?'

"Then, like I knew he would, he started getting hot, going into one of his real gorilla acts. He was one of them silverback gorillas, strong, like in the jungle, or on TV. A silverback gorilla, that's what he was.

"He started cursing, saying he was going to make me his bitch, stick his whatever in my ass, and he'd do the same to my mama, too. Well, as of now, he's dead. My mama is a quiet church lady and I can't have that sort of talk about her. No question, a dead man. But I let him talk. A dead man should be able to say anything he wants to. It is his right. Last will and whatever. Now there's a crowd, the whole fucking block is out there. They want to see what's gonna happen, if I'm going to pussy out, you know. He was still yelling. So I said to him, 'When you get through, let me know.'

"Then the motherfucker knows I'm going to kill him. So he broke for me. But he was too late. I shot him. Four times, bam, bam, bam, bam.

"Yeah, it was right there," says Frank Lucas thirty-five years after the shooting, pointing out the car window to the curbside to where a man in coveralls is sweeping up in front of the Canaan Baptist Church, Wyatt Tee Walker, senior pastor.

"Right there . . . the boy didn't have no head in the back. The whole shit blowed out. . . . That was my real initiation fee into taking over completely down here. Because I killed the baddest motherfucker. Not just in Harlem, but in the world."

Then Frank laughs.

Frank's laugh: It's a trickster's sound, a jeer that cuts deep. First he rolls up his slumped shoulders and cranes back his large, angular face, which despite all the wear and tear remains strikingly handsome, even empathetic in a way you'd like to trust, but know better. Then the smooth, tawny skin over his cheekbones creases, his ashy lips spread, and his tongue snakes out of his gatewide mouth. Frank has a very long, very red tongue, which he likes to dart about like a carny's come-on for real good loving. It is only then the aural segment kicks in, staccato stabs of mirth followed by a bevy of low rumbled cackles.

Ha, ha, ha, siss, siss, siss. For how many luckless fools like Tango was this the last sound they ever heard on this earth?

Frank's laugh translates well on tape. Listening to a recording of our conversations, my wife blinked twice and leaned back in her chair. "Oh," she said, "you're doing a story on Satan. . . . Funny, that's exactly how I always imagined he might sound." She said it was like hearing a copy of the real interview with a vampire.

"After I killed that boy," Frank Lucas goes on, gesturing toward the corner on the other side of 116th Street, "from that day on, I could take a million dollars in any kind of bag, set it on the corner, and put my name on it. *Frank Lucas*. And I guarantee you, nobody would touch it. Nobody."

Then Frank laughs again. Ha . . . ha . . . ha. He puts a little extra menace into it just so you don't get too comfortable with the assumption that your traveling partner is simply a limping old guy with a gnarled left hand who is fond of telling colorful stories and wearing a five-dollar acetate shirt covered with faux-NASCAR logos.

Just so you never forget exactly who you are dealing with.

When asked about the relative morality of killing people, selling millions of dollars of dope, and playing a significant role in the destruction of the social fabric of his times, Frank Lucas bristles. What choice did he have, he demands to know. "Kind of sonofabitch I saw myself being, kind of money I wanted to make, I'd have to be on Wall Street. From the giddy-up, on Wall Street. Making a damn fortune. But I couldn't have gotten a job even being a fucking janitor on Wall Street."

Be that as it may, there is little doubt that when, on a sweltering summer's afternoon in 1946, Frank Lucas first arrived in Harlem, which he'd always been told was "nigger heaven, the promised land," his prospects in the legitimate world were limited. Not yet sixteen years old, he was already on the run. Already a gangster.

It couldn't have been any other way, Lucas insists, not after the Ku Klux Klan came to his house and killed his cousin Obedai. "Must have been 1936, because I was born September 9, 1930, and I wasn't more than six. We were living in a little place they call La Grange, North Carolina. Not even La Grange. Way in the woods. Anywise, these five white guys come up to the house one morning, big rednecks. . . . And they're yelling, 'Obedai, Obedai . . . Obedai Jones . . . come out. Come out you nigger . . .'

"They said he was looking at a white girl walking down the street. 'Reckless eyeballing,' they call it down there.

"Obedai was like twelve or thirteen, and he come out the door, all sleepy and stuff. 'You been looking at somebody's daughter. We're going to fix you,' they said. They took two ropes, a rope in each hand, they tied him down on the ground, facedown on the porch, and two guys took the rope and . . . pulled it tight in opposite directions. The other guy shoved a shotgun in Obedai's mouth and pulled the trigger simultaneous."

It was then, Lucas says, that he began his life of crime. "I was the oldest. Someone had to put food on the table. My mother was maxed out. I started stealing chickens. Knocking pigs on their head, dragging them home. . . . It wasn't too long that I started going over to La Grange, mugging drunks when they come out of the whorehouse. They'd spent their five or six bucks buying ass, getting head jobs, then they'd come out and I'd be waiting with a rock in my hand, a tobacco rack, anything. . . .

By the time he was twelve, "but big for my age," Lucas says, he was in Knoxville, Tennessee, on a chain gang, picked up by the police after breaking into a store. In Lexington, Kentucky, not yet fourteen, he lived with a lady bootlegger. In Wilson, North Carolina, he got a truck driver job at a pipe company, delivering all over the state, Greenville, Charlotte, and Raleigh. The company was owned by a white man, and Lucas started in sleeping with his daughter. This led to problems, especially after "Big Bill, a fat, 250-pound beerbelly bastard," caught them in the act. In the ensuing fight, Lucas, sure he was about to be killed, managed to hit Bill on the head with a piece of pipe, laying him out.

"They didn't owe me but a hundred dollars for the work I done, but I took four hundred and set the whole damned place on fire." After that, his mother told him he better get away and never come back. He bummed northward, stopping in Washington, which he didn't like, before coming to Harlem.

"I took the train to Thirty-fourth Street. Penn Station. I went out and asked the police how you get to Fourteenth Street, what bus you take. I had only a dollar something in my pocket. I took the bus to Fourteenth Street, got out, looked around. I went over to another policeman on the other side of the street. 'Hey,' I said, 'this ain't Fourteenth Street. I want to go where all the black people are at.' He said, 'You want to go to Harlem . . . *one hundred* and fourteenth street!'

"I got to 114th Street. I had never seen so many black people in one place in all my life. It was a world of black people. And I just shouted out: 'Hello, Harlem . . . hello Harlem, USA!'"

If he wanted any money, everyone told him, he better go downtown, get a job as an elevator operator. But once Frank saw guys writing policy numbers, carrying big wads, his course was set. Within a few months he was a one-man, hell-bent crime wave. He stuck up the Hollywood Bar on Lenox and 116th Street, got himself six hundred dollars. He went up to Busch Jewelers on 125th Street, told them he needed an engagement ring for his girl, stole a tray of diamonds, and broke the guard's jaw with brass knuckles on the way out. Later he ripped off a high-roller crap game at the Big Track Club on 118th Street. "They was all gangsters in there. Wynton Morris, Red Dillard, Clarence Day, Cool Breeze, maybe two or three more. I just walked in, took their money. Now they was all looking for me."

The way he was going, Frank figures, it took Bumpy Johnson, the most mythic of all Harlem gangsters (Moses Gunn played Johnson in the original *Shaft,* Lawrence Fishburne did it twice, in *The Cotton Club* and the more recent *Hoodlum*) to save his life.

"I was hustling up at Lump's Pool Room, on 134th Street. I got pretty good with it. Eight-ball and that. So in comes Icepick Red. Now, Icepick

Red, he was a fierce killer, from the heart. Tall motherfucker, clean, with a hat. Freelanced Mafia hits. Had at least fifty kills. Anyway, he says he wants to play some pool, took out a roll of money that must have been that high. My eyes got big. I knew right then that wasn't none of his money. That was MY money . . . there's no way he's leaving the room with that money.

"'Who wants to shoot pool?' Icepick Red keeps saying. 'Who wants to fucking play?' I told him I'm playing but I only got a hundred dollars . . . and he's saying, what kind of sissy only got a hundred dollars? All sorts of shit. The way he was talking, I wanted to take out my gun and kill him right there, take his damn money. I just didn't care what happened.

"Except right then everything seemed to stop. The jukebox stopped, the poolballs stopped. Every fucking thing stopped. It got so quiet you could have heard a rat piss on a piece of cotton in China.

"I turned around and I saw this guy—he was like five-ten, five-eleven, dark complexion, neat, looked like he just stepped out of *Vogue* magazine. He had on a gray suit and a maroon tie, with a gray overcoat and a flower in the lapel. You never seen nothing that looked like him. He was another species altogether. You could tell that right away.

"'Can you beat him?' he said to me in a deep, smooth voice.

"I said, 'I can shoot pool with anybody, mister. I can beat anybody.'

"Icepick Red, suddenly he's nervous. Scared. 'Bumpy!' he shouts out, 'I don't got no bet with you!'

"But Bumpy ignores that. 'Rack 'em up, Lump!'

"We rolled for the break, and I got it. And I wasted him. Just wasted him. Icepick Red never got a goddamn shot. Bumpy sat there, watching. Didn't say a word. But when the game's over, he says to me, 'Come on, let's go.' And I'm thinking, who the fuck is this Bumpy? But something told me I better keep my damn mouth shut. So I got in the car. A long Caddy I think it was. First we stopped at a clothing store; he picked out a bunch of stuff for me. Suits, ties, slacks. Nice stuff. A full wardrobe. Bumpy never gave the store guy any money, just told them to send it up to the house. Then we drove to where he was living, on Mount Morris Park. He took me into his front room, said I should clean myself up, sleep there that night.

"I wound up sleeping there for about six months after that. . . . You see, Bumpy had been tracking me. He figured he could do something with me, I guess. After that night, things were different. All of a sudden the gangsters stopped fucking with me. The cops stopped fucking with me. I walk into the Busch Jewelers, look right at the man I robbed, and all he says is: 'Hello, can I help you, sir?' Because now I'm with Bumpy Johnson—a Bumpy Johnson man. I'm seventeen years old and I'm *Mister Lucas*.

"Bumpy was a gentleman among gentlemen, a king among kings, a killer among killers, a whole book and Bible by himself," notes the still-reverent Lucas. "He showed me the ropes—how to collect, how to figure the vig. Back then, everybody, every store, business, landlord above 110th Street, river to river, had to pay Bumpy. It was the Golden Rule: You either paid Bumpy or you died. Extortion, I guess you could call it. Everyone paid except the mom-and-pop stores, they got away for free. . . ."

After a while, Frank moved up. Three or four days a week he'd drive Johnson downtown, to the Fifty-seventh Street Diner across from Carnegie Hall, and wait outside while the boss ate breakfast with Mafia stalwart Frank Costello. On another occasion, around 1950, Bumpy told him to pack his bag, they were taking a trip. "We're on the plane, he says we're going to see Charley Lucky in Cuba. Imagine that! A Country Boy like me, going to visit Lucky Luciano!" reports Lucas, who spent his time guarding the door, "just one more guy with a bulge in his pocket."

"There was a lot about Bumpy I didn't understand, a lot I still don't understand," Frank reflects. "When he was older he'd be leaning over his chessboard up there at the Lenox Terrace, with these Shakespeare books around, listening to soft piano music, Beethoven—or that Henry Mancini record he played over and over, 'Elephant Walk.' Then he'd start talking about philosophy, read me a passage from Tom Paine, the *Rights of Man*. . . . What do you think of that, Frank, he'd ask . . . and I'd shrug, because I wouldn't know what to say. What could I say? What did I know? About the only book I remember reading was Harold Robbins's *The Carpetbaggers*."

In the end, as Frank tells it, Bumpy died in his arms. "We was eating at Wells Restaurant on Lenox Avenue, talking about day-to-day stuff. Chitchat. I think Billy Daniels, the singer, might have been there. Maybe Cockeye Johnny, JJ, or Chickenfoot. When Bumpy was around, there was always a crowd, people wanting to talk to him. All of a sudden Bumpy started shaking and he fell over, right up against me. Never said another word."

Two months after Martin Luther King's assassination, the headline of the front-page account of Bumpy Johnson's funeral in the *Amsterdam News* headline read, BUMPY'S DEATH MARKS END OF AN ERA. Bumpy had been the link back to the wild days of Harlem gangsterism, to people like Madame St. Clair, the French-speaking Queen of Policy, and the wizardly rackets magnate Casper Holstein, who reportedly aided the careers of Harlem Renaissance writers like Claude McKay. Also passing from the scene were characters like Helen Lawrenson, former managing editor of *Vanity Fair* (and mother of Joanna Lawrenson, who would marry Abbie Hoffman), whose tart, engrossing account of her concurrent affairs with Condé Nast, Bernard Baruch, and Ellsworth "Bumpy" Johnson can be found in the long-out-of-print *Stranger at the Party*.

Lucas says, "There wasn't gonna be no next Bumpy. You see, Bumpy, he believed in that 'share the fortune' thing. Spread the wealth. I was a different sonofabitch. I wanted all the money for myself. . . . Besides, I didn't want to stay in Harlem. That same routine. Numbers, protection, those little pieces of paper flying out of your pocket. I wanted adventure. I wanted to see the world."

A few days after our Harlem trip, watching a Japanese guy in a chef hat dice up some hibachi steak in a fake Benihana place beside an interstate off-ramp, Frank told me how he came upon what he refers to as his "bold new plan" to smuggle thousands of pounds of heroin from Southeast Asia to Harlem. It is a thought process Lucas says he often uses when on the verge of "a pattern change."

First he locks himself in a room, preferably a hotel room on the beach in Puerto Rico, shuts off the phone, pulls down the blinds, unplugs the TV, has his meals delivered outside the door at prearranged times, and does not speak to a soul for a couple of weeks. In this meditative isolation,

Lucas engages in what he calls "backward tracking . . . I think about everything that has happened in the past five years, every little thing, every nook and cranny, down to the smallest detail of what I put on my toast in the morning."

Having vetted the past, Lucas begins to "forward look . . . peering around every bend in the road ahead." It is only then, Frank says, "when you can see all the way back to Alaska and ahead as far as South America . . . and decide that nothing, not even the smallest hair on a cockroach's dick, can stand in your way"—that you are ready to make your next big move.

If he really wanted to become "white boy rich, Donald Trump rich," Lucas decided he'd have to "cut the guineas out from above 110th Street." He'd learned as much over the years, running errands for Bumpy over to Pleasant Avenue, the East Harlem mob enclave, where he'd pick up "packages" from Fat Tony Salerno's guys, men with names like Joey Farts and Kid Blast. "I needed my own supply. That's when I decided to go to Southeast Asia. Because the war was already on and people were talking about a lot of GIs getting strung out over there. So I knew if the shit is good enough to string out GIs, then I can make myself a killing."

Lucas had never been to Southeast Asia, but felt confident. "It didn't matter about it being foreign," Frank says, "because I knew it was a street thing over there. You see, maybe I went to school only three days in my life, but I got a Ph.D. in street. I am a doctorate of street. When it comes to a street atmosphere, I know what I'm doing. I know I'm going to make out."

Once in town, Frank checked into the swank Dusit Thani Hotel, where he often spent afternoons watching coverage of the war being waged a couple of hundred miles to the east. Lucas soon hailed a motorcycle taxi to take him to Jack's American Star Bar, on the edge of the then-notorious Patpong sex district. Offering hamhocks and collard greens on the first floor and a wide array of hookers and dope connections on the second, the Soul Bar, as Frank calls it, was run by the former U.S. Army master sergeant Leslie (Ike) Atkinson, a Country Boy from Goldsboro, North Carolina, which made him as good as family.

"Ike knew everyone over there, every black guy in the army, from the cooks on up," Frank says. "A lot of these guys, they weren't too happy to

be over there, you know. That made them up for business. . . ." It was what
Frank calls "this army inside the army, that was our distribution system."
According to Lucas, most of the shipments came back on military planes
routed to eastern seaboard bases like Fort Bragg, and Fort Gordon in Georgia, places within easy driving distance of his Carolina ranch. Most of
Frank's "couriers" were enlisted men, often cooks or plane maintainance
men. But "a lot of officers were in there, too. Big ones, generals and colo-
nels, with eagles and chickens on their collars. These were some of the
greediest motherfuckers I ever dealt with. They'd be getting people's asses
shot up in battle, but they'd do anything if you gave them enough money."

Acting on information given him by a woman called "Nurse" whom he
met in a Mott Street restaurant in New York's Chinatown, Lucas located
his main overseas connection—a youngish, English-speaking Chinese
gentleman with a buzz cut who went by the sobriquet 007. "When he drove
up in a Rolls and a white linen jacket, I knew he was my man. . . . Double-
O-Seven, that was all I ever called him because he was a fucking Chinese
James Bond." Double-O-Seven took Lucas upcountry, to the Golden Triangle, the heavily jungled point where Thailand, Burma, and Laos come
together, the richest poppy-growing area in the world. By Lucas's account,
it was an epic journey.

"It wasn't too bad getting up there," says Lucas, who recalls being dressed
in his uptown attire, with a brim hat and tailored pants. "Maybe a ten-day
thing through the bush. We was in trucks, sometimes on boats. I might have
been on every damn river in the Golden Triangle. When we got up there,
you couldn't believe it. They've got fields the size of Newark with nothing
but poppy seeds in them. There's caves in the mountains so big you could
set this building in them, which is where they do the processing. . . . It was
beautiful, mist hanging on the green hills. I'd sit there, smoking a cigarette,
and watch these Chinese paramilitary guys come out of the fog carrying these
rifles that looked like they hadn't been fired in twenty years. When they
saw me, they stopped dead. They'd never seen a black man before."

More than likely dealing with soldiers who had fought with Chiang Kai-
shek's defeated Kuomintang army in the Chinese civil war (Lucas recalls
seeing Nationalist Chinese flags flying over several buildings), Frank

purchased 132 kilos on that first trip. At $4,200 per unit, compared to the $50,000 that Mafia dealers were charging Harlem competitors like Nicky Barnes and Frank Moten, it would be an unbelievable bonanza. But the journey was not without problems.

"On the way back, that's when our troubles began," Lucas says. "Right off guys were stepping on these little green snakes. A second later they were dead. Then, guess what happened? Them banditos. Those motherfuckers, they came out of nowhere. Right out of the trees. Stealing our shit. Everyone was shooting. I was stuck under a log firing my piece. The guys I was with—007's guys—all of them was Bruce Lees. Those sonsofbitches were good. They fought like hell. But the banditos, they had this way of sneaking up, stabbing you with these pungi sticks. All around me these guys were getting shot. You'd see a lot of dead shit in there, man. It was like a movie. A bad B-movie. A month and a half of nightmares. I think I ate a damn dog. It was the worst meat I ever tasted in my life. Very uncomfortable. I was in bad shape, lying on the ground, raggedy and stinking, crazy with fever, barfing. Then people were talking about tigers. Like there were tigers and lions up there. That's when I figured, that does it. I'm out of here. I'm gonna be ripped up by a tiger in this damn jungle. What a fucking epitaph. . . . But we got back alive. Lost half my dope, but I was still alive."

Embroidered at the edges or not, it is a fabulous cartoon, an image to take its place in the floridly romantic, easy-riding annals of the American dope pusher—Superfly in his Botany 500 sportswear, custom leather boots, and brim hat, clutching his hundred keys, Sierra Madre style, as he shivers in malarial muck, bullets whizzing overhead.

"It was the most physiological thing I ever done and hope not to do again," says Lucas, who would like it known that through all his wartime smuggling gambits, he never felt less than "100 percent true blue red, white, and blue, a patriotic American." To this end, Lucas swears that details concerning the dope-in-the-body-bags caper have been wildly misrepresented. The story that he and Ike Atkinson actually stitched the dope inside the body cavities of dead soldiers is nothing but "sick cop propaganda" put out to discredit him, Lucas insists. "No way I'm touching a dead anything. Bet your life on that."

What really happened, Lucas recounts, was that he flew a Country Boy North Carolina carpenter over to Bangkok and had him "make up twenty-eight coffins identical to the ones the government was using. Except we fixed them up with false bottoms, compartments big enough to load up with six, maybe eight kilos. . . . It had to be tight, because you couldn't have shit sliding around. We was very smart in that respect because we only used mostly heavy guys' coffins. We didn't put them in no skinny guy's."

Still, of all his various Asian capers, Frank still rates "the Henry Kissinger deal" as "the scariest and the best." To hear Frank tell it, he was desperate to get 125 keys out of town, but there weren't any "friendly" planes scheduled. "All we had was Kissinger. I don't know if he was secretary of state then. He was on a mercy mission on account of some big cyclones in Bangladesh. We gave a hundred thousand dollars to some general to look the other way and we was in business; I mean, who the fuck is gonna search Henry Kissinger's plane?

". . . Henry Kissinger! Wonder what he'd say if he knew he helped smuggle all that dope into the country? . . . *Hoo hahz poot zum dope in my aero-plan?* Ha, ha, ha. Good thing he didn't know or maybe he would have asked us for carrying charges. . . . Ha, ha, ha . . . fucking Henry Kissinger."

Asked how he invented these schemes, Lucas leans back in the dim light of the Japanese restaurant and, after a couple of Kirins, unleashes his most jocularly macabre smile. "When did I come up with these ideas? On September 9, 1930, at about four o'clock in the morning, that's when. The moment I was born . . . Instinct, man . . . Everyone's born to do something, and smuggling dope was it for me. To me that's the thrill, more than even the money. Beating the cops. Beating the feds. Beating everybody . . . ha, ha, ha."

Back issues of the *Amsterdam News* from the late sixties and early seventies are full of accounts of what 116th Street was like during the reign of Frank Lucas. Lou Broders, who ran a small apparel shop at 253 West 116th, says, "We here are being destroyed by dope and crime every day . . . it's my own people doing it, too. That's the pity of it. This neighborhood is dying out." It was Fear City time, when the feds were estimating that out of all the heroin addicts in America, more than half were in New York, 75 percent of those in Harlem. In a city that would soon be on the brink of financial collapse, the plague was on.

In the face of such talk, Frank, who remembers the Harlem riots of the 1960s as being "no big deal" exhibits his typically willful obliviousness. "It's not my fault if your television got stolen," he says. "If everything is going to hell, how can I be responsible for all that? I'm only one guy. Besides, Harlem was great then. It wasn't until they put me and Nicky Barnes in jail that the city went into default. There was tons of money up in Harlem in 1971, 1972, if you knew how to get it. And I did. Shit, those were the heydays. That was the top."

To hear Frank (who never touched the stuff himself) tell it, life as a multimillionaire dope dealer was a whirl of flying to Paris for dinner at Maxim's, gambling in Vegas with Joe Louis and Sammy Davis Jr., spending $140,000 on a couple of Van Cleef bracelets, and squiring around his beautiful mistress—Billie Mays, stepdaughter of Willie, who, according to Lucas, he'd sneaked away from Walt "Clyde" Frazier. Back home there were community businessman's lunches and fund-raising activities for the then-young Charles Rangel. The gritty 116th Street operation was left in the hands of trusted lieutenants. If problems arose, Lucas says, "we'd have 250 guns in the street so fast your head would spin off your neck."

Frank was always the boss, handling all the cash, albeit idiosyncratically. His money-laundering routine often consisted of throwing a few duffel bags stuffed with tens and twenties into the backseat of his car and driving up to a Chemical Bank on East Tremont Avenue in the Bronx where he knew the branch officers. Most of the money was sent to accounts in the Cayman Islands, but if Frank needed a little extra cash, he sat in the bank lobby reading the newspaper while the bank managers filled one of the duffels with crisp new hundred-dollar bills. For their part in the laundering scheme, the Chemical Bank would eventually plead guilty to 445 violations of the Bank Secrecy Act.

As Bumpy had once had the Palmetto Chemical Company, a roach-exterminating concern, Frank opened a string of gas stations and dry cleaners, but this did not suit his temperament. "I had a dry cleaning place on Broadway, near Zabar's. I don't remember what happened, but there wasn't no one to watch the place. I had to go myself. Now, you know I ain't no nine-to-five guy. And these old ladies kept coming in, screaming, 'Look at this spot. . . . Why can't you get this out? . . . shoving the damn shirt in my face. I couldn't take it anymore. I ran out of the place, didn't lock up, didn't even take the money out of the cash register, just drove away."

Show business was more to Frank's taste, especially after he and fellow gangster Zack Robinson put "a bunch of money" into Lloyd Price's Turntable, a nightclub at Fifty-second Street and Broadway that soon became a must hangout for black celebrities. "There'd be Muhammad Ali, who was a friend of Lloyd's, members of the Temptations, James Brown, Berry Gordy, Diana Ross," says Frank, who calls the Turntable, "a good scene, the integration crowd was there, every night."

In 1969, Price, a Rock & Roll Hall of Famer who'd had huge hits with tunes like "Personality" and "Lawdy Miss Clawdy," got the idea to make a gangster movie set on the streets of New York. "There'd been lots of gangster movies before, but not too many black gangster movies, and none of them ever had real, practicing gangsters in them," says Price, always a sharp article when it came to cultural margins between white and black culture (now in his late sixties, he still looks good in a gold lamé suit). "We needed a guy to play the Superfly, the guy with the sable coat and the hat, so I thought, why not get Frank? He was real handsome in those days. A real presence. So he played the bad-guy romantic lead. He was a natural, really."

"It was like *Shaft* before *Shaft*—the first *Shaft*," reports Lucas, who sees a "young and dangerous" Morgan Freeman Jr. ("You know, in that movie *Street Smart*, when he terrorizes that reporter") in the prospective *Frank Lucas Story*. "We had this scene where I was chasing Lloyd down the street, shooting out the window of a Mercedes somewhere up in the Bronx. I put a bunch of money into the picture, seventy, eighty grand. It was real fun. Real fun."

Alas, never finished, the footage apparently disappeared. *The Ripoff* qualifies as the "great lost film" of the so-called blaxploitation genre. "A lot of strange things happened making that movie," says Lloyd Price, who recalls a trip to the film editor's office with Frank, whom the singer seems to regard with much affection and a touch of fear. "Frank didn't care for the way the cut was going," Lloyd says. "Some words were said, and then Frank is pulling out his knife. I had to tell him, Frank, man, I don't think this is the way it is done in the movie business."

A drug kingpin attracts a degree of attention from the police, but according to Frank, it wasn't the "straight-arrow types" who caused him undue problems. His trouble came from repeated shakedowns run by the infamously corrupt and rapacious Special Investigations Unit, NYPD's "elite" detective squad. Collectively known as the Princes of the City for their unlimited authority to make busts anywhere in New York, the SIU wrote its own mighty chapter in the wild street-money days of the early seventies heroin epidemic; by 1973, forty-three of the sixty officers who'd worked in the unit were either in jail or under indictment.

Lucas's relations with his fellow drug dealers were more congenial. "It wasn't one of those gang-war, fighting-over-territory things. There was plenty of customers to go around." Disputes did come up, such as the one that, according to Special Narcotics Prosecutor Sterling Johnson, once caused Lucas to take out a contract on his famous Harlem rival, Leroy (Nicky) Barnes. Frank denies this, but says he never liked the grandstanding Barnes, who Lucas thought brought unneeded heat by doing things like appearing on the cover of the *New York Times Magazine* wearing his trademark goggle-like Gucci glasses, bragging that he was "Mr. Untouchable." The assertion soon had then-president Jimmy Carter on the telephone demanding that something be done about Barnes and the whole Harlem dope trade.

According to Lucas, it was Barnes's "delusions of grandeur" that led to a bizarre meeting between the two drug lords in the lingerie department of Henri Bendel. "Nicky wanted to make this Black Mafia thing called The Council. An uptown Cosa Nostra. The Five Families of Dope or some shit.

I didn't want no part of it. Because if we're gonna be Genoveses, then before long, everyone's gonna think they're Carlo Gambino. Then your life ain't worth shit. Besides, I was making more money than anyone.

"Anyway, I was shopping with my wife at Henri Bendel's on Fifty-seventh Street, she's in the dressing room, and who comes up? Nicky fucking Barnes! 'Frank . . . Frank,' he's going . . . 'we got to talk . . . we got to get together on this council thing.' Talking that solidarity shit. I told him forget it, my wife is trying on underwear, can't we do this some other time? Then before he leaves, he says, 'Hey Frank, I'm short this week. Can you front me a couple of keys?' That's Nicky."

Asked if he ever thought about quitting when he was ahead, Lucas says, "Sure, all the time." He says his wife, Julie, whom he met on a "backtrack-ing" trip in Puerto Rico, always begged him to get out, especially after Brooklyn dope king Frank Matthews jumped bail in 1973 and disappeared, never to be heard from again. ("Some say he's dead, but I know he's living in Africa, like a king, with all the fucking money in the world," Lucas sighs.) "Probably I should have stayed in Colombia. Always liked Colombia. But I had my heart set on getting a jet plane, learning how to fly it . . . there was always something. That was the way I was, addicted to action, addicted to the money. . . ."

For Lucas, the end, or at least the beginning of the end, came on January 28, 1975, when a strike force of the DEA feds and NYPD operatives, acting on a tip from two low-level Pleasant Avenue guys, converged on the house where Frank was living at 933 Sheffield Street in leafy Teaneck, New Jersey. The raid was a surprise. In the ensuing panic, Lucas's wife, Julie, screaming "Take it all, take it all," tossed several suitcases out the window. One of the suitcases hit a hiding DEA agent square on the head, knock-ing him out. The case was later found to contain $585,000, mostly in rumpled twenty dollar bills. At the time it was the second largest "cash re-trieval" in DEA history, behind only the million dollars dug up in the Bronx backyard of Arthur Avenue wiseguy Louie Cirillo. Also found were several keys to Lucas's safe deposit boxes in the Cayman Islands, deeds to his North Carolina land, and a ticket to a United Nations ball, compliments of the ambassador of Honduras.

"Those motherfuckers just came in," Lucas says now, more than twenty-five years later, as he sits in a car across the street from the surprisingly modest split-level house where, prior to his arrest, he often played pickup games with members of the New York Knicks. For years Lucas has contended that the cops took a lot more than $585,000 from him when he was busted. "585 Gs . . . shit. I'd go to Vegas and lose $485,000 in a half hour." According to Frank, federal agents took something on the order of "nine to ten million dollars" from him that fateful evening. To bolster his claim, he cites passing a federally administered polygraph test on the matter. A DEA agent on the scene that night, noting that "ten million dollars in crumpled twenty-dollar bills isn't something you just stick in your pocket," vigorously denies Lucas's charge.

Whatever, Frank doesn't expect to see his money again. "It's just too fucking old, old and gone."

Then, suddenly snickering, Lucas addresses my attention to the trunk of a tree in the front yard of the house. "See that little gouge there, where it goes in? Aretha Franklin's car made that dent. I think maybe King Curtis was driving. They had come over for a party and just backed up over the grass into it."

"Funny," Lucas says, looking around the innocent-seeming suburb, "that tree has grown a lot since then, but the scar's still there."

A few days later I brought Lucas a copy of his newspaper clip file, which almost exclusively details the Country Boy's long and tortuous interface with the criminal justice system following his Sheffield Street arrest, a period in which he would do time in joints like Otisville, Sandstone, Trenton, Rahway, Lewistown, Tucson, Elmira, the Manhattan Correctional Center, and Rikers. Squinting heavily, Lucas silently thumbed through yellowed, dog-eared articles that had heads like "Country Boys, Called No. 1 Heroin Gang, Is Busted," "30 Country Boys Indicted in $50 million Heroin Operation," "Charge Two Witnesses Bribed in Lucas Trial; Star Murder Trial Witness Vanishes." There was also an October 25, 1979, story in the *New York Post* titled "Convict Lives It Up with

Sex and Drugs," which quotes a Manhattan Correctional Center pris-
oner named "Nick," convicted hit man killer of five, who whines that
Lucas had ordered prostitutes up to his cell and was "so indiscreet about
it I had to have my wife turn the other way . . . he didn't give one damn
about anyone else's feelings."

In between bitching that the mugshot of him looking "like I ain't slept
in two weeks" Lucas, who likes to point out that "biography is history,"
said it figured that "the whiteboy press" only covered him in relation to
his dealings with the cops. "Once they get you and think you're tame, then
it's safe to say a bunch of shit about you."

One clip, however, did engage Lucas's attention. Titled "Ex-Assistant
Prosecutor for Hogan Shot to Death in Village Ambush," the November 5, 1977, *Times* clip tells how Gino E. Gallina, onetime Manhattan
D.A. turned Pelham Manor mouthpiece for "top drug dealers and organized crime figures," was rubbed out "mob style . . . as many passers-by
looked on in horror" one nippy fall evening at the corner of Carmine
and Varick streets.

Lucas reckons he must have spent "millions" on high-priced criminal
lawyers through the seventies and early eighties, people like Ray Brown
Sr., counselor for Rubin "Hurricane" Carter, and John H. Gross, a former
southern District D.A. under Rudolph Giuliani, who represented Frank
in a series of cases. Gino Gallina, however, was the only lawyer Lucas ever
physically assaulted, the incident occurring in the visiting room of the
Rikers Island prison. According to later testimony, Lucas had given
Gallina $400,000 to fix a case for him, and $200,000 became "lost." It was
upon hearing this news that Frank, the *Daily News* wrote, "leaped across a
table and began punching him [Gallina] savagely, knocking him to the
floor before prison guards were able to subdue him. . . . Gallina wore the
scars from that assault for weeks" but "significantly . . . filed no charges
against his client."

For his part, Frank acknowledges "beating the dogshit out" of Gallina.
He also allows that the lawyer "stole my money," that "I told him he was
a dead man if he didn't get it back to me," and that "the man did not deserve to live." However, Frank pointing out that there's no statue of limi-

tations on murder steadfastly maintains he has "no idea, no idea at all" about how and why Gallina was killed, a crime that remains unsolved to this day.

Despite offering "little tidbits" like how he often talked boxing with Frankie Carbo and politics with Black Panther Joanne Chesimard while in prison, the Country Boy offers scant details about what he's been up to in the past twenty-five years of his life. Whole decades are dismissed with a shrug or wave of a hand.

What Lucas will absolutely not talk about is how he got out of jail, the stuff described in clips like the April 24, 1978, *Daily News* story, "Jailed Drug King Turns Canary to Cage 13 Old Pals," or a *Newark Star-Ledger* piece from 1983 titled "'Helpful' Drug Kingpin Granted Reduced Term," in which Judge Leonard Ronco of Newark is reported as cutting in half Lucas's thirty-year New Jersey stretch "because of the unprecedented co-operation he has given authorities" in the making of cases against other drug offenders. This followed the previous decision by U.S. District Court Judge Irving Ben Cooper, who "granted the unusual request of Dominic Amorosa, chief of the Southern District Organized Crime Strike Force, to reduce Lucas's forty-year New York prison sentence to time already served."

"I am not talking about none of that Witness Protection shit," Frank declared in our first meeting. It was part of the oral contract between Lucas and myself. "I ask two things," the Country Boy said evenly: "One, if they are slamming bamboo rods 'neath your fingernails with ball peen hammers, you are not to reveal my location, and two, none of that buddy-buddy crap with the cops. That is out."

Staying to the bargain has been frustrating since, in law enforcement circles, Lucas's "unprecedented cooperation" is nearly as legendary as his stuffing bricks of heroin into dead soldiers' coffins. Dominic Amorosa, long in private practice, estimates Frank made "maybe a hundred cases all told. . . . I don't know if anyone made more."

All Frank offers on the topic is "anything I said about anyone they would have said the same about me if they had the chance." As for anyone he gave evidence against, Lucas adds, "I've made my peace with them."

Well and good, but how was I, the journalist, supposed to explain how he, the drug kingpin, had come to serve less than nine years—barely double the time routinely handed out on shitty little possession charges under the loathsome Rockefeller drug laws, which were partially enacted in (over)reaction to big dealers like himself?

"You're the writer, you'll think of something," was Frank's response. Failing that, Frank suggested I could just "leave the whole fucking thing out . . . stop at 1975 and make everything else into a cliffhanger . . . if anyone asks what I been doing since then, just say I was in the oil business."

I'd been told this would be the most difficult part, that gangsters (or gangstas, for that matter) will go on forever about people they killed, how much dope they'd moved, but as for the inevitable "giving up"— Richard Roberts, former head of the Essex County Narcotics Task Force that would successfully prosecute Lucas, says, "In this business, everybody in this business cooperates, everybody, sooner or later"—no one wanted to talk about that.

"The betrayal, that's the thing you won't hear," said a writer well known for writing about criminals who inform on their fellows. And, soon enough, Frank Lucas, the Country Boy who insisted on blood loyalty, lost patience with my persistent attempts to get him to talk about flipping. Asked to tell "the worst thing he'd ever done," he said balefully, "You already know the answer to that so I won't dignify that with a reply." Later, hoping to get him to open up, I proposed a scenario in which Frank, ever the pragmatist, faced with the extreme "pattern change" of being in the joint for the rest of his life, entered into perhaps the most intense "backtracking" trance of his long career. Was it the simple arithmetic of being in his late forties and "forward-looking" into the black hole of a seventy-year sentence that made him decide to talk?

"Listen, I told you before," Lucas said, stone-faced, his voice halfway between a threat and plea, "I have hurt my mother and family before with this and I will not do it again. So don't go there, now or ever . . . don't cross me, because I am a busy man and I have no time, no time whatsoever, to go to your funeral."

Still, I couldn't give it up. Nicky Barnes, who'd also cooperated, making many cases, had only just been released after serving twenty-one years. How was it possible that when he was asked for a name in a repair shop, Frank said with appalling matter-of-factness, "Frank Lucas . . . my name is Frank Lucas." How could he just be *out there*? It was a mystery.

Finally, Frank said, "Look, you want to know what the bottom line is on a guy like me? It is that I am sitting here talking to you right now. Still walking and talking. That is all you need to know. That I am right here when I could have, maybe should have, been dead and buried a hundred times. And you know why that is?

"Because: people like me. People *like the fuck out of me*." This was his primary survival skill, said the former dope king and killer: his downright friendliness, his upbeat demeanor. "All the way back to when I was a boy, people have always liked me, wanted to do things for me. I've always counted on that."

That much had become apparent a few days earlier, when I went over to the Eastern District Federal Court to visit with Judge Sterling Johnson. During the plague year of 1976, when government alarmists claimed that junkies were stealing a billion dollars' worth of property a year, Johnson, a former NYPD beat cop and head of the Civilian Review Board, took several congressmen and local politicians on a walking tour of 116th Street, then still Frank Lucas territory. Events of the tour were noted during a hearing of the 94th Congress Select Committee of Narcotic Abuse and Control, a group that would make many key appropriations in the nascent War on Drugs. According to the testimony, at the corner of Eighth Avenue, some of Frank's "block workers," in addition to "flinging their heads into windows of passing cars hawking their wares," came over to outraged congressmen Charles Rangel, Fortney Stark, and Benjamin Gilman and told them, with all due respect, "If you're not buying, get out of here."

Frank had told me to look up Johnson, whom he refers to as "Idi Amin."

"Judge Johnson likes me a lot. You'll see," Lucas said. "I'm lucky for him, because if he didn't put me in jail, he wouldn't be a judge to begin with."

When I first called his office, Johnson answered the phone with a burnished dignity befitting a highly respected, distinguished public official. "This is Judge Johnson," he said. Yet when I mentioned the name Frank Lucas, Johnson's voice rose a couple of octaves and became notably more familiar. "Frank Lucas? Is that *mother* still living?!" A few days later, while talking in his stately chambers, the judge told me to call Lucas up.

"Get that damn old gangster on the phone," Johnson demanded, turning on the speakerphone.

Lucas answered with his usual growl. "This is Frank. Who's this?"

Johnson mentioned a name I didn't catch, someone apparently dead, likely due to some action involving a Country Boy or two. This got Lucas's attention. "What are you talking about? Who gave you this number?"

"Top!"

"Top who?"

"Red Top!" Johnson said, invoking the name of Lucas's beloved chief dope cutter.

"What the—Red Top don't got my number." It was at around this point that Frank figured it out.

"Judge Johnson! You dog! You still got that stick?"

Johnson reached under his desk and pulled out a beat cop's nightstick and slapped it into his open palm loud enough for Lucas to hear it. "Better believe it, Frank!"

"Stop that! You're making me nervous now, Judge Johnson!" Lucas exclaimed, before somewhat gingerly inquiring, "Hey Judge, they ever get anyone in that Gallina thing?"

Johnson laughed and said, "Frank. You know you did it."

Ignoring Lucas's effusive denials, Johnson said, "Well, come around and see me. I'm about the only fly in the buttermilk down here."

After he hung up, Johnson, who still has a rustic dope-weighing machine in his office, a souvenir bought on an investigation/field trip to the Golden Triangle, and says many of his recent cases can be "a snore," added "That damn Frank. He's a pisser. He always was a pisser."

"You know, when we were first investigating him, the feds, the FBI, DEA, they didn't think he could pull off that Southeast Asia stuff. They wouldn't let themselves believe a black man could come up with such a sophisticated smuggling operation. In his sick way, he really did something."

The memory clearly tickled Johnson, who quickly added: "Look, don't get me wrong, Frank was vicious, as bad as they come. But what are you going to do? The guy was a pisser, a pisser and a killer. Easy to like. A lot of those guys were like that. It is an old dilemma."

A couple of days later, Lucas and I stop for lunch at a local TGI Friday's. TGI Friday's isn't the Oak Bar, where he never tipped less than two hundred dollars, but at least it's better than Bennigan's, Lucas says, picking at his bowl of pasta and shrimp, which he pronounces "swimph." Scowling through the glare-proof glass to the suburban strip beyond, Frank deplores "this crummy shit" he finds himself surrounded by these days.

The giant Home Depot down the road especially bugs him. Bumpy Johnson himself couldn't have collected protection from a goddamned Home Depot, Frank says with disgust. "What would Bumpy do? Go in and ask to see the assistant manager? That place, it's so big, you're lost once you pass the bathroom sinks. That's the way it is. You can't find the heart of anything to stick the knife into. The independent man don't stand a chance. It is a sign of the times."

Then Frank turned to me and asked, "So what do you think? You gonna make me out to be the devil or what? Am I going to heaven or am I going to hell?"

As far as Frank was concerned, the issue of his place in the hereafter was a foregone conclusion, settled since he joined the Catholic Church while imprisoned at Elmira. "The priest there was recommending early parole if you confessed your sins, so I signed up," he says. If this didn't pan out, Frank had backup, since he was also a Baptist. "I have praised the Lord," Frank says. "I have praised Him in the street and I have praised Him in the joint. So I know I'm forgiven, that I'm going to the good place, not the bad."

But what did I think, Frank wanted to know, taking another swig of his Sam Adams. How did I see it going for the Country Boy after he left this world?

It was a vexing question, like Sterling Johnson said, an old dilemma. Who knew about these things? Catch him on a good day at the home and even the Führer might have seemed a charming old guy, with hilarious stories of the *putsch* times. Frank was a con man, one of the best. He'd been telling white people, cops, and everyone else pretty much what they'd wanted to hear for two and a half decades, so why should I be different? I liked him. Liked the fuck out of him. Especially when he called his church lady, wrestling fan, ninety-one-year-old mother, which he did about five times a day.

But that wasn't the point. Cool copy was beyond Like and Dislike, beyond Good and Evil. Frank Lucas was, and is, cool copy. Braggart and trickster, he was nonetheless a living, breathing historical figure, tapped into a highly specialized font of secret knowledge, more exotic and certainly less picked over than any Don Corleone. Frank was a fucking gold mine, worth at least a couple of seasons of the Black Sopranos, Old School division. The idea that a backwoods Country Boy could somehow maneuver himself into a position to tell at least a plausible lie about stashing 125 kilos of *zum dope* on Henry Kissinger's plane—much less actually do it—mitigated a multitude of sins. Plague vector or not, Lucas filled an indispensable cultural niche. Who knows, if it weren't for vicious opportunistic crumbums like Frank, Lou Reed might never have written "Waiting for My Man," not to mention Marvin Gaye doing "Trouble Man." On some level, morality didn't have anything to do with it.

In the end even Lucas's resounding unrepentance didn't matter. Former Essex County prosecutor-turned-lawyer Richie Roberts, who remains a great friend of Frank's despite the fact that the Country Boy once took a contract out on his life ("He busted my mom and dad, what else could I do?" Frank says), likes to tell how Lucas cried in his courtroom. "We had this woman testify," Roberts says. "She was the mother of a drug addict. Her family had been destroyed by heroin, Frank's dope. It was really heartbreaking. A lot of people in the courtroom were crying, sobs all around.

I was crying myself. Then, I looked over at Frank. He was crying, too. Huge tears were rolling down his cheeks. There he was, Mr. Big, who had come into the courtroom like Al Capone, with Joe Louis and Johnny Sample from the Jets, this whole entourage—and he was bawling louder than anyone. I never saw anything like it."

"There Richie goes again, telling that story about me crying," remarks Lucas, who says, "but all I cared about was the mother. What she was going through, seeing her daughter suffer like that. It reminded me of my mom." As for the daughter herself, Frank has no sympathy at all. "Look, I gave strict orders to all my people, no selling to kids, no selling to pregnant women. She was old enough to know what she was doing. She did what junkies do. What happened was her problem."

Indeed, about the only flicker of remorse I'd ever seen Frank emit occurred one afternoon following a lunch we ate with one of his brothers, Vernon Lee, who is known as Shorty. Known as a particularly vicious Country Boy, Shorty, a squat, bespectacled man now in his early fifties and taking computer courses after a ten-year stretch, followed Frank to Harlem in 1965. "We came up from Carolina in a beat-up car, the brothers and sisters, Mom and Dad, with everything we owned shoved in, like the Beverly Hillbillies coming to the Land of Plenty," Shorty recalls. Frank was still working for Bumpy at the time, not the giant deal he would become, but Shorty knew what he wanted. "Diamond rings, cars, women, those things. But mostly it was the glory. Isn't that what most men really dream of? The glory."

Then Shorty reached across the table and touched his older brother's hand. "We did make a little bit of noise, didn't we?" Shorty said. To which Frank replied, "A little bit, all right."

A few minutes later we dropped Shorty off at the low-rise apartment development where he was living. It was early spring then and there was still ice on the ground. Frank watched his younger brother make his way across the frozen puddles in the late afternoon light and sighed. "You know, if I'd been a preacher, they would have all been preachers. If I'd been a cop, they'd have all been cops. But I was a dope dealer, so they all became dope dealers. I don't know, I don't know if I'd done right or not."

Later on, driving around the funky suburban landscape, Frank says if he wanted to start up dealing again, "it would take me until about this afternoon." He says it is a rare week that someone doesn't come "looking for the connect . . . but that's not happening. I'm out . . . you know, people might see my shitty clothes, shitty car, and think, Hey, bigshot, you're nothing now. How's it feel to be down? Well, fuck them. I had my day."

Then Frank said he was late. He had to go pick up his three-year-old son. Frank has several other children, including a "stockbroker in Texas" and a daughter in Georgia who's already got her MA and soon will have her Ph.D. "They're all smart but she's the really smart one," says Frank, who says, "If things had been different" he would have studied hard and gone to MIT like he always wanted to instead of getting his GED in a federal joint in Minnesota. Of all the kids, though, Frank says his son, sharp-eyed and handsome, like a chip off the old Country Boy block, is "my heart . . . I really love that boy." The other day Frank said, "You know, he can read. He's just so little and he can read. He says to me, 'Look: C-A-R-T-O-O-N . . . cartoon network.'" Can you believe that? You know how long it took me to read?"

Not that parenting is a snap for the Country Boy. Frank's son, quick afoot, "gets into everything." For sure, he is not intimidated by his gangster dad. When Frank lurches for the top drawer of the bureau, blustering about "getting my belt," the boy just laughs. Luckily Frank doesn't have far to chase the kid. The former resident of the Regency Hotel currently resides in a two-room, haphazardly furnished apartment. The cleanup lady was due that day but didn't show, so Frank apologizes if the place is a little messy. If there is any suspicion that Lucas has held on to any of his millions, the busted chair in the corner dispels that. "Shit," Frank says, "my living room used to be bigger than this whole damn building."

"From the King of the Hill to changing diapers," Lucas says in the middle of his bedroom, which just about fits his bed and dresser.

We sat around for a few hours, waiting for the kid to go to sleep, watching *The Black Rose*, an old swordfight movie with Tyrone Power and Orson Welles. Lucas, a big fan of old movies, likes Welles a lot, "at least before he got too fat." Then, when it was time for me to go, Lucas insisted I call him on the cell phone when I got back to New York. It was late, rainy, and a long drive. Lucas said he was worried about me. So, back in the city, driving down the East River Drive, by the 116th Street exit, I called Lucas up, as arranged.

"You're back, that's good," the Country Boy croaks into the phone. "Watch out. I don't care what Giuliani says, New York is not as safe as they say. Not so safe at all. You never know what you might find out there." Then Frank laughed, that same chilling haint of a laugh, spilling out the car windows and onto the city streets beyond.

2

The Most Comfortable Couch
in New York

The small pleasures of the Big City. From New York *magazine, 1999.*

The couches in the lobby of the Sherry-Netherlands hotel are comfortable. The Algonquin lobby couches are pretty plush. The couches at the old Mudd Club, the erstwhile punk Mecca, were not uncomfortable. Once, I sat down on a couch in a Maurice Villency showroom and fell asleep. When I woke up, I said, "I'll take it." The ugly thing sits in my living room to this day, covered with dog hair, never as comfortable as during that first sitting. That said, the most comfortable couch in all New York can be found in a storefront on Sixth Avenue, between Twenty-fifth and Twenty-Sixth streets.

This most comfortable couch belongs to Marta Bravo, who, along with her husband, Enrique Peña, is the proprietor of PB Cuban Cigars, an oasis of gentlemanly pleasure in the Flower District. When Marta and Enrique first opened their place on the premises of a former pizza parlor three years ago, they had no couch. "I did not think to have a couch," says the courtly, diminutive Marta, who was born in Colombia around fifty years ago and soon moved to Santiago in the Dominican Republic, where she met Enrique, a large, smiling man with double-thick glasses. Enrique worked as a cigar roller for several big tobacco farms around Santo Domingo before the couple came to this country in the 1970s. Here they realized their dream: to slip the pale-orange-and-gold ring of their own brand around hand-rolled Cuban-seed cigars, the only kind they sell.

To Marta and Enrique, the storefront on the heavily trafficked stretch of Sixth Avenue seemed perfect. The mural on the wall was "a good omen." Left over from the pizza place, the painting depicts a flock of seagulls soaring over the Statue of Liberty, the Twin Towers, and other New York landmarks. The painting celebrates a sense of giddily unabashed hometown spirit, a sentiment that Marta and Enrique, immigrants to the great metropolis, fully endorse. Still, the couple never supposed their modest premises, where the tobacco leaves are stored in the basement in big cotton-wrapped bundles, would become the marvelously serendipitous New York hangout that it has.

"We thought people would come into this small store, buy a few cigars, and then leave," says Marta with a sly smile the Mona Lisa could only envy. But Marta, a natural hostess, was not happy to have people just come and go. "When you work hard to make something, it is a good thing to be able to see them enjoy it," she says.

This is especially so since the vast majority of Marta's customers are not the sort likely to turn up in the pages of *Cigar Aficionado* or talking on cell phones at Nat Sherman, where the business class slavishly plunks down $13 apiece for Monte Cristos, Cohibas, and other Dominican-grown knockoffs of the famous Cuban brands. These suspenders-wearing junior brokers and their walk-in humidors almost killed cigar smoking as a regal, if stinky, bad habit in the Big Apple.

Thankfully, none of these foul airs sully the dense smoke inside PB Cuban. Here, all cigars—be they robusto, corona, or perfecto—are $5 or less, a suitable price to the minions of the Flower District, one of the few remaining local trade neighborhoods in midtown, a blue-collar stomping ground for Jamaican bus drivers, Bangladeshi computer repairmen, and Ukrainian electrical contractors with vivid memories of the day Chernobyl melted down.

"People come in on their lunch hour and relax for a moment," Marta reports, remembering the day she first decided to bring a couple of metal-frame chairs from her apartment on Twenty-first Street and set them up on the linoleum floor between the cigar display case and the storefront's neon-lit plate-glass window. Martha soon began brewing up potent, thickly sugared espresso, which she serves free of charge to her customers in thimble-sized plastic cups. A coatrack was soon installed, so customers need not sit about in their heavy outer garments. Should a lunch-hour regular care to bring a bit of Scotch to accompany his corona, Marta cleared a shelf. Now perhaps a dozen bottles sit there bearing handwritten labels, such as ALAN'S—NO TOUCH.

How the couch in question arrived under the water-stained ceiling at PB Cubans is "a funny story," Marta says. Seems that one of her "good customers," Andrew DeForrest, formerly of southern Tipperary and currently an installer of midtown-office-building bathrooms, happened to be passing his lunch hour in his preferred manner, letting his mind go while puffing on one of PB Cuban's "brilliant" robustos.

"Nothing could be better," says DeForrest, an impressively huge man known for carrying a five-inch curved blade on his ample belt. One day it occurred to DeForrest, whom Marta refers to as "Mr. Le Florist," that however perfect life inside PB Cubans might be, it could still be more perfect.

"Martha," said DeForrest, "if you only had a comfortable couch here, I'd never leave. I'd live here and sleep on it."

Then, "like magic, with the words barely out of my mouth," DeForrest recounts, a man wearing a stocking cap stuck his head in the door of PB Cuban. "Hey," he said with a surreptitious hiss, "anyone wanna buy a couch?"

"How much?" replied DeForrest without pause.

"Twenty bucks," said the man.

DeForrest rose and went with the seller around the corner. A few moments later, DeForrest returned with the couch on his back, Paul Bunyan style. He set the couch against the wall to the right of the cigar case and sat down.

"This is a comfortable couch," DeForrest said in his manly brogue. "I think it might be the most comfortable couch in all of New York." With that DeForrest closed his eyes and slept for the rest of his lunch hour.

More than two years later, Marta's couch remains, exactly where DeForrest placed it. And true, it doesn't look like much. It is bulbous in the manner of a half-deflated blow-up doll, and its linty variety of fake Naugahyde is not recommended for prolonged contact with bare skin. But to sit on it! To sink into its squishy pillows! Perhaps it's the presence of swaying palm fronds outside the storefront window (this is the Flower District, after all), but sitting on Marta's couch, bathed in the pink-and-blue light of the PB Cuban neon sign, following the curl of smoke snaking from the end of a short corona is to be transported. As has been noted by a number of smokers, the awning of the gypsy fortune-teller next door offers "a true vision of the past, present and future—your choice." To sit on Martha's couch goes this several steps better, offering, for a nicotine-enabled moment, accessibility to all states, at the same time.

Today, a good group has assembled. Present is Tom the computer man, sad about breaking up with his girlfriend. DeForrest, back from Ireland, is here in his wide-brimmed outback hat. Chris the painter has come over from F.I.T. Steve, the stand-up comic, commandeers the left side of the couch. Recently, Steve got a job coaching public speakers. According to polls, Steve announces, public speaking is the third-greatest fear held by mankind, right behind drowning. "Incredible," he says. "People would rather be shot in the head than talk in front of a crowd."

For each regular, Marta offers both cheeks to be kissed and a cigar. In her canny, sphinxlike way, she knows everyone's particular passion.

This doesn't mean an occasional wrong number doesn't turn up. This afternoon, a beefy, cajoling man from Budapest brought discord to PB Cuban. Speaking in the hushed but insistent tones of a post Soviet black-marketeer, the man was under the impression that Marta sold "real Cuban" cigars, not this "Dominican crap which is not even worth smoking." Rudely declining Marta's offer of a cup of espresso, the Hungarian kept up this harangue, even disparging Enrique's impeccable rolling technique.

This was the last straw. One cannot simply enter Marta's pleasure salon and sling around this bullshit.

"Hey, shut the fuck up, Martha got the best cigars in New York!" screams Steve. "Better than your shit *Fidelista* Cohibas!" Several other regulars join in, holding up the honor of PB Cuban. It takes a lot to rouse a smoker once settled on Martha's couch, but this Hungarian has managed it. DeForrest has now joined the discussion, jacket thrown open to show off the pearl handle of his knife. No one here has ever seen the laconic Irishman mad, nor have they cared to. Eventually, the muttering Hungarian stalks out, much to everyone's relief.

The assembled smokers notice our hostess has a tear in her eye. She has been touched by this defense of PB Cuban. "I feel such a love from my good customers," Martha says, her hands upon the cigar case. "It is such a love I feel I do not deserve." But as anyone who has ever spent a blissful half hour sitting on Martha's couch, the most comfortable in New York, knows: of course, she does. All that love and more.

3

The Wounds of Christ

Nothing stirs the heart more than the possibility of the miraculous among us. Father Zlatko Sudac came from Croatia to the Bronx, and to Brooklyn, bearing the stigmata, the mysterious wounds of Christ. Or did he? From New York *magazine, 2002.*

"Which one is he," asked the seventy-year-old lady from Yonkers. "Near blind" seeing "only gray shadows," the woman was one of twenty-five hundred souls who had come to the Immaculate Conception Church in the north Bronx on this rainy, windswept evening, hoping to be healed.

"The one in the purple vestments," said the lady's companion, leaning on her cane. "The one who looks like God."

Truly, there was no mistaking the presence of Father Zlatko Sudac, who now sat in a velvet-covered chair to the right hand of the altar at the Capuchin Roman Catholic church. In his early thirties, the young priest from the island of Krk, off the Adriatic coast of northern Croatia, his long russet hair pulled tightly away from a parched, pasty complexion, thick brows arched above deep-set, mournful brown eyes, appeared as a vision of sorrow. Only moments before he had spoken of love, and the unsurpassed joy of ultimate devotion, but now everything about the body language of his frail frame, the way he alternatively rested his head in his spidery hands and craned his long neck so as to scan the crowded church, suggested an otherworldliness of suffering.

"Can you see *it*?" the half-blind woman asked her companion.

"Yes. On his head . . . I see . . . *a notch*," replied the second old lady, squinting hard behind her thick glasses.

This much was visible: an indentation perhaps an inch long, like a coin slot, in the middle of Father Sudac's (pronounced Soo-*dots*) wide, flat forehead. It very well could be, as many in the church commented upon, the horizontal plane of a Cross that, it is said, appeared on Sudac's brow in October of 1999. This was followed a year later by markings on the wrists, feet, and side, five in all, outward signs that the former philosophy student and Croatian soldier had received the *stigmata*: wounds corresponding to those suffered by Christ on the Cross.

In what has been a most difficult time for the Church, with seemingly another appalling headline of sexual and financial abuse every week, news of Father Sudac's stigmata has been greeted with both skepticism and a hopeful expectancy. The first widely accepted stigmatic since the revered Padre Pio (the Italian priest who will officially canonized this June), Father Sudac has become the hottest ecclesiastic ticket in town since his arrival in the New York area last fall. At the Immaculate Conception those unable to fit into the standing-room-only chapel huddled on the church steps where, in forty-degree weather, they listened to the three-hour mass through a loudspeaker. Two masses at Our Lady of Pompeii in Greenwich Village attracted upward of four thousand people. At St. John the Baptist in Paterson, New Jersey, fire marshals, fearful of the seriously overcrowded conditions, attempted to clear the room, leading one firefighter to grouse, "I'll run into any burning building, but throwing people out of mass? They don't pay me for that. . . . The man could be a saint, for chrissakes."

It was no surprise God had chosen this particular time, in the horrific wake of 9/11, to send a messenger like Father Sudac, said Patty Fioreillo, a thirty-year-old secretary who had driven from Peekskill to the Immaculate Conception mass. The world was a mess, Patty said, more so than we were willing to admit. People had deluded themselves into thinking the materialism of TV commercials, the rat race of work , and "me-first ethics" were the actual state of things. It was like the movie *The Matrix*, she said, where the consensus reality was generated by computers. "We, as human beings, have two choices," Patty said. "We can either accept the soulless here and now, and a lot of lazy people will do that. Or we can fight against it, try to be who we are supposed to be: those made in God's image."

"9/11 raised the stakes," Patty asserted. The terrorist attacks "punched a hole in the fake reality," she said, drenched from two hours of waiting in the rain to see Father Sudac. The battle wasn't between "political versions of Good and Evil the way Bush says." After all, Patty continued, what did someone like Bush know about Good and Evil? Goodness was Truth, Evil was lies—what the world needed wasn't more armies, killing innocent people. It needed messengers like Father Sudac, those "gifted in the Spirit."

The fact that Father Sudac was in the world, now, was "very hopeful," said Patty. "I pray for him, every day."

According to *The Catholic Encyclopedia,* compiled in 1912 and still a commonly used source, the first known receiver of the mystical stigmata was Saint Francis of Assisi, afflicted while in deep prayer inside a hut on Mount Averna in 1227. Suddenly, according to Felix Timmerman's re-telling of St. Francis's experience, "it was as if the heavens were exploding and splashing forth all their glory in millions of waterfalls of colors and stars." Inside the "whirlpool of blinding light" was "a fiery figure with wings nailed to a Cross of fire." It was Jesus Christ. His wounds were "blazing rays of blood" that pierced Francis's hands and feet with nails and his heart with "the stab of a lance." The fiery image, "like a mirrored reflection, im-pressed itself into Francis's body, with its love, its beauty, and its grief." Then, "with nails and wounds, his soul and spirit aflame, Francis sank down, unconscious, in his blood."

Sudac, whose wounds have been declared "not of human origin" by Vatican doctors at the Gemelli Clinic in Rome, has a somewhat less dramatic description of his holy affliction. It happened at "a friendly get-together in one family's house," the priest said in his only interview avail-able in English, adding only that events generated "a tremendous fear of the Lord" that "surpasses myself." Asked if he has pain from the Cross on his forehead, Sudac says, "It doesn't hurt me, except when I am in prayer, then I feel it pulsing. On first Fridays and other certain times, it's known to bleed and leak as though it is crying."

Sudac has also spoken of the other "gifts of the Spirit" he has received since his stigmatization. These include "levitation, bilocation, illumination, and knowledge of upcoming events." Bilocation is particularly "interesting gift," Sudac says. "You have the feeling you are in one place, but your heart and imagination are somewhere else." The priest says he didn't exactly know he'd been in two places at the same time until "some people had come forward and confirmed it all."

One would like to engage Sudac on these matters, to discuss how and why, as with other stigmatics, the skin around his wounds never blackens or putrefies. Or whether his stigmata smells "like roses and tobacco," as witnesses said Padre Pio's did. But this conversation will have to wait as Sudac, who speaks no English, does not give interviews to the American press. Nor does he display his wounds of Christ, save the "notch" on his forehead. Perhaps this is why the archdiocese is vague at best concerning Sudac. The only thing they'll say is, "Father Sudac is a priest in good standing."

Asked if Sudac's refusal to display his wounds created any doubt in his mind, Tom Robles, a postal worker from Flushing, says no. "The Vatican says he's legitimate. I go with that. I am a man of faith. If I didn't have faith I couldn't believe in anything. Then where would I be? Where would any of us be?"

This was the general opinion of many of the people standing in Bronx rain waiting to get inside Immaculate Conception Church. Gathered across the street from Dunkin' Donuts and the burger joint called Sloppy Buns are bus drivers, maintenance men, manicurists, teachers, and retirees. Many of the seekers were born in Croatia, but others hail from the Philippines, Mexico, Russia, Korea, and all of Latin America, wherever souls have been touched by the historical reach of the Roman Catholic Church, wherever the black-robed missionaries and armored clank of conquistadors strode with Scripture and sword. Standing with the faithful, you hear the usual

New York Babel, five languages going at once. But this will soon change, says Tom Robles. Soon another tongue, transcendent of national origin and neighborhood, a language of the heart, will be spoken tonight inside the church.

It is something he found in his reading, Tom says: that stigmatics, due to their unique relationship with God and Christ, can somehow "communicate with each other through meditation across the ages." Since so many stigmatics have been declared saints, that means, Tom supposes, Father Sudac will not be alone in saying mass tonight. "Saint Francis will there too. . . . Saint Francis, and Saint John of God, and Saint Catherine of Siena and Saint Catherine de' Ricci, and Saint Clare, and Padre Pio too. Saints from six hundred years ago, right here, on Gunhill Road in the Bronx."

"No church is big enough for Sudac now," says Father Giordano Belanich, the fifty-three-year-old pastor of St. John's Church in Fair View, New Jersey, an industrious if slightly scruffy home to several thousand Croatian and Latin immigrants a few miles south of the George Washington Bridge. Born in the Adriatic town of Mali Losinj before fleeing the Tito regime with his family as a young boy, Father Gio, as he is called, has been charged with the responsibility of "looking after" Father Sudac during his stay in the United States. An amply proportioned man with a stern, down-to-earth manner that gives him a Karl Malden waterfront cleric aspect compared to Sudac's Montgomery Clift etherealness, Father Gio acts as the stigmatic's interpreter. He stands beside the younger priest during mass translating his sermons into both English and Spanish, a language Gio has mastered recently so as to better serve his largely Latin flock. Father Gio also arranges Father Sudac's schedule (he's been in Kansas City, Vermont, and Louisville in the past couple months) and compiles long lists of e-mailed "healing petitions," which he prints out for Sudac to bless en masse.

Looking after Father Sudac was becoming "a full-time job," said Father Gio, who has plenty to do already with his regular pastoral duties and running Croatian Relief, the organization he founded 1991 to provide spiritual and material aid in the wake of the ruinous Yugoslavian war. But Belanich was not complaining. God's work was God's work, plus, he said, with a sly smile, it was "always like that with these mystics, they're so much trouble."

This was because, Gio said, people like Sudac were not like everyone else. They were under "a lot of stress." On one hand everyone wanted to see them, seek their counsel and blessing; on the other hand, they needed repose, time for introspection. In an urban setting, with so many needy people, this created a serious management problem, said Father Gio. Maybe once Saint Francis could talk to the birds without interruption, but that was eight hundred years ago, before faxes requesting interviews were piling up on the desk. Prophets were no longer free to sit in caves to receive divine revelation. They tended to be "confused young people like other young people." People with "special gifts" needed to be "kept in line," lest they "lose focus, fall prey to distraction." Already Sudac has had to move out of the rectory house in Fair View, to some "undisclosed" place in the metropolitan area. His whereabouts are not discussed. Father Gio personally drives him to masses around the City in his Toyota Avalon with the Croatian flag hanging from the rearview mirror. When the mass is over, Sudac, Elvis-like, leaves the church immediately.

As a Croatian, he had some knowledge of the handling of potential saints, Father Gio said, in an offhand way. Croatia has had a long history of millennialism. Medjugorje, a village on the Bosnian border where in 1981 several students reported a visitation from Mary, Mother of God, is one of the foremost Christian pilgrimage spots in the world. (Indeed, for around $2,300, Gio could sign you up for a five-day summer retreat in Medjugorje, including air, hotel, and an audience with Father Sudac.)

But there was also a temporal aspect. "Things are bad now in Croatia," Gio said, as we sat in the stark white kitchen behind his office, with its shelves full of china cups decorated with Balkan coats of arms. "As bad as the war was, we knew things would get worse once Ted Koppel forgot who we were. World crises are like that. When you are at the top of the news, relief comes in. Then, you are forgotten and on your own. Our economy is very bad now. People are depressed, the suicide rate is very high. Perhaps

God recognizes such things. Perhaps that is why we have Father Sudac now."

Asked what sort of fellow Sudac was, on an everyday basis, Gio cocked his giant Easter egg–shaped head and said, "Oh, I'd say he's pretty normal." What did this mean? Did the stigmatic like to watch the Croatian soccer team in the Olympics? Did he like to laugh, sharing Father Gio's stated belief that "God is a great comedian, sitting up there in His rocking chair, making fun of the mess we make for ourselves?" Was he a pragmatic and an activist like Gio, who was driving a forklift truck in street clothes when we first met, moving relief supplies he planned to send to Bolivia and El Salvador?

Father Gio shrugged. "I am not here to tell you that he is a regular fellow. These people, they are not like you or me, or the guy you might run into in the next pew or at the corner bar. . . . Let's say he spends a lot of time in his room thinking about the Eucharist."

When talk turns to skepticism and why Sudac does not display the wounds, however, Father Gio grows testy. "This is why I can't stand the media. I read in the newspaper, 'Sudac *claims* to have the stigmata. He doesn't *claim* to have it. He *has* it. That's what people don't understand about Father Sudac. He is not a rock star. He is not a television actor, something stupid like that. The devil is alive in this world and Sudac, being full of God's love, is a weapon, a special weapon, to fight against the enemy."

A week or so later, another two thousand or so people wait in another rainstorm, trying to get inside St. Athanasius Church on Bay Parkway and Sixtieth Street in Bensonhurst, where Father Sudac will conduct mass. In an article in the Brooklyn section of the *Daily News* titled "Abuzz Over Stigmata Priest," St. Athanasius monsignor David Cassato expressed concern over the size of the turnout. Consequently, the cops have shut down Bay Parkway, snarling traffic for blocks around.

"Hope, I feel a lot of hope," says a woman in her fifties, wearing a black dress and high heels. Her daughter, who has cancer, is undergoing chemotherapy. She had a picture of the teenage girl, taken at the beach in Bermuda. She planned to hold the photo up for Sudac to bless, but fears the church will be filled by the time she gets to the front of the line and she'll have to watch the mass on closed-circuit TV from the school auditorium on the other side of the street. "I got to make eye contact. If I make eye contact, then I know Father will pray for me."

"This is really something," remarks an older Italian woman, who says her mother once saw Padre Pio near Naples. "Now I get my turn. . . . I am so excited." The woman's sons, both Wall Street workers who still live in the neighborhood, are less convinced. "Let's just see, Mom," says one. "Let's wait and see. You don't know who he is, if he's for real."

"Yes, I do," says the woman.

Inside the church, a '50s modern-looking place without a choir or any of the medieval ambiance the soul hungry *tourista* of such occasions craves, Father Gio is translating Father Sudac's sermon. Sudac, usually quite soft-spoken and conversational, is raising his voice, screaming in Croatian, sounding almost like a Baptist or Pentecostal preacher.

"Don't look into politics! Don't look into ideologies! Don't look into magics!" Sudac shouts, a roar of urgency in his voice, Father Gio following him with matching fervor, a mighty, rising call and response. "Don't look into spiritism! Don't look into Santeria! Don't be afraid of the Truth! Don't be afraid of sin! There is no sin! Jesus Christ died to banish sin from this world! Open yourself! Leave yourself open. Make room in your heart. Then He will come in there. He will come *real fast!*"

Sudac, who usually does not allude to the stigmata in his sermons, now draws attention to it. Speaking in a tone of harsh rebuke, he says, "You have heard of me, you know who I am, perhaps that is why you are here . . . but that is the *only* reason, you must think again. Look to the giver, not the gift. Come for Christ, not for me."

Then, quieter, almost inaudibly, he went on. "I am a young priest. Only thirty-one, which is very young for a priest. But I am not so young not to see that many crazy things go on in this world. Things beyond explaining. Does it matter if I am a saint? I don't think so. Only Jesus matters."

With that, Sudac slumped down in a thronelike chair to the right of the altar. For a moment there was a hush in the room as Sudac, seemingly spent, took a Kleenex from his vestments and wiped his eyes.

"He's crying," said a young girl, in a voice that could be heard for several pew rows around. Several flash cameras went off. Visibly angry, feeling that "the infernal snapping" demeans the Spirit, Father Gio rises in protest. "This is not a show! Not a circus!" he yells. Yet, you wonder, why not take Sudac's picture? Last year, in Chicago, someone took a snapshot in which Sudac appears to be transparent. A few days later, the shot was all over the Internet.

Now, in the strobing light, you could watch Sudac, hone on his wan, almost desperate-looking face. A few days earlier I called up a priest friend who also practiced as a university psychologist. What would he do, I asked, if someone had come into his office bearing the wounds of Christ. "Well," the priest said, "as a psychologist I'd probably give him the Minnesota multiphasic test and then treat him as a hysteric . . . as a priest I'd pray for him. Pray hard. Because I'd think, *better him than me.* God chooses who he wants. But in the end, what really matters is: does it help people, make their burden in this life any lighter? If this Sudac is stigmatic, or if people just think he is stigmatic, does it matter?"

At St. Anthanasius's, however, rationalities and doubts could be discarded. For a moment it was possible to stop trying to see if the sleeves of Sudac's vestment were about to blot red from wounds made by "blazing rays of blood." His face, mournful, tortured, was enough. You knew, whatever anyone else might think, *he* believed it.

Moments later, Father Sudac was holding the monstrance, the sun burst–shaped symbol of Eucharist in front of his face, walking through the church, blessing the faithful. One by one, people reached out for him as he walked down the aisle, some falling back into their seats after touching his robe. Then he walked out into the rainy night, across Bay Parkway, to bless those who couldn't fit inside the church. The cops formed a corridor through the crowd for Sudac and Father Gio to pass. The lights from police cruisers swept across the slick streets, reflecting off the golden monstrance in front of Sudac's face. He looked electric, on fire. For the moment a Brooklyn block, as prosaic as any Brooklyn block, was transformed, lifted from the everyday.

People surged toward Sudac. Two men pushing a wheelchair barged through the crowd, the tires running over an older woman's feet.

"Father! Father! Our brother! Bless him!" the men screamed to Sudac, indicating a teenage boy in the chair. The boy was crippled, his dense black eyes crossed. The boy had been paralyzed since he was born, the men shouted. "A stroke . . . a stroke since birth," the men declared in heavily accented broken English. One reached over the police line and grabbed Sudac's garment.

"You have the stigmos!" the man yelled. "Bless him. We are Greek! Bless him! He has always been like this! Please, Father . . . *the stigmos* . . . help him . . . there is nothing else that can be done! Please!"

Father Sudac turned and, Eucharist in front of his face, bowed once, turned both left and right, and walked on. Immediately, the men, now crying, kissed the boy in the chair. "He blessed you," they weeped. "Now you have hope."

One of the men sprinted after Father Sudac, again reaching for his garment. Falling to his knees, the man said, "Bless you, Father. *Bless you.*" Whether Father Sudac, afflicted of the wounds of Christ, heard this was hard to tell. He just kept walking, into the night.

4

Zombies in Da Hood

When I first wrote this piece, it sat around for a while because it was sup-posed to go in the "culture" section and the editor felt it "had nothing to do with culture." What's culture then, I yelled, "spending fifty dollars to see Mark Morris dance around?" This exchange did not do wonders for our relationship. From New York *magazine 2005.*

The usual Saturday afternoon merchants lined the sidewalk across 125th Street from the Apollo Theatre: the shaved-ice lady, the roots-and-incense dealers, the Senegalese peddlers of ersatz Rolexes. Also there was the zombie, machete protruding from the side of his bullet-hole gouged head. An invader from Brooklyn, the zombie was in sell mode, lurching toward passersby, product in hand.

"*Dead Roses!* Independent film! Shot in Brooklyn! Not a bootleg! *Dead Roses!*" the zombie droned, his voice muffled beneath several pounds of latex and stuffed cotton. "*Dead Roses!* Only ten dollars!"

A chunky shopper with headphones slapped on her ears strolled by, blissfully oblivious to the urban tumult. She never saw the bum-rushing zombie.

"*Dead Roses!*" the zombie grunted, shoving the DVD box in the shopper's face.

"Ahhhh!" the shopper shrieked, dropped her plastic bags, and ran down the street.

The zombie followed. "Wait, lady . . . wait! I'm not a real zombie! I'm only a *promotional* zombie!" The woman kept running, into the crowd.

This was the downside of direct marketing, allowed Robert McCorkle, the director and writer of *Dead Roses*, almost certainly the most ornately plotted full-length zombie movie ever shot exclusively on location in the housing projects of Bedford-Stuyvesant. (Hence the film's tagline: Brooklyn Has a New Evil!!!) Until recently a financial analyst's assistant cooped up in a cubicle at a Midtown investment-banking firm, it has always been the ambition of McCorkle, a thirty-five-year-old monster movie freak, to make his own "epic horror films . . . you know, that end-of-the-world stuff with millions dying." Alas, McCorkle's budget was decidedly less than epic (it was, as he says, "less than indie, it was sub-sub indie"). This was a problem since even if rappers producing their own discs in their bedroom and selling them out of the back of a car are a dime a dozen these days, a brother making his own movie, with his own money, was a whole other, much more complicated affair. For one thing, you needed a camera, which McCorkle did not have. And you needed to know how to operate that camera, which McCorkle only kind of did. You also needed a distribution method, which is what the foray to 125th Street was about. As McCorkle says, his layers of latex starting to peel, "Who better to sell a zombie movie than a zombie?"

Then again, as an auteur of street cinema, McCorkle's *mise-en-scène* has never been less than gung ho. "People told me, all the zombies needed was a little talcum powder on their faces," says McCorkle, who personally designed and applied all the film's makeup. "To me a zombie isn't a zombie unless he's decayed. Putrefied. Mutilated. All messed up. Totally fucked. I mean, they're *dead*, right? So I taught myself how to put this stuff on, from reading *Fangoria* magazine and on the Internet. Just because we're low-budget doesn't mean it can't be realistic—at least movie realistic."

Whether or not *Dead Roses* is movie realistic—or at least *Plan 9 from Outer Space* realistic—depends on how you look at those kinds of things.

Shot and edited in digital video for $6,000 over a year's time, the film has pithy dialogue that's occasionally inaudible, an unsettling obsession with dismembered body parts, and lighting that goes blooey every so often. But *Dead Roses* is still imbued by a defiant sense of the verisimilitude.

"*Night of the Living Dead* in the projects? Now that's a concept I can get behind," said *Dead Roses* producer and star Johnathan Tucker when he first met McCorkle at the aforementioned banking firm where Tucker ran the mailroom. Having grown up in Bed-Stuy wanting to be an actor—and having acquired some street cred for an (uncredited) part in the pioneer hip-hop film *Krush Groove*—Tucker, a large-voiced guy with a rakish look and demeanor, had tried writing for TV and taken several film-production classes. But he was frustrated.

"I had that pay-bill frustration, that work-at-Home-Depot-on-the-weekend frustration. Robert changed that. He was kind of quiet around the office, kept to himself. I didn't know what to make of him at first. But we got to talking. He's kind of what you'd call a dreamer. Head in the clouds. Really out there, man. He told me about *Dead Roses* and I said: *Yeah, screw the system. Do it ourselves.*"

Sharing McCorkle's fervor for slasher/sci-fi/horror movies, especially the moment when Linda Blair's head does that 360 thing before spitting up a pint of pea soup in the first *Exorcist*, Tucker, a thorough-going pragmatist who spent ten years selling real estate in Park Slope, recognized the zombie genre as exceedingly budget-friendly. "What you need, in the end, is a bunch of screwed-up-looking people stumbling around with their hands held out in front of them."

"We shot mostly at night," Tucker recounts. "A lot of it was done at the low-rise project where Reevse Bobb (*Dead Roses'* cowriter and cinematographer) lives near Boys and Girls High School. We got the zombies from the neighborhood. We saw people hanging out and asked them, 'Hey man, you want to be a zombie?' They'd stand there for a while and then say, 'Huh?' We say, 'you're perfect.'

"Robert wanted each zombie to be unique, you know, with their own distinctive running sores and stab wounds. So it took a while for each of them to get made up. After an hour or two these street guys would have, like, five pounds of junk on, and they'd begin asking, 'Hey, what I'm getting paid for this?' We'd tell them, 'Well, nothing.' Some got testy and start yelling, 'You put all this shit on my head and I ain't getting paid?' We told them they could have points. On the back end. That shut 'em up.

"All sorts of strange stuff happened. We had a scene with fifteen zombies and wham, our generator blows out. I convinced this old lady to let us run an extension cord through the window. Robert says, 'Action,' and the electricity goes out again. I ran up to the lady's apartment and her granddaughter is standing there with the cord in her hand looking really pissed off. She just got off the swing shift cleaning office buildings and pulled the plug. She's screaming, 'You'll not be stealin' my grandma's 'lectricity!'

"Another night, we were doing this scene where a bunch of zombies get their head blown off with sawed-off shotguns. I guess maybe we should have done it indoors, not out on the street. It's like two in the morning and these people are hanging out the windows. This guy was yelling, *they're blowing the fuck out of zombies down there*. They thought it was real. Then, out of nowhere, these cop cars are coming up from every direction. Lights. Sirens. The whole deal. They got their guns drawn, spread-eagling us against parked cars. Then one of the cops is pointing at the street and says, 'What's that?' I told him it was brains.

"'Brains?'

"'Zombie brains.'

"Now there's six cops with their guns out at Troy and Decatur, looking at a pile of fake brains. We were using beef fat from the Spanish butcher's. One of the cops is knocking at the fat with his foot. It kind of oozed. I thought he'd lose it right there. Finally they told us to get a permit and left."

It is no small tribute to cross-cultural, semiprofessional horror-fan mania that *Dead Roses* came out more than watchable—way more watchable, say, than Melvin Van Peebles's *Sweet Sweetbacks*. McCorkle has a way with cheesy FX, and Tucker's final confession of remorse (he plays the gang leader who has wronged the heroine) is kind of touching, at least until he's ripped apart, limb from limb, by a gaggle of underfed zombies.

But creation is only the outset of art. It must be brought to the market-place. "We weren't exactly going the Sundance route," says Johnathan Tucker, unloading a stack of DVDs from the back of his Chevy Tahoe in front of the Target department store on Flatbush Avenue. Business is brisk; in an hour, Tucker and McCorkle (sans makeup this time) move sixty "units," for a total of near twelve hundred now. "Keep this up and we'll be in profit soon enough," says Tucker.

Just then a guy in a Nissan Pathfinder comes wheeling around the corner near the Williamsburg Savings Bank building. "Saw the movie, man!" he shouts. "Scared the shit out of me!" Watching the Nissan head down Atlantic Avenue, the filmmakers agreed, you couldn't ask for a better review than that.

5

Chairman of the Money

Charlie Rangel has been Harlem's representative to the United States Congress for the past thirty-six years and counting. This is the story of the dean of New York delegate's most impeccably American journey. From New York magazine, 2007.

When Charlie Rangel, DeWitt Clinton High School dropout, first became a congressman from Harlem in 1971, beating the iconic Adam Clayton Powell Jr. by 150 votes, he would drive to Washington from his home on 132nd Street and Lenox Avenue in a beat-up Buick. "It was cheaper," says Rangel in his quarry-pit voice. But mostly Rangel has flown the shuttle. Figuring how many times he'd made the trip, Rangel said multiply 36 (the years he's been in office) times 52 times 2 (round-trips per week). From that, subtract the time Congress wasn't in session. Still, it's a lot of flights. But never had Dan Rather risen from his window seat to greet him.

"Mr. Chairman," Rather said, with a slight nod of the head.

This is how it is for Charlie Rangel post-11/7, since the Democrats won Congress and the seventy-six-year-old Harlem rep became the chairman-to-be of the House Ways and Means Committee, a body usually prefixed by the adjective *powerful*. Delineated in the Constitution, the committee has the power "to lay and collect taxes, duties, imposts and excises, to pay the debts," that is, Ways and Means is where the deals are cut on taxes, borrowing funds, Social Security, and control of trade and tariff legislation.

In other words, Rangel rasps, "the money."

The Chairman of the Money tends to be a popular guy. Then again, Charlie Rangel has always been popular in Harlem, where many residents have never known another congressman. What is now called the Fifteenth District has been represented by exactly two men since 1945—Rangel and Powell. Asked if this was democracy, two guys in sixty-two years, Rangel honks, "The people know what they want." Rangel has been reelected seventeen times, usually with more than 90 percent of the vote. Since "the chairmanship," however, on One-Two-Five Street and up in Dominican Washington Heights (Hispanics make up 46 percent of the district now), wherever Charlie shows up, silvery hair swept back, iris shock tie and pocket handkerchief matched up just right, he is shown an extra helping of love.

"People come up to me saying, 'We did it, we finally made it,'" reports Rangel, who's been on Ways and Means since 1975, the last ten excruciating years as ranking member of the minority Democrats. "It's like the whole neighborhood's moving up."

Ride with Rangel for a few days and congratulations come from every angle. They're lining up to kiss the outsize green opal ring on his finger. One minute State Assembly strongman Shelly Silver is calling him "my great friend, one of our own . . . whom we can trust to do the right thing." Then Mickey Kantor, former U.S. trade representative, is on the phone. Congrats on the chairmanship, says Kantor, and, by the way, maybe Rangel might want to talk a bit about U.S.-China trade relations? Mary Landrieu, senator from Louisiana, adds her good wishes, but what about that offshore-drilling bill?

And here comes Hillary, charging down the buffed hallways of the Capitol Building, with a hearty "Mr. Chairman!" Just the other day, Rangel ate breakfast with the senator in Harlem. Rangel figures he'll overlook Hillary's early prowar stance. "If I swallowed John Kerry, I can swallow that," he says. Rangel (who told Barack Obama to "go for it if you want; if you don't, you'll wind up hating yourself") doesn't think Rudy Giuliani's running ("He's just building up his billings") but hopes he does because "it'll be fun, kicking the crap out of him."

The whiplash over the power shift from lily-white Houston boardrooms to Sugar Hill has only begun. The other day, men from Pfizer dropped by Rangel's 125th Street office. "He just wanted to say hello," Rangel recounts. As for those nasty details about drug pricing ("gouging," Rangel calls it) and exactly how the new chairman—a harsh critic of the status quo "health-care disaster"—was likely to view the role of big-time pharmaceutical companies, well, that was another conversation.

"I've got so many new friends these days," Rangel says with mock amazement.

Rangel's new status was clear enough during the recent dustup over the draft. Appearing on *Face the Nation*, Rangel kept to less sexy Ways and Means issues, like the alternative minimum tax currently draining middle-class 1040s. As Charlie Rangel performances go, it was fairly uneventful. At no time did Rangel call Dick Cheney "a son of a bitch" or suggest the vice president check into "rehab [to deal with] whatever personality deficit he may have suffered." Nor did Rangel, as he did following Hurricane Katrina, refer to George W. Bush as "our Bull Connor," a man who "shattered the myth of white supremacy once and for all." Then host Bob Schieffer asked Rangel if he still believed in reinstating the draft.

Military conscription has little to do with Ways and Means, but Charlie Rangel, the most canny of loose cannons, has never been one to underplay his hand in a big spot. "You bet your life," said Rangel, who has long opposed the volunteer army, saying politicians would think twice about starting wars if their own children had to fight them.

Rangel told Schieffer: "If we're going to challenge Iran and challenge North Korea and then, as some people have asked, to send more troops to Iraq, we can't do that without a draft. . . . How can anyone support the war and not support the draft?"

The reaction in the blogosphere and every other "-osphere" was loud and unanimous: Rangel was bonkers. The limp liberals of the *New York Times* editorial page, haven to who knows how many recipients of 2-S college deferments, said a draft would not achieve the aim of making "the armed forces more equitably representative of American society." The chicken hawks of the right wing lambasted Rangel's assertion that the military was inordinately composed of "people who can't get a job doing anything better." There were plenty of potential Rhodes scholars and Hardee's CFOs slogging through the Iraqi sands, angry radio voices declared. To suppose otherwise was downright unpatriotic. As a testament to Rangel's runaway moonbatism, commentators pointed out that when he introduced his draft bill in 2004, it was defeated 402 to 2.

"Rangel didn't even vote for his own bill!" complained an eye-rolling Dick Cheney to Fox News' Sean Hannity. (Rangel says he voted nay to protest Republican procedural finagling.)

Rangel, who has that raised-bushy-eyebrow *who me?* thing down pat, purports to be "flabbergasted by the fuss" caused by his draft statements. "I've been talking about this for years and no one paid attention. I guess that's the power of the majority."

Gee, you think?

A world-class press hound, Rangel was soon wall-to-wall on the tube. "I want to push the debate, make them think about what exactly war means," says Rangel, with the assurance of a man whose position on the issue has been impeccable for the past fifty-six years, ever since November 30, 1950, which was when he found himself, along with forty or so other members of the all-black 503rd Field Artillery Battalion of the Second Infantry Division, hunkered down in a foxhole near the Yalu River.

"We had these ten thousand crazy-ass Chinese coming down on us," recalls Rangel. "All I could hear was bugles, screams, and gunfire. Dead, bloated bodies were everywhere. Guys' toes were falling off from frostbite. I thought we were deader than Kelsey's nuts. The Chinese dropped leaflets saying they were colored people like us, and when we got back to the States we weren't going to be allowed to swim in pools in Miami Beach and how could that be worth fighting for?

"In a situation like that, you don't think about saving the world from communism, you think about surviving," says Rangel, who despite shrapnel wounds managed to lead several soldiers to safety, for which he got the Bronze Star and Purple Heart, both of which now sit on a shelf in his

125th Street office. "People who haven't been in war don't understand what a difference a wrong step here, a bad decision there makes. . . . That's the question in Iraq. How long can you wait? By tomorrow it's gonna be too late for someone. It is a matter of time . . . time running out."

It makes sense that time would be on the mind of someone past his seventy-sixth birthday, even a workaholic (sixteen tightly scheduled hours per day is routine) who looks fifteen years younger and plans to keep going forever. Rangel gives you his happy-warrior line about how he's "never had a bad day" since getting out of that foxhole, but he admits to feeling "the claustrophobia" of time. He says the chairmanship "couldn't have come any later for me."

Fact is, if the Democrats hadn't won this time, Rangel would have retired. It would have solved a lot of problems; his wife, Alma, had been after him to stop for years. Mostly, though, "I couldn't take it anymore, how the Republicans were running things. Someone like Tom DeLay has no interest in legislating. He just wants to push through policy. This wasn't the Congress I'd grown up in. The House of Representatives was being destroyed right in front of me. Sending people to prison camp without trial, wiretapping without warrant. This was another kind of America. I didn't want to be part of it."

Word that Rangel might quit sent a chill through Harlem. It isn't that he doesn't have his rivals. The Reverend Calvin Butts, who has Adam Powell's old job at the Abyssinian Baptist Church, has sniped at Rangel for years, once calling him "a timid politician" willing to "settle for crumbs." But no one wanted to see all that seniority (some might say pork) go down the tubes. Local papers ran pleading headlines: BROTHER CONGRESSMAN! DON'T GO!

A thoroughgoing secularist, rare among old-school black politicians in not bearing the honorific "Reverend" (his Catholicism once had Harlem Baptist ministers debating whether he should even be allowed to speak from the pulpit), Rangel has greeted the Democratic victory as tantamount to being born again. "For me, it's a reprieve. My grandfather told me about seeing people getting lynched, how it haunted him, thinking what he could have done about it. I didn't want to have my grandchildren ask, 'What did you do when the Constitution got ripped up?' and have to answer, 'I quit.'"

So there he is, getting called Mr. Chairman, living what he calls "my honeymoon," which figures to go on through the first week of the 110th Congress. That's when, Rangel says, "The clock will start ticking again. We got two years to turn things around." It is, as Rangel says, "a short fuse."

Once it seemed as if Charlie Rangel had all the time in the world. "Growing up in Harlem, I didn't think much about the future. My father left when I was six. I was just drifting around." Indeed, it isn't hard to find Harlem codgers willing to boast, "Charlie Rangel? *Shit.* I used to take his lunch money." The army changed that. "When I came out of the service in 1952," Rangel says, "I had so much self-esteem."

Back home, however, was not all that different. "I had a hundred jobs. I worked in a drugstore. The Adler Shoe Store. Sold vacuum cleaners." He also worked down in the garment center, where he had the epiphany that set him on his life path. "I was unloading a truck, and these boxes fell out, spread all over the street. This cop came over and said, 'You better clean that up, boy.' I started picking up the boxes, and I'm thinking, *I'm pretty sick of this crap.* I thought I'd reenlist, go back into the army. Then I thought to myself, '*No.* I'm Sergeant Charles Fucking Rangel. *Who are these people to treat me like this?*'"

Rangel went back to high school, at age twenty-three. He took a job-aptitude test that indicated he'd make a swell mortician, a classic race-based track for black men. Rangel's response was "Screw that." He used the GI Bill to pay for school, getting his degree at NYU in three years, then enrolled at St. John's law school. Becoming a lawyer seemed logical.

"The most important person in my life was my grandfather," Rangel relates. "He was an elevator operator at the court buildings downtown. He wore a neat uniform and was always talking to men in slick suits. I got the idea that being a lawyer or a judge was the most magnificent thing a human could do. It was funny, though, when I told my grandfather I was going to be a lawyer; I thought he'd never stop laughing."

He put himself through school as a desk clerk on the night shift at the Hotel Theresa, sometime home to Joe Louis, Sugar Ray Robinson, Duke Ellington, Jimi Hendrix, and Moms Mabley. Moms defended Rangel when he was caught reading his law books on the job. "Let the boy study," the old chitlin-circuit comic snorted. Rangel was at the Theresa when Fidel Castro came to the U.N. after the Cuban revolution. "They said he got thrown out for plucking chickens in his room, but I never heard about that," says Rangel, a longtime opponent of the U.S. embargo of the island. Once, meeting with Castro, Rangel said the United States might see things differently if he held "free and fair elections." Castro said he did have "free and fair elections."

"But you get all the votes," Rangel said. Castro replied, "Don't *you?*"

Rangel started his career as an assistant U.S. attorney in the Southern District. Later came a term in the State Assembly, which set him up to run against Adam Clayton Powell Jr. in what remains the most pivotal election ever held in Harlem.

"I knew Charlie could beat Adam; all he had to do was listen to me," says former Manhattan borough president and Ur-Harlem businessman Percy Sutton, who along with Basil Paterson and David Dinkins and Rangel (who calls Sutton "my mentor") formed the so-called Gang of Four, young-Turk Harlem politicians chafing under Powell's increasingly erratic suzerainty.

"In the beginning I called him Pretty Boy Rangel, to denigrate him, because he was one of those handsome types, hair pushed down and that mustache. But he had a way about him, with that great humor, an ability to influence people," recalls Sutton, who, like Rangel, lives at the Lenox Terrace apartments, Harlem's revered power address. (As a young pol, Rangel was summoned to the Terrace apartment of the aging Bumpy Johnson. Harlem's most famous gangster wanted to look at the new guy in town. "He said I looked okay and I left, fast," Rangel says.)

"Adam was a great man, but he didn't understand the new Harlem," Sutton continues. "He went down to Wyatt Tee Walker's church on 116th Street and condemned Martin Luther King Jr. That's when I knew he was slipping, ego getting the best of him. We told Charlie to go down to Selma to march. When he came back, we said here's the man who wears the orange vest of courage, which is what the marchers wore. . . . Adam thought it was all in the bag. How could anyone beat him?"

Dead since 1972, Powell still casts a shadow. Rangel's office is in the Adam Clayton Powell Jr. State Office Building. In a 1994 primary, Adam Clayton Powell IV, running almost exclusively on his father's name, held Rangel to a spindly 58 percent. Not that you'll ever hear Charlie Rangel utter a bad word about Adam Clayton Powell Jr. He says, "I keep the faith, always, baby."

Ask Rangel how come it seems like every black politician in New York is another politician's son or daughter, and he cackles. "I call that the 'no child left behind' school of politics. . . . My mother was a seamstress, there was no family business to go into." So he rolls on, secure in his mottled skin, the self-made wise old head, dean of the delegation. "Talking to Charlie is like getting the lottery numbers early, because if history repeats itself, who's seen more history than him?" says state assemblyman Ruben Diaz Jr., one of those politicians' sons.

Retirement talk aside, Rangel never gets tired of being the congressman from Harlem. "I've always lived in Harlem. Never wanted to go anywhere else." The most cosmopolitan of neighborhood guys (he can be seen cruising down St. Nicholas Avenue at the wheel of his own car, sans a single bling-encrusted bodyguard), Rangel says he's never wanted any other office. Standing in front of the Capitol Building, he says, "Couldn't be a senator—going all around the state, talking to farmers, taking pictures with pigs and cows? Forget that." Likewise, he's never been tempted to be mayor. "Staten Island? No."

All this raises the question, if Rangel really is Harlem, and vice versa, what's he really done for the uptown ville in his long tenure? The answer to this is a matter of perception. During the dope plagues of the seventies and eighties, Rangel was on the front lines of the *farkakta* war on drugs, chairman of the congressional committee on narcotic abuse. He visited South American countries, made tough-love speeches, set up programs. Yet 125th Street was still overrun by crack. Despite much legislation aimed at job creation, unemployment in his district remained among the highest in the country. After years of talking about upgrading neighborhood schools, now he says he's "all but given up on public education. I see no relationship between what our kids get in school and the ability to make a life for themselves."

Detractors—hard to find these days—say Rangel's legislative activism is really "a cover," since no one ever solves massive sociological problems like drug use and unemployment. "It's a failure-proof, no-blame situation for him," says one close observer. "He can always say, 'Look, I'm only one guy. What do you expect?'" Others disagree. "In Harlem, you're always going to have your cynics—people who say he's done nothing, he's only in it for himself. But that's wrong," says Kenny Knuckles, head of the Upper Manhattan Empowerment Zone, part of the $500 million infusion of public and private capital that has changed the face of Harlem in the past few years. "Charlie Rangel wrote the empowerment legislation. He made it happen," says Knuckles.

Argue all you want whether a new condo development on every block, Home Depot, and latter-day white hipsters getting off the A train at 145th rank with Countee Cullen and Minton's Playhouse when it comes to a Harlem Renaissance. Gentrification is a citywide conundrum. Why should Harlem be any different? There's some irony that Rangel, a link to an earlier, more flamboyant uptown, will be remembered as a prime mover of this shinier, corporate version. It is a legacy that will no doubt preclude the rise of another Charlie Rangel, the new Harlem figuring to be full of competing power interests, not the sort of place that elects the same guy for thirty-six years.

Rangel says, "Housing prices are a problem. But its better than boarded-up buildings. Everything changes. Harlem will stay Harlem."

Rangel's ardor for his uptown vote bank was on display at a recent holiday turkey giveaway held by the Martin Luther King Jr. Democratic Club. In the interests of decorum, you had to sign up in advance. There was to be no walk-up largesse. Told this, a grizzled man in a Florida Marlins baseball cap and using a golf putter as a cane said, "I can't have no turkey?" Since he'd lived in Harlem all his life and always voted Democratic, he felt entitled. Hearing Rangel would be there, the man scoffed.

"Oh, Mr. Draft," he said. "That's the stupidest fucking thing that ever came out of that man's mouth." The guy said being in the military was the worst experience of his life and anyone who advocated "sticking a gun in a young man's hand" was "sick in the head." He'd tell Rangel exactly that, too, straight to his face.

When the congressman arrived, the man engaged him in animated conversation. Later, standing behind a table piled high with bags of Arnold herb stuffing, Rangel said there was a man outside who'd signed up for a turkey but his application was unfortunately lost. The man had a sick mother to boot. The guy in the Marlins cap came in, got his turkey. Clutching cans of cranberry sauce, he turned to say it was "his valuable military service" that earned him his holiday dinner. In the army, he said, "they teach you to speak up for yourself." Informed of all this, Rangel could only smile and shake his head.

Today, in the final throes, so to speak, of the 109th Congress, it is moving day at Rayburn, the House office building. Hallways are lined with desks and chairs. "Losers' furniture," says a mover, pushing a "Republican watercooler" on a dolly. Rumpled features pushed forward like the hood ornament of an old DeSoto, Rangel trundles through the electoral detritus without comment. He sees no reason to rub it in.

Not that Rangel didn't allow himself "a period of gloating." This largely centered on his plan to "repossess" H208, an office traditionally used by the Ways and Means Committee but loaned out by the Republican majority to Dick Cheney. Eschewing sending an exterminator to give the place a quick spray, Rangel says he decided to "be gentle as I restore the dignity of that office. . . . But still: When you gotta go, you gotta go."

Rangel says he's tired of Democrats standing around with goony looks on their faces, "pinching themselves" to make sure the Wicked Witch is really dead. The other day, when his colleagues from the Congressional Black Caucus, the group he helped found, cheered his ascension to chairman, he was heard to say, "Knock it off already."

"The election's over. We won," he says. "Let's do business."

In 1975, when Rangel switched from the Judiciary Committee to Ways and Means, Charles Diggs, a thirteen-term black congressman from Detroit, said he was nuts. "He said no one ever leaves Ways and Means, that I'd be a freshman for thirty years." After just a few years, however, through some unexpected attrition—including longtime chairman Wilbur Mills's being caught in the midst of an affair with stripper Fanne Foxe—Rangel found himself the committee's third-ranking Democrat.

"Only Sam Gibbons and Jake Pickle were ahead of me," Rangel recounts. He didn't become the ranking Democrat until 1996, after Newt Gingrich's Contract With America. It has been a decade of fronting an increasingly marginalized minority.

The past six years, sitting beside Republican chairman Bill Thomas, have been particularly vexing. Hearing that Thomas had once been named the House's "meanest" and "second brainiest" man in a poll of congressional aides, Rangel says, "Right on both . . . All those years, he never once asked me for a vote. He did everything he could to stifle debate and the democratic process in general." Plus, Rangel says, "the man has no personality. None."

The animosity came to a head most infamously in July 2003, when, as Rangel puts it, "Thomas called the cops on me."

As Rangel tells it: "Thomas came in with a revision of this giant pension bill. A big thick thing. He says we're going to vote on it. I said we haven't even read it, how can we vote? He said too bad. . . . I told my guys, that's it. We went into the library, said we weren't coming out until we were done reading. Thomas went bananas. He said if we didn't get out of the library he'd call the Capitol Police, which he did. The sergeant at arms knocked on the door and said, 'I'm sorry, but it seems as if the chairman has called the police.' He says you're trespassing. We looked at him like you must be kidding."

Days later, citing his "poor judgment," Thomas tearfully apologized on the House floor. "I felt bad for him," Rangel says. "I didn't think he was going to cry."

It was a lot of heavy water under the bridge, Rangel says as he passes through the Capitol Hill tunnels to 1100 Longworth, the Ways and Means hearing room. It's a trek Rangel has made thousands of times over the years. But this one is different. This is the last hearing of the 109th Congress, the final time Rangel would sit in the smaller leather chair directly to the left of Thomas's big one.

"Hey, Charlie, just don't let the door hit him on the way out," says a woman in the elevator. The fact that she's a Republican bears out Rangel's contention that many in Congress, conservatives included, are pleased autocrats like DeLay are gone, that people are sick of thinking of the opposing party as mortal enemies.

"You'll see," Rangel says, turning to the woman. "I'll be nicer than you'd think."

As far as Rangel's concerned, the restoration of civility is part of his job as chairman. "Most of the younger people in Congress have never experienced working in a bipartisan way," he says. Just the night before, he attended a party for Nancy Johnson, one of the five Ways and Means Republicans who lost in the election. Clearly touched, Johnson said, "One of the worst things about losing is not getting the chance to work with you."

Mr. Congeniality stuff aside, the Hill is abuzz as to what Rangel will do as chairman. Far more of a policy wonk than most suspect, often burning the midnight oil studying arcane trade packages, Rangel can be expected to fight off any dead-ender Republican action on Social Security privatization. He will also push for a repeal of Bush's tax cuts. Asked if he thought any of the cuts deserved to be renewed, Rangel said, "I can't think of one." This doesn't mean the business community sees no silver lining in Rangel's rise. A recent story in the neo-con *Weekly Standard*, "Harlem Globetrotter," detailed Rangel's fondness for free trade, making the case for him as a "pragmatist," a "deal-maker," and potential closet globalizer.

What being chairman will do to Charlie Rangel is something else again. People talk about how he'd better watch his back, that Cheney and henchmen like Alberto Gonzalez are likely doing a fine-tooth job to see what dirt they can find on him. "Let them look," Rangel says. In 1999, New York State attorney general Dennis Vacco charged Rangel and old pal

Percy Sutton with financial malfeasance and mismanagement of the Apollo Theatre. Vacco's successor, Eliot Spitzer, exonerated Rangel, with the proviso that he remove himself from the board of the Harlem landmark. This aside, few accuse Rangel of being in it for the money. Rangel's more concerned about "my routine." Known to run his office like a fifties City Council member, Rangel says he'll be a little less hands-on. "Someone else will have to return all these calls."

Job one is filling the committee with people he likes, that is, as many New Yorkers as possible. "I'll try this on an equity basis," he tells some power trader on the phone. "If not, I'll make it happen politically." In other words, down in the trenches. Whatever, it works. Rangel got Queens County leader Joe Crowley on the committee, the guy he wanted all along.

A chairman has to multitask, Rangel explains. To wit: He begins telling a story about how he was working in his office one night when Jorge Mas Canosa, leader of the anti-Castro Cuban American National Foundation, showed up unannounced. Mas Canosa told Rangel it might be healthier if he gave up his opposition to the Cuban embargo. "What are you implying?" Rangel wanted to know.

Rangel is interrupted in mid-story. Costa Rican president Óscar Arias Sánchez has arrived with a large entourage.

"Mr. President!" Rangel shouts, greeting Arias and his ministers. A farreaching discussion of U.S.–Costa Rican economic relations ensues, including much talk about the Central American Free Trade Agreement, which Rangel voted against. A half hour later, after calling Rangel "one of the most powerful people on the globe," Arias leaves. He's barely out the door when Rangel picks up the Mas Canosa story exactly where he stopped.

However it goes on Ways and Means, depend on Rangel to be in charge. Case in point was a recent Capitol Hill breakfast for the New York congressional delegation with then governor-elect Eliot Spitzer. Chuck Schumer was extolling Rangel as "a straight shooter," saying how proud everyone was that "Charlie had finally reached the promised land," when Rangel, impatient to start the meeting, let forth with an eardrum-rattling whistle. "Now," he shouted, in Sergeant Rangel mode.

"He also can whistle really loud," Schumer added, skulking off to his seat.

Rangel's last hearing in the minority—on Medicare payments for "end-stage renal disease"—goes off without incident. Acknowledging that it's outgoing chairman Thomas's birthday that very day, Rangel says he wants the record to show that "regardless of what many may think," he has "never had an unpleasant conversation with Bill Thomas, *outside this room.*"

Later, Rangel is still in the now-empty 1100 Longworth. It is a large, impressive room hung with portraits of former Ways and Means chairmen. Some, like Wilbur Mills (1957–1974) and Dan Rostenkowski (1981–1994), served a long time, then went down in flames. Others like Harold Knutson, Republican of Minnesota (1948–1949), are largely forgotten. James K. Polk, Millard Fillmore, and William McKinley became president. Now the portrait of Charles B. Rangel, Democrat of New York, will join them.

"Never had my portrait painted before," Rangel croaks. His likeness will, of course, be the first of a black man to adorn the stately walls of 1100 Longworth. Noting that a number of other Americans of color, old colleague John Conyers and Brooklyn's Nydia Velasquez among them, would be chairing committees in the 110th Congress, Rangel says he is "honored that the descendants of slaves might have their chance to restore the Constitution in this great nation of ours during this time of need."

To sit in the big chair at the front of 1100 Longworth, where he's spent so much of the past three decades, seems a fitting end to Rangel's particular American journey. Looking around, he says, "I've always thought this was a beautiful room."

DOWNTOWN

6

Is This the End of Mark Zero?

A saga of the artist in a landscape of brutal change. What will a man do to save a life's work? From New York *magazine, 1998.*

Mark Zero, street video artist and filmmaker, was asleep at his girlfriend's house in Williamsburg two Saturdays ago when the call came from Rockets Redglare, noted downtown personage. Rockets said something "really bad" was happening at 172 Stanton Street, the century-old Lower East Side tenement where Mark Zero has resided for the better part of the past decade. The place was swarming with cops. Fire engines were everywhere. They were evacuating the building.

This didn't seem particularly strange to Mark Zero—*nom de art* of Mark Friedlander. Something was always wrong at 172 Stanton Street. The place was a pit. Hot water was intermittent, the pipes leaked nonstop. In winter torrents of cold air flew through rotting window frames, in summer it was a sweatbox. But when you live the Art Life, especially on the outskirt occupied by Mark Zero, a rough edge or two is to be expected. Indeed, Mark Zero, thirty-five, whose father expected him to be a doctor when he was growing up in Harrisburg, Pennsylvania, felt he'd be happy enough to live the rest of his days in the fourth-floor walk-up at the corner of Stanton and Clinton.

"It was home, if you can understand that," he said.

Before Mark Zero arrived that Saturday night, Mayor Rudolph Giuliani had already been to 172 Stanton Street. Standing in the snow, Rudy assured everyone not to worry, things were well in hand, public safety issues were being addressed. This did not appear to be the case as far as Mark Zero could see. Many of his longtime and (mostly) well-loved neighbors—the elderly Mr. Kleinkopf, twenty years a waiter at Ratner's on Delancy Street; the Bangladeshi family upstairs; the Spanish people from down the hall—were standing out in the freezing cold, many of them crying. Officials from the City Department of Buildings had issued a "vacate order" for 172 Stanton Street, declaring it an unsafe structure.

Years of shoddy maintenance and the previous night's two and half inches of freezing rain had taken its toll. Former home to untold numbers of Lower East Side immigrants (the address is mentioned in Jacob Riis's famous tome of the dispossessed, *How the Other Half Lives*), 172 Stanton Street had seen its last sunset. No more matzo balls would be boiled on stove tops here, not another plantain would be fried under the harsh light of a fluorescent ring, never again would a junky would climb up the fire escape to steal a rabbit-eared TV. The tenement was ordered to be torn down that very day. Orange-outfitted demolition crews were already on the scene.

Commanded by Jerry Hauer, the flinty-eyed head of Office of Emergency Management, City officials promised residents they would be allowed in the building one last time to retrieve their possessions and pets. Then, suddenly and without explanation, the City's position changed. No one would be permitted back into 172 Stanton. The building would be torn down immediately.

This is when, Mark Zero said, he began to lose it. "Everything I had was in that apartment. My entire archives, fifteen years of shooting videos and film on the streets of New York. Twenty hours of documentary footage from the Men's Shelter on Third Street, a hundred party shoots. All my paintings, my screenplays, a thousand songs I wrote, my guitar, albums full of family photographs of old Nazis I found in East Germany. Who knows how many autopsy photos. Everything! My entire life's work."

Mark Zero tried to explain this to the cops on the scene, but they wouldn't listen. They told him to get back, for his own safety. "My own safety!" Mark Zero exclaimed. "You knock down that building without letting me get my stuff, you might as well be killing me right here and now. Go ahead, take a gun, shoot me. It'll be the same thing."

When the cops just looked at him "like I was fucking crazy," Mark Zero said he had no other choice. He waited until no one was looking and slipped into 172 Stanton Street. "I ran up the stairs, trying to decide what to do," he recounts. "I had this giant duffel bag in the closet. I had to figure out what to save and what to leave. I had to be organized. To triage. I knew I couldn't get all. Top priority was the edit masters of my most recent work and my cameras. Except when I got into the apartment, everywhere I looked was something that meant a lot. Something I created out of nothing. It was like some totally sick TV show: you know, you've got like three minutes, what out of an entire existence do you save?

"Then I heard this really loud noise. Like: *bam!* The whole building shook. I looked out the window. They had this giant machine out there, with a big metal ball. *A goddamn wrecking ball right outside my window, coming right at me*. I figured I had two choices then. I could stay quiet and hope the ball didn't hit me. That way I could save some more stuff. On the other hand, I thought, well, I could die. They could cave the place in on my head. So I went to the window and started screaming, *Stop! I'm in here!*"

A few hours after the cops from the Seventh Precinct hauled Mark Zero away on criminal trespass charges for unlawfully entering his own building, 172 Stanton Street started to come down. Demolition crews worked through the snowy yet strangely thunder-and-lightning-filled Saturday night. Lit by huge vapor lamps, plumes of water arching across the narrow street, it was quite a sight, in a Dresdenesque sort of way. Apartment after apartment in the five-story tenement was chewed open by a low-slung triceratops-looking device called "the rake." Bathrooms with archaic pull chain toilets were crunched to dust. Grayish looking walls bearing dozens of coats of paint and crucifixes tumbled. Who knew how many people had lived in those apartments, from what countries they'd come from, what hopes, dreams, and disappointments they'd harbored?

Then the machine got to the fourth floor, in the back, where the plaster was hued electric green, purple, and orange. This was Mark Zero's apartment. The numerous paintings still hung on the walls were scooped up with the rest of the debris and tossed into a massive dumpster, to be hauled off to a landfill on Varick Avenue in Brooklyn.

Two days later, 172 Stanton Street is a fenced-off vacant lot. Splayed out on the street like a low-rent thieves' bazaar is a pile of "recovered" items: a few pair of water-logged pants, a flattened cassette player, a 1993 Playboy calendar, a stack of old *Cue* magazines. Mr. Kleinkopf's canceled checks flutter in the breeze. Meanwhile, at the Lotus Club, a faux-beatnik café diagonally across from where his home once stood, Mark Zero sits sucking on a Winston Light. Making clear he isn't comparing his situation to the loss suffered by the poor, now-homeless families of 172 Stanton, Mark Zero reports himself to be "totally devastated, emotionally and physically, absolutely in a daze."

He is also angry. "They're saying the building collapsed, like it just keeled over and died. You saw what they had to go through to knock the place down. It took all day and night. There were guys up there with sledgehammers on the roof. What were they doing up there if the building was supposed to be so unsafe? I was in there, it didn't seem any worse than usual to me. That building did not fall down, it was dragged down."

This being the Lower East Side, where (wholly justified) paranoia concerning every beady-eyed landlord's gentrification plans strikes deep, there has been much talk about who decided to pull the plug on 172 Stanton Street and why. There have been several instances of buildings coming down in similar fashion of late, as if late-night condemnation is one more typically heavy-handed Giuliani administration method of so-called urban renewal.

For sure, someone's gonna get sued. But Mark Zero says no settlement, however large, can make up for his loss. "I'm a collector. I keep everything, even old tapes off my answering machine, you know like Herbert Hunke calling up saying, 'Like, fuck off, asshole.' How do you put a dollar value on that?"

Every minute he winces, remembering another irreplaceable item. "My letter of recommendation from Allen Ginsberg, my signed copy of *Tulsa*, footage of Stiv Bator's last show. If I'd only gotten another ten minutes in the apartment before they started knocking it down . . . I could have saved a lot. A whole museum got buried in that building."

There have been black moments since the building's demise, times when he contemplated that "this might be the end of Mark Zero," but the artist finds himself strangely buoyed. Running into 172 Stanton as the wrecking ball flew might well turn out to be his greatest single statement. "Can't top it for performance art. It shows what I'll do," he notes, with a mournful pride. 172 Stanton might still have an artisitic function, Mark Zero says. The blank wall might make an excellent canvas for a video installation. Some footage of Rudolph Giuliani "with flames around his head" would fill the space nicely.

Mark Zero decides he needs some more Winston Lights, so he gets up and moves toward the Lotus Club door, intending to go over to the bodega across the way, like so many times before. "Shit," he says, stopping. The bodega, open very late, used to be so convenient, right there on the ground floor of 172 Stanton Street. Now that's gone too.

7

Ghost Shadows on the Chinatown Streets

The compelling saga of Nicky Louie, leader of the Ghost Shadows youth gang, which for a brief and bloody time in the 1970s ruled about two hundred yards of sidewalk in New York City's Chinatown. A thousand years of history crushed into an immigrant story. A personal favorite. From the Village Voice, 1977.

Midnight in Chinatown, everyone seems nervous. The old waiters look both ways before going into the gambling joint on Pell Street. Ladies bleary from a ten-hour day working over sewing machines in the sweatshops are hurrying home, and restaurants, usually open until four in the morning, are closing early. At the Sun Sing Theatre on East Broadway, underneath a hand-painted poster of a bleeding kung fu hero, a security guard is fumbling with a padlock. Ask him how business is and he shakes his head, "No good." Ask him why and he points his finger right between your eyes and says, "Bang!"

"Low Tow," which is what the Cantonese call New York's Chinatown, is on edge. A couple of blocks away, in front of the coffee shop at 56 Mott Street, Nicky Louie, the twenty-two-year-old leader of Chinatown's currently most powerful street gang, the fabulously monikered Ghost Shadows, looks no less relaxed. Pacing up and down the ruddy sidewalk in his customary green army fatigue jacket, Nicky has good reason to be watchful. It is only Wednesday, and according to the cops, there have already been two separate assassination attempts on Louie's life this week. Facing such heat, most gang leaders would stay inside and play a few hands of Chinese thirteen-card poker. Or maybe leave town altogether, go up to Toronto or out to Chicago. But not Nicky. When you are the leader of the Shadows, with so much money and turf at risk, it is a matter of face to show your face. You've got to let them know—all those other twenty-two-year-old killers—that Mott Street is yours. Yours and yours alone.

Born Hin Pui Lui in the slums of Hong Kong's Kowloon district, Nicky came to Low Tow in the late 1960s. The old Chinatown people called America "Gum Shan," which means Gold Mountain. But Nicky arrived on a 747 rather than a boat and is a different kind of immigrant. Older neighborhood residents might be content to work out their tiny sliver of the so-called American Dream serving up bowls of *yat kaw mein* to Queens tourists, but Nicky had different ideas. No way he would end up a faceless waiter ticketed for the TB ward. He was born for greater things. When he got into the gangs half a dozen years ago, first as a foot soldier in the penny-ante protection rings, selling firecrackers to the undershirt-clad Italians on the other side of Canal Street, people say Nicky already had the biggest set of balls in Chinatown. He was the gun-wielding wild man, always up for action, willing to do anything to get attention. His big break came in the winter of 1973, when the Shadows' first chief, twenty-four-year-old Nei Wong, got caught with a Hong Kong cop's girlfriend. The cop, in New York for a surprise visit, ran across Wong and his betrothed in the Chinese Quarter Nightclub beneath the approach ramp to the Manhattan Bridge and blew off both their heads with his police revolver.

Since then Nicky's rise in the Chinatown youth gang world has been startling. He has piloted the once ragtag Shadows from the bleak days when they were extorting a few free meals and dollars from the greasy spoons over on East Broadway to their current haunt, Mott Street, Low Tow's main drag, in other words, the big time.

Controlling Mott Street means that the Shadows get to affiliate themselves with the On Leong tong, the richest and most influential organization ("tong" means association or organization) in Chinatown. In addition to securing the protection racket on Mott, the gang also gets to guard the gambling houses the On Leong operates in the musty lofts and basements along Mott and Bayard streets, some of them taking in as much as $75,000 a week. The Shadows also act as runners in the Chinatown Connection heroin trade, bringing the stuff across the Canadian border and spreading it throughout New York. The money filters down to Nicky and his lieutenants; they, in turn, spread the spoils to the younger Shadows.

For Nicky this adds up to a weekly check that ranges from $200 to $2,000 depending on who you talk to. In any event, it's enough to buy a swift $7,000 Peugeot to tool down Canal Street in.

But tongs are fickle. If another group of Hong Kong teenagers—say their archenemy White Eagles or the hard-charging Flying Dragons, who bide their time taking target practice on the pigeons down by the East River—should show the On Leong that they're smarter or tougher than the Shadows, Nicky's boys could be gone tomorrow.

No one knows this better than Nicky Louie. Two years ago Nicky and the Shadows pushed the surly Eagles off the street. In September, after licking their wounds over in Brooklyn and down in Florida, the Eagles with their leader Paul Ma—Nicky's main rival—returned. And they were not going to be satisfied with crummy Elizabeth Street. Soon the Eagles started appearing on Bayard Street, part of Shadowland. Paul Ma set up his own gambling house on the block, a direct affront to Nicky.

Several weeks ago the Shadows struck back, shooting a bunch of Eagles, including Paul Ma and a gang member's wife, in front of Yuen Yuen Snack Shop on Bayard Street. This set off the most hair-raising month of street-fighting in Chinatown history; no weekend went by without a major incident. The infamous Wong Kee chop-chop was the highlight of the war. According to cops, the Shadows, including Nicky himself, crashed through the door of the Wong Kee Rice Shop on the Italian end of Mott and carved up one Eagle with chef's kitchen cleavers and stabbed another with a fork.

Everyone figures the Eagles will try some kind of revenge, which is the major reason, people say, Nicky has spent the past two weeks pacing up and down in front of 56 Mott. His presence keeps things cool. In the long history of Chinese crime, a saga that goes back at least to the founding of the thousand-year triad 14K, Nicky Louie is the newest legend. He is, as they say, no one to fuck with.

Fifty years ago, chances are Nicky might have been lying around the "joss houses" and streetfighting alongside the hatchetmen and gunmen of Chinatown's "tong wars." In those days, the two big tongs, the On Leong and the Hip Sing of Pell Street, battled on the sidewalks over the few available women, the opium trade, and out of sheer boredom. Back then there were legendary *boo hoy dow* (warriors): like Mock Dock, the great gambler known as "the Philosophical Killer," and Yee Toy, "the Girl-Faced Killer." Most famous of all, however, was the plain-faced Sing Dock, "the Scientific Killer." Once, after hearing of an outbreak of war in New York, he rode in the baggage compartment of a train (Chinese weren't allowed to ride up front) for six weeks from San Francisco. That was when Pell Street was called "Red Street" and the crook on Doyers Street was known as "the Bloody Angle."

Today the Chinatown warrior has changed. The young gangs are not respected tong members, as Sing Dock was. Like most late-twentieth-century gangs, they're in for the bucks and the fact that none of them can figure out what else to do with their lives, especially considering the dismal choices confronting those entering the fiscal crisis job market with little or no English-language skills. There is also the whole style thing. Nicky and the Shadows have eschewed tong warrior black overcoats in favor of pegged pants and puffy hairdos. (Asked if their hair is a Hong Kong fashion, one gang member said, "No, man, it's cause we dig Rod the Mod, man." Meaning Rod Stewart.) In this world everyone must have a good nickname, a *nom de street guerre*. Hanging with Nicky tonight are old-time Shadows "Mongo," the wild-man enforcer who got his name from *Blazing Saddles*, and "Japanese," who shaved his head after he heard that things might go easier for him in jail if he looked like a "Muslim." There are some guys with grade-B movie monickers like Lefty and Four-Eyes, but most of the kids go for names like "Stinkybug,"

"White-Faced Tiger," "Pointy Lips," "Porkupine," and "Nigger Choy." There must be twenty kids called "Apple Head" running around Chinatown.

Strangely enough, the Ghost Shadows themselves got their unbeatable name from that bastion of street culture, the *New York Times*. It happened about four years ago when the Shadows were functioning as the "junior auxiliary" of the now-defunct Kwon Ying gang of Pell Street. A *Times* reporter was in Chinatown to cover an incident in which some of the young Kwon Ying were involved. The reporter wanted to know what "Kwon Ying" meant. (It means "not the Eagles," a reference to the rival gang, the White Eagles.) One wiseguy—likely an Eagle—said, "It means ghost shadow." This, unbeknownst to the *Times* reporter or just about any white person, was a terrible insult. Proceeding from the metaphor that a bamboo stalk is empty in the middle, Chinatown residents have long called white people *bak guey*, meaning a white piece of empty bamboo, or, more derogatorily, a "white ghost." Blacks are called *hak guey*, meaning "black ghost." The gist is that these people are incomplete—not all there. Being a "ghost shadow" went double. The *Times* reporter dutifully filed "ghost shadow" with his copy. The next morning, after reading about themselves in the paper, Nicky Louie and the rest of the Ghost Shadows decided they liked their new name. It was so born to lose.

Yet through all this posturing nomenclature, Nicky has no nickname. He remains, simply, Nicky.

Some say Nicky has nine lives. The estimates of how many slugs he carries around inside his chest vary. According to an ex-gang member, "When he turns over at night, he can hear them bullets clank together."

Last May teenage hit men from the San Francisco–based Wah Ching gang flew across the country just to kill Nicky. Some say it was an Eagle contract. For whatever reason they pumped a dozen bullets into the middle of a Saturday afternoon shopping crowd on Mott Street while Nicky disappeared across Canal Street. The Chings missed everyone and wound up getting pinched by two drug cops who just happened to be eating won ton in the nearby Joy Luck Restaurant.

The *ging cha* (police) have arrested Nicky for everything from robbery to extortion to murder to rape, but he's never been convicted.

Detective Neal Mauriello, who is assigned full-time to the Fifth Precinct's Chinese gang section, is a smart cop. He realizes he's got a crazy
and hopelessly complicated job. Chinatown gangs aren't like the bruisers
fighting over street corners and ghetto reps up in the Bronx. There's piles
of money and politics behind what Nicky and his guys are doing. And since
it's Chinatown, they'd rather do it quietly—which is why the Shadows don't
wear dungaree coats with hard-on things like SAVAGE SKULLS emblazoned
on the back.

Neal makes it his business to memorize all the faces on Mott Street. He
also writes down the names and birthdays of the gang members so he can
walk down Mott Street and say, "Hey, happy birthday Pipenose; seen Dice
around?" This blows the gang members' minds, Mauriello says. "Because,
the world they live in, a Chinese guy is supposed to be invisible. They're
supposed to all look alike. That's what we think, right? Well, they know
that and that gives them a feeling of safety, like the whities have no idea
who we are. I try to break through that curtain. It freaks them out."

About Nicky Louie, Neal, with typical cop insouciance, says, "That kid
is okay really. But I've been chasing him for five years and I'll nail him. He
knows it, too. We talk about it all the time." Neal remembers the time
he came upon Nicky lying facedown in a pool of blood near the Bowery.
He said, "Nicky, come on, you're gonna die, tell me who shot you." Nicky
looked up at Neal, his eyes blazing arrogance, and said, "Fuck you."

"That's Nicky," said Mauriello, shaking his head with a smile, because
what else can you say or do when confronted with someone who lives his
ethic to the end like that? (Of course, Louie would survive his wounds and
be back on the streets within weeks.) It is more than that, because, as
Mauriello, from an immigrant culture himself, says, "That's not just Nicky
Louie, some kid gangster telling me to fuck myself. There's a lot of history
behind that 'fuck you.'"

Toy Shan is a village in the mountainous region of Canton from which
the great majority of those who settled New York's Chinatown came in
the mid-1800s. It's possible that this Toy Shan settlement in New York
was as closed a community as has ever existed in urban America. Much
of this is bounded in mutual racism, including the horrendous series of

"exclusion acts" that severely limited Chinese immigration to the United States for the better part of a century.

Probably the most draconian of these "yellow peril" fear laws prohibited immigration of Chinese women to the United States. Males were allowed, in small numbers, to enter the country to maintain existing businesses. But they could not raise families or live anything approaching a normal life. Chinatowns became essentially male-only gulags of indentured restaurant workers and the like. By the 1940s, when the laws finally began to ease, the ratio of men to women in Chinatown ranged as high as ten to one. The havoc these laws wreaked on the Toy Shan consciousness is difficult to overestimate. Drinking and gambling, both venerable Chinese passions, became endemic. Apart from the neighborhood gambling dens where one could lose a month's pay in an hour of fan tan playing, Chinese faces became familiar at the city's racetracks—probably the only place they were, outside restaurants and laundries—which prompted wags to dub the Belmont subway special "the Shanghai Express." Prostitutes from uptown were frequent visitors to Toy Shan back then. Chatham Square was one of the best nonhotel beats in the city. "The money's always been good down there," said one current lady of the night. "They come in, say nothing because they can't speak English, shoot their load, and go."

It was a society within a society, not that most of the Toy Shans were complaining. They were not eager to mingle with the people they called *lo fan* (foreign devils) in any event. Determined to survive, they built an extralegal society based on furtive alliances, police bribes, creative bookkeeping, and immigration scams. The aim was to remain invisible and separate. To this day, few people in Chinatown are known by their real names; most received new identities—such as the Lees, Chins, and Wongs—from the family associations, who declared them "cousins" in order to get them into the country.

In place of the "Western government," they substituted the Chinese Consolidated Benevolent Association (CCBA), an organization to which the neighborhood's sixty-five-odd family and merchant associations belong. To this day every other president of the CCBA has to be a Toy Shan descendant.

In reality, it was the tongs, Hip Sing and On Leong, Chinatown's so-called "night mayors," who dominated much of the economic and social power in the neighborhood. They controlled the illegal activities in a community where everyone felt outside the law. Their spokesmen, with hatchetmen behind them, grew in power at the CCBA. Between themselves, they struck a parity that still holds. On Leong has always had more money and connections, mostly owing to their ongoing relationship with Chiang Kai-shek's Kuomintang Party, which has ruled Taiwan since its expulsion from the mainland by Mao's victorious Communist army in 1949. The more proletarian-minded Hip Sing, which is known as "the friend of the seaman" for its ability to sneak Chinese off boats and into waiter jobs, has more members and branches throughout the United States.

But in 1965 the Toy Shan traditions were seriously threatened. Federal laws were altered to allow open Chinese immigration to this country. Since then more than two hundred thousand Hong Kong residents have emigrated to America, with more coming all the time. Half settled in the New York area.

Chinatown is in the midst of a gut-wrenching change. The population is edging toward seventy-five thousand, a fivefold increase since the law change. It's one of the fastest-growing neighborhoods in New York and without a doubt the most densely populated. Once confined to the familiar pentagon bounded by Canal Street, Worth, and the Bowery, Chinatown is now sprawling all over the Lower East Side. Already Mott Street—above Canal up to Grand, once solidly Italian—is 70 percent Chinese. To the east, Division Street and East Broadway, formerly Jewish and Puerto Rican, have become centers of Chinese business and residence. Chinatowns have begun to appear in Flushing, Queens, and parts of Brooklyn.

Transition is under way. On one hand a good deal of the old Toy Shan separatism remains. Most Chinatown residents do not vote; currently there are fewer than three thousand registered voters in the area. In marked contrast to the Asian community in California, no Oriental has ever held major office in New York. The Chinatown Democratic Club has been repeatedly busted as a gambling house. Chinatown activists say this neglect is responsible for the compromised stand in the zoning fight with the Little

Italy Restoration Association, which is seeking to ward off the Chinese in-flux and zone large portions of the area for the dwindling Italian population.

Yet changes are everywhere. Chinatown now functions for Chinese; it looks like Hong Kong. Investigate the brand-new Silver Palace Restau-rant on the Bowery—it breaks the mold of the cramped, no-atmosphere Chinatown restaurant. An escalator whisks you up to a dining room as big as a football field. Almost all the thousand or so people eating there will be Chinese, many middle-class couples who've motored in from Queens to try a more adventurous version of Cantonese food than this city is ac-customed to. (Many Chinese will tell you that the "exotic" Szechuan and Hunan food is "American" fare.)

The mass migration has transformed Chinatown into an odd amalgam of boomtown and ghetto. Suddenly half the businesses here are no longer in the hands of the old *lo fa kew*, the Cantonese Toy Shans. In their place have come Hong Kong entrepreneurs and Taiwanese investors, who are fearful about the future of their island. A Taiwanese combine, the Sum-mit Import Corporation, has already done much to change shopping habits in Chinatown by opening two big supermarkets, Kam Wah on Baxter Street and Kam Kuo on Mott.

The Taiwanese money is an indication that even though the National-ists appear on the verge of international political eclipse, their influence in American Chinatowns, especially New York's, is on the rise. A Taiwan concern is also behind the proposed block-long Golden Pacific National Bank on Canal Street. It's one of the several new banks opening in this neighborhood of compulsive savers. The gold rush, prodded by extraordi-nary greed, has pushed real estate values here to fabled heights as Taiwan-ese businessmen seek to hide capital in the United States. The defeat of South Vietnam, where Chinese interests controlled much of the economy, has brought untold millions into the local market. According to Mott Street scuttlebutt, the day Saigon fell, three Chinese restaurants were supposedly purchased in Chinatown. Tumbledown warehouses on East Broadway are going for Upper East Side prices.

All this has the Toy Shan powers hanging on for dear life. The new-comers, filtered through Hong Kong, come from all over China. The old

Toy Shan loyalties don't apply. These people got here without the help of the associations and owe them little. The tongs and the CCBA are beginning to feel the crunch. They've begun to see more and more store owners break away. Suddenly there are publicly funded social service agencies, most prominently the Chinatown Planning Council, to challenge CCBA rulings. And the younger Chinese, sons and daughters of the *lo fa kew*, have been openly critical.

But one hundred years of power isn't something you give up without a fight. Recently the CCBA held a meeting to discuss what to do about Nicky Louie and his Ghost Shadow buddies shooting up the neighborhood. Chinatown has traditionally been one of the safest areas in the city. Crime figures are remarkably low here for a place with so many new immigrants. That's what made the recent violence all the more shocking. Especially in a neighborhood so dependent on tourism. Although the battles were being waged among the various Shadows, Dragons, and Eagles around, merchants were reporting a 30 percent drop in business. Places that stayed open late were doing even worse.

The streetfighting is "disfiguring" Chinatown, said one merchant, referring to the April shootout at the Co-Luck Restaurant on the Bowery. That night, according to the cops, a couple of Shadows roared up in a late-model blue Ford, smashed through the glass door, and started spraying .32 automatic slugs in the general direction of some Dragons who were *yum cha* (drinking tea and talking) in the corner. One of the Dragons, who may not have been a Dragon at all, got clipped in the leg. For the rest of the people in the restaurant, it was grimmer. By the time the Shadows were through, they had managed to hit three New York University law students, a waiter, and a lady from Queens who later died on the floor, her daughter crying over her body. The cops said, "The place looked like a slaughterhouse; there was blood all over the linoleum."

Since then Co-Luck has been considered bad luck for prospective buyers. It remains vacant, rare in a neighborhood where no storefront is empty for long. On the door is a sign: CLOSED FOR ALTERATIONS.

"Perhaps we keep it that way," said a merchant, "as a scar to remind us of our shame."

Restaurant owners say there won't be so many wedding banquets this summer because of an incident in the Hung Gung Restaurant a few months ago. Gang members crashed the banquet hall, stationing sentries outside to make sure no one came or went, and instructed a hundred celebrants to drop their valuables into shopping bags. "It was just like the Wild West," says someone close to the wedding guests.

The police don't see things looking up. In October they made sixty gang-related arrests, the most ever in a single month. They say there are more guns on the street than ever before and estimate gang membership—before the recent crackdown—at about two hundred, an all-time high. The gang kids are younger, too—fourteen-year-olds from Junior High School 65 are common these days.

Pressured by editorials in the Chinese press, the CCBA lurched into action. It called a public gathering at which the community would be free to explain its plight to Manhattan district attorney Robert M. Morganthau.

This was quite a change in tactics for the CCBA. Until quite recently one of its major functions had been to keep the lid on Chinatown's considerable and growing urban problems. The fact that Chinese women sew garments for twelve cents apiece, that more than one-third of the area's males work as waiters (toiling as much as sixteen hours a day, seven days a week), that Chinatown has the highest rate of TB and mental illness among city neighborhoods—all that was dirty linen better kept under wraps. But Nicky and the Shadows, they make noise. They get picked up for killing people and get their sullen pictures in what the Chinese still call "the Western press." Keeping that quiet can make you look awfully silly, such as when Joseph Mei, the CCBA vice president, told the *New York Times*, "We have no problem at all about youth gangs in Chinatown," the day after Nicky's people allegedly shot five White Eagles in front of the Yuen Yuen Snack Shop.

The meeting was held in the CCBA's dank auditorium (underneath an alternating string of American and Nationalist Chinese flags). Yut Yee, the seventy-year-old CCBA president, who reportedly has been known to fall asleep during meetings, was unusually awake that night. He said, "Chinatown will become a dead city" if the violence continues. He urged residents to come forward and "report cases of crimes: We must be witnesses." This seemed unlikely, for in a culture where the character for "revenge" means literally "report a crime," the act of informing tends to be a complicated business. This confuses and angers the *lo fan* cops, who say that even though just about every restaurant in Chinatown has been robbed or extorted from in the past few years, the incidence of reporting the crimes is almost nil. Despite the fact that gang members have been arrested for more than a dozen murders in Manhattan, there has been only one conviction: that of Yut Wai Tom, an Eagle who made the mistake of putting a bullet through the throat of a Shadow in front of a couple of Puerto Rican witnesses.

Morganthau sighed during the debate of Chinese businessmen, looked at his watch, said he'd "help," and left. By this time, however, many people were openly restive. "My God, when will this bullshit stop?" asked a younger merchant.

No one talked about the tongs and their relationship to the gangs. How could they? Of the seven permanent members of the CCBA inner voting circle, one is the On Leong, another the Hip Sing. No wonder people tend to get cynical whenever the CCBA calls a meeting at which the tong interests are at stake. Perhaps that's why, when a Chinese reporter asked what the D.A. was planning to do to help the community, one of Morganthau's people said, "What do you want? We showed up, didn't we?"

But, if you wanted to see changing Chinatown in action, really all you had to do was watch Benny Eng. Benny is director of the Hip Sing Credit Fund (which drug cops figure is a laundry room for dirty money). He is also an officer of the Chinese-American Restaurant Association, an organization that deserves blame for keeping waiter wages in Chinatown at about fifty dollars a week for the past twenty years.

As people entered the CCBA hall, Little Benny—as he is called, in deference to Big Benny Ong, the old Hip Sing bossman recently arrested while sneaking out of the tong's venerable gambling house at 9 Pell Street—greeted everyone with a grave face. "So happy you are interested in the security of Chinatown," Little Benny said. But later, after the meeting, Benny, now attired in a natty hat and overcoat, could be seen nodding respectfully to the skinny-legged honcho pacing in front of 56 Mott Street.

Part Two

A pockmark-faced guy who nowadays spends ten hours a day laying bowls of congee in front of customers at a Mott Street rice shop remembers the day the White Eagles, the original Chinatown youth gang, ripped off their first *cha shu baos* (pork buns).

"It was maybe ten years ago. We were hanging out in Columbus Park, you know, by the courthouse, feeling real stupid. Most of us had just got to Chinatown. We couldn't speak English worth a shit. The *juk sing* (American-born Chinese, a.k.a. ABCs, or American Born Chinese) were playing basketball, but they wouldn't let us play. We didn't know how to anyway. I remember one of our guys said, 'Shit, in Hong Kong my old man was a civil servant—he made some bread. Then he listened to my goddamned uncle and came over here. Now he's working as a waiter all day. The guy's got TB; I can hear him coughing. And I ain't got enough money for a goddamned *cha shu baos*.'"

Even then the *juk tuk* (Hong Kong–born Chinese) were sharp to the short end of the stick; they looked around the Toy Shan ghetto and sized up the possibilities for a sixteen-year-old immigrant. The chances had a familiar ring—what the tourists call "a Chinaman's chance," which, of course, is no chance at all. There might be moments of revenge, like lacing a *lo fan*'s sweet-and-sour with enormous hunks of ginger to watch his lips pucker. But you knew you'd wind up frustrated, throwing quarters into the "Dancing Chicken" machine at the Chinatown Arcade. You'd watch that stupid Pavlovian-conditioned chicken come out of its feeder to dance and you'd know you were watching yourself.

So the eight or nine kids who would become the nucleus of the White Eagles walked up the narrow street past the Italian funeral parlor and into the pastry shop, where they stole dozens of *cha shu baos*, which they ate—and got so sick they threw up all over the sidewalk.

Within the next week the Eagles got hold of their first pieces—a pair of automatics—and began to terrorize Toy Shan. They beat the daylights out of the snooty ABCs, who were just a bunch of pussies anyway. They ripped off restaurants. They got tough with the old men's gambling houses.

It seemed so easy. In Hong Kong, try anything shifty and the cops would bust up your ass. They would search an entire block, throwing pregnant women down the stairs if they got in the way, just to find a guy they suspected of boosting a pocketbook from the lobby of the Hyatt Regency. Here the cops were all roundeyes—they don't know or care about Chinese. Besides, the old guys kept them paid off. The fringe benefits included street status, fast cars to cruise uptown and watch the *lo-fan* freaks, days to work on your "tans" at Coney listening to the new Hong Kong–Filipino platters, plenty of time to go bowling, and the pick of the girls—in general, the old equation of living quick, dying young, and leaving a beautiful corpse.

It took the Toy Shans a while to comprehend what was happening in their village. By the late sixties, several *juk tuk* "clubs" began to appear. Foremost was the Continentals, a bunch who spent a good deal of time looking in the mirror, practicing complex handshakes, and running around ripping the insignias off Lincoln Continentals. In the beginning the family associations did their best. They marshaled the new kids into New Year's dragon-dancing. For the older, more sullen ones, they established martial arts clubs. But these kids didn't seem interested in discipline; besides, they smoked too many cigarettes. That's when the tongs intervened. Within weeks of the first extortion report, several White Eagles and representatives of the On Leong tong were sitting in a Mott Street restaurant talking it over. When they were done, a pact was sealed that would establish the youth gang as a permanent fixture of "New Chinatown."

It was agreed that the Eagles would stop random mayhem around the community and begin to work for the On Leong. They would "guard" the tong-sponsored gambling houses and make sure that no one ripped off restaurants that paid regular "dues." In return, the Eagles' leaders would receive a kind of salary, free meals in various noodle houses, and no-rent apartments in the Chinatown area.

It seemed a brilliant arrangement, especially for the tongs. The On Leongs and Hip Sings no longer struck fear in the heart of Chinatown. With warriors like Sing Dock barely a misty reminiscence, the tongs had become paunchy, middle-aged businessmen who spent most of their time competing for black-mushroom contracts. The Eagles brought them the muscle they felt they would need in changing times. It was like having your own private army, just like the good old days.

. But the tongs weren't used to this kind of warrior. The kids mounted a six-foot-tall statue of a white eagle on top of their tenement at Mott and Pell. One night ten of them piled into a taxicab and went uptown to see *Superfly;* afterward they shot up Pell Street with tiny .22s for the sheer exhilaration of it. They went into tailor shops, scowled, and came away with two-hundred-dollar suits. Once Paul Ma—Eagle supreme commander—showed up for an arraignment wearing a silk shirt open down the front so everyone could see his bullet holes.

During eight or so years on top in Chinatown, the Eagles set the style for the Chinese youth gang. Part was savagery. Eagle recruiting practices were brutal—coercion was often used to replenish their street army. They kidnapped merchants' daughters and held them for ransom. They also set the example of using expensive and high-powered guns. No Saturday-night specials in Chinatown. The gangs used Mausers, Lugers, and an occasional M-14. One cop says, "You know, I've been on the force for twenty-two years, and I never saw nothing that gave me nightmares like watching a fifteen-year-old kid run down Bayard Street carrying a Thompson submachine gun."

But there was another side to this. A new style was emerging in Chinatown. Chinese kids have had a tough time of it in schools like Seward Park. Blacks and Puerto Ricans as well as meanies from Little Italy would vamp Chinese students for sport. Groups like the Eagles were intent on changing this. It was a question of cool. In the beginning they copied the swagger and lingo of the blacks—it is remarkable how closely a Chinese teenager can imitate black speech. From the Puerto Ricans they borrowed souped-up car styling as well as the nonfashion of wearing army fatigues, which they added to their already zooty Hong Kong–cut shirts.

But it was Bruce Lee, the Hong Kong sex-symbol kung fu star, who did the most for the Chinese street presence. Gang kids ran around Chinatown carrying *nunchahas*—kung fu fighting sticks—which few of them knew how to use, and postured like deadly white cranes. When "Kung-Fu Fighting" became a number one hit on WWRL, being Chinese was in. They became people not to mess with (although the police report there has never been a gang incident in which martial arts were used). "It was like magic," says one ex-Continental. "I used to walk by the Smith projects where the blacks live, and those brothers would throw dirty diapers out the window at me and call me Chinaman. Now they call me *Mr. Chinaman*."

The image of the Chinese schoolgirl was changing, too. Overnight they entered the style show on the subway. A lot of the fashion—airblown hairstyles, mucho makeup, and tiny "Apple jacket" tops—came from the Puerto Ricans. Classy tweezed Oriental eyebrows produced a new "dragon lady" look. Openly sexual, some of the Hong Kong girls formed auxiliary groups. Streaking their hair blond or red to show that their boyfriends were gangsters, they were "ol' ladies," expected to dab their men's wounds with elixirs swiped from Chinese apothecaries. Who can blame them? More than half of Chinatown's women work in the three-hundred-odd garment factories in the area, buzzing through the polyester twelve hours a day, trying to crack a hundred dollars a week. Hanging with the bad kids risked an occasional gang bang, but it was a better risk than dying in a sweatshop.

It seemed only a matter of time before the youth gangs would get into dope, especially since drug dealing has been the key staple of the Chinese underworld for centuries. The present-day version of the Chinatown connection dates back to the end of the Chinese civil war in 1949. Several Nationalist units were cut off in the poppy-rich area known as the Golden Triangle near the Burmese/Thai/Laotian border as the rest of Chiang Kai-shek's army fled to Taiwan. A large smuggling route was then established, with the Nationalist government reaping the benefits. This was not unprecedented, as many historians cite Chiang's involvement with the notorious dope-peddling Shanghai-based Green Gang during the 1920s.

According to the federal Drug Enforcement Agency, with Mao's takeover on the mainland, several KMT officials with drug-selling connections soon found their way to New York, where they eased into the On Leong power structure. It wasn't long after that, the DEA says, that the On Leong people went across Canal Street to strike a bargain with Italian organized crime. Soon a new adage was added to Mafia parlance: "If you want the stuff, get yourself a good gook."

The connection—which is believed to be kept running by a manager of an On Leong restaurant who is also believed to be the only Chinese ever admitted to the Carlo Gambino crime family—works well. While most of the country is flooded with Mexican smack, in New York the percentage of Golden Triangle poppy runs high. The dope money is the lucrative tip of Chinatown's pyramid crime structure. DEA people say the gangs are used as runners to pick up dope in the Chinese community in Toronto and then body-carry it across the border. But they may play a greater role. Chinese dope hustlers have always felt on uneasy ground when dealing with flashy uptown pushers. Now, however, street sources say the gutterwise gangs are dealing directly with black and Puerto Rican dealers.

Then again, junk has always been an issue in Chinatown. Even now you can walk by the senior citizen home on East Broadway and see eighty-year-old Chinese men and women who still suffer from the effects of long-ago opium addiction and live out their lives on methadone. They're probably the oldest addicts in America. The specter of the opium days is still horrifying down here, where landlords continue to find ornate pipes in basements.

That's why the sight of fourteen-year-old Eagles nodding on Mott Street during the smack influx of the early '70s was so galling to the old men. It was a final indiscretion, a final lack of discipline. Actually, the Eagles had been tempting fate for some time. They insulted tong elders in public. They extorted from restaurants they were supposed to be protecting. They mugged big winners outside of the gambling houses. It was playing havoc with the tong's business as usual. Often the old men threatened to bring in sharpshooting hit men from Taiwan to calm the kids down.

So in 1974, when Quat Kay Kee, an aging street hustler looking for a handle in the tong hierarchy, told the On Leong of a new and remarkable gang leader, the old men were ready to listen. Nicky Louie and his Ghost

Shadows were not only tougher than the Eagles, but they knew how to do business. To show their style, Nicky and his top gun, Philip Han (known as Halfbreed), supposedly put on masks and pulled off a ballsy submachine-gun holdup at the Eagle-guarded gambling house in the local VFW post, knocking off a pair of sentries to boot.

Soon after, in another gambling house, a drunken Eagle poured a water glass of tea down the brocade jacket of an On Leong elder. The word came down: the tong was formally withdrawing its support of the Eagles; the Shadows could make their move. A few nights later, the 4:00 A.M. quiet on Mott Street was broken by Shadows honking the horns of their hopped-up cars. They rode around the block, screeching their tires. The Eagles tumbled out of bed clutching their pieces. The shooting woke up half the neighborhood. Amazingly, no one was injured. But the change had come. The Eagles fled to Brooklyn. And Nicky Louie was pacing back and forth on Mott Street.

A relationship was forged. For the most part, Nicky's Shadows have been model rulers during their stay on Mott Street. "I'm a businessman, and I know how to stay in business," Nicky once told Neal Mauriello. The gang takes its cut and protects the status quo. Would-be neighborhood reformers have learned to be fearful of visits from gun-wielding gang members; one lawyer who spoke out against the Chinatown establishment woke up the next morning to find Mott Street plastered with wall posters telling him to get out of town.

It is a strange reign of terror that could flourish only in a limbo-land like Chinatown. One hundred years of neglect have distorted the links to the *lo fan* power. The cops and tongs have maintained a nonaggression pact well oiled with palm grease. One On Leong insider says, "Those guys are crooks. I was pit boss at a gambling house and gave two hundred a week to the same sergeant for two years." It goes on. Fifth Precinct cops are not allowed to make gambling arrests unless they actually see money on the table. But since the chance of a *lo fan* getting into a Chinese gambling house unnoticed is akin to a snowcone in hell, they might as well not bother. "When you do raid the houses, it's almost like they've been tipped," says one detective. "By the time you get through all the trick doors, there's no one there but a couple of one-hundred-year-old men smoking cigarettes."

For years there was only one Chinese cop, the fabulous Johnny Kai. Kai walked a thin line between American and Chinese law and did a good job for both. Today, however, with the Chinese making up the majority of the Fifth's constituency and youth crime skyrocketing, there is still only one Chinese cop on the beat, Barry Eng, who once said with a straight face, "Of course, everyone knows the associations disowned the youth gangs a long time ago."

One thing that Nicky Louie makes fairly clear is that he is not interested in talking to reporters, especially this reporter. No, he says, when approached in front of 56 Mott Street, he is not up for a little *yum cha* to discuss his life and times. Avoiding eye contact, he claims to speak "no English!" For sure he doesn't want his picture in the paper. In fact, he says, he doesn't even know who the fuck this Nicky Louie is and, in any event, he is not him. So maybe you should get the fuck away, like now.

Not that you could blame the Ghost Shadow for wanting to keep a low profile. The past several months have been a kind of hell for the gang leader. It was only a few Saturdays ago that he reportedly saw an old Eagle enemy gesturing in his direction from across the street. Nicky was being fingered. He stood like a freeze frame, looking at the two strangers drawing down on him. One had a Mauser, the other a Colt .38. The first gunshot whistled by his ear and broke him out of his trance. He ran down Mott, pushing aside the tourists and the old ladies, turning down Canal until he was safe, panting against a wall.

That afternoon haunted Nicky. Battling Paul Ma made sense. But these unknown hitmen had no reason to shoot except money.

It was scary; things were getting out of control. Eagle Yut Wai Tom had been convicted—the first gang kid to be sent up for murder. Word was around that Tom had cracked up when he got to Rikers Island. The cops were doing a suicide watch on him. Quat Kay Kee, Nicky's old sponsor at On Leong, had been flipping out, too. Shot at in the Wiseman Bar on Bayard Street by a group of Eagles wearing ratty wigs they had bought from a hasidic shop on East Broadway, Quat railed that he'd tell all. He managed to compose himself just before the drug cops got there with their tape recorders.

Being a Chinatown warlord was a tough gig. To keep up their street army, the Shadows had been forced to recruit younger and younger kids. But what exactly do you say to a fourteen-year-old when you're a twenty-two-year-old legend? The young Shadows were griping about their wages. In the early part of the year some of the kids had broken away from Nicky to ally themselves with the scuzzy Wah Chings. For a couple of nights in January, they had actually succeeded in pushing Nicky off the street. It took all of his negotiating prowess to fix things again.

For months he'd let it be known that he was tired of being a youth-gang leader, but the tong gave little indication that they'd allow him to move up in the organization. Quitting was out of the question. First of all, he knew too much and had far too many enemies. It wouldn't be enough to leave Chinatown, or even New York City. Anyplace there was On Leong— like Toronto or Chicago—or Hip Sing, which is just about everywhere, he'd be known and fair game. Anyway, if he did get out, what was waiting? He knew lots of ex-gang guys who'd "retired" and now broke their humps for their families in the old restaurant grind.

Ironically, it was the old men who provided Nicky and the other gang kids with an escape from street-fighting. Despite Chinatown's traditional reluctance to look for outside help, poverty money is beginning to find its way down here. Funding scams may not be as venerable as gambling houses, but in a modern world, there must be modern hustles. People had been telling the old men about a Harlem incident in which the *hak guey* youth gangs had given up their arms. The federal government had laid a sizable chunk of cash on groups promising to reform the kids. The old men saw an opening; if they could get the gangs to call "peace," they could get the uptight merchants off their backs as well as pick up a large grant.

The plan was laid out to Nicky. He liked it and promised to set it up. He contacted Eagle Paul Ma and Dragon Mike Chen—who hated each other more than they both hated Nicky—and got them to say "Cool."

Next step was to make it respectable. The gangs contacted one of the old Continentals, now a well-known Chinatown social worker, and told him they wanted to give up their evil ways. The worker, eager to be known as the man who stopped Chinatown gang warfare, went for it. Everything was set.

But somewhere along the line, Nicky began to forget that it was all a scam. Suddenly he liked the idea of "reforming," learning English for real and getting a decent job. And he wasn't the only one. Around *lo tow*, guys were still packing rods, but they also were talking about what they'd do when they went "legit."

The first "peace" meeting was at the Kuo Wah Restaurant on Mott Street. Kids embraced each other, saying it was crazy for Chinese guys to kill other Chinese guys. Nicky sat down with Paul Ma. They'd been trying to wipe each other out for years; but now they spent hours reminiscing about their favorite extortion spots on Mott Street.

The old men were flabbergasted. What a double cross! If these kids were on the level, then the whole vice structure could go down the tubes. Then again, it could be a trick. The gangs might be pulling a power play to cut Chinatown up for themselves. Either was disaster. After that the tongs did everything they could to sabotage the peace. They spread mistrust among the merchants; they tried to bribe the gang leaders. The old men unsuccessfully tried to cancel the press conference formally announcing the "peace." But, on August 12, Nicky and the other gang leaders read their joint statement. They didn't expect to be forgiven, but then again they weren't apologizing. They had become wiser; being a gangster wasn't so great. Other kids shouldn't get into it. It was moving; several of the old family association leaders wept. Even Nicky looked a little misty.

But time had run out on Nicky's peace: the old Toy Shan forces of secrecy and mistrust were working overtime. The merchants, brutalized so often, never believed the gangs were sincere and offered no support. The social service agencies failed to come up with concrete programs. The cops offered a ten-day amnesty period for the gang kids to turn in their guns, nothing else. "Oh yeah," said one Shadow. "I'm gonna turn in my gun so they can do a ballistic and fingerprint check on it? Sure." No weapons were turned in.

Of course, it is not possible to know if Nicky was ever truly sincere about declaring peace in Chinatown. The cops, cynics that they are, said, "They might have called it peace, but they spelled it 'p-i-e-c-e.'" Still, no one disputes the fact that three weeks went by without anyone getting shot at around Mott and Bayard. Nicky must have known it was over the night the Eagles ripped off a restaurant at the other end of Mott Street. He ran over to find Paul Ma and see what was up. An Eagle told him that Paul was "out" and laughed. After that, Nicky kicked chairs in a Mott Street rice shop. Gang members say the sear was back in his eye. By then it was just a matter of time. Within the next week the Shadows, Eagles, and Dragons were shooting at each other; the two-month-long war would prove to be the bloodiest in Chinatown history.

The tongs, fearing total loss of control, responded to the madness by calling in some old friends from across Canal Street. According to the Chinese newspapers, a couple of Shadows walked into the wrong restaurant at the wrong time. Five smashnoses imported from Mulberry Street were waiting for them. Reportedly the kids wound up in a meat grinder, their remains dumped into a plastic bag and driven to Newark.

This got the gangs' attention. Except for a few gun violations, the cops say Chinatown's been quiet for the past few weeks. However, reports of gang extortions in local Massapequa and northern New Jersey Chinese restaurants have begun to come in.

But in fanning out of Chinatown, the gangs broke a New York City rule: Don't mess with the rich white people. Someone goofed when they rubbed out the young couple who ran the Szechuan D'or on East Fortieth Street. It mobilized whole armies of uptown cops. Determined to strike Chinese crime at its root, the police have shut down the gambling and extortion rackets in Chinatown. This has caused widespread panic. Word is, big gamblers walk around in a daze at the OTB, trying to latch on to private *pi gow* games uptown. Nicky and the Shadows, seeing no percentage in hanging around for the onslaught, split for greener fields in the On Leong–run towns of Toronto and Chicago.

No one, of course, expects this to last. Balances of power are constantly shifting downtown. Just the other day the cops busted Flying Dragon Mike Chen with a 12-gauge shotgun and 150 rounds of ammunition hidden in the ceiling of his apartment. Paul Ma, Philip Han, and Big Benny Ong are on their way to the slammer. And some even say that the good people at Hip Sing could stage a takeover in Benny's absence.

But much more remains the same. Go tonight to a restaurant on Mott Street and look out the window. Across the street you're likely to see a good-looking skinny guy in a green fatigue jacket pacing back and forth. Nicky Louie is back in town, vigilant as ever. Look into his eyes and wonder what he's thinking. But, then, remember . . . it's Chinatown.

8

From the Annals of Pre-gentrification: Sleaze-Out on East Fourteenth Street

A case study from before the invention of the two-thousand-dollar studio apartment. Back in 1977, the so-called Summer of Sam, soon after the near bankruptcy of the city, there were many contenders for the title of "sleaziest street corner in New York." Fourteenth Street and Third Avenue was closest to my home, and I like to walk to work. Now East Fourteenth Street is "redeveloped." Jullian's, once the most picturesque pool hall in the city, is now an NYU dorm. Ditto the Academy of Music. The Gramercy Gym, where fighters good and bad trained, is long gone. So is the studio where Bettie Page took her famous bondage pics. This is called progress. Even if it is a perverted nostalgia to long for the bad old days when the city's major thoroughfares were lined with nodding junkies, it is hard to dismiss the lingering (loitering?) feeling that something has been lost. From the Village Voice, *1977.*

All the popcorn pimps, penny-ante pross, nickel-and-dime pill-pushers, methadone junkies, and doorway-living winos felt the hawk wind as it blew down East Fourteenth Street. It's late October, the time of the year when one night, all of a sudden, you know you better break out the warmer coat. Except that on East Fourteenth Street, who has a warmer coat? One creep— a downer-selling vermin—knows the raw of it all. He stands in front of the pizza joint on Fourteenth and Third Avenue, begging for eye contact. "Robitussin, man, Robitussin." Robitussin? "Robitussin," he croaks. He's selling cough syrup. Over-the-counter cough syrup.

It is enough to stop you in your tracks. "Robitussin, man? Don't you got no Luden's or Vicks VapoRub?" I mean: Two-dollar Placidyl is low enough. But Robitussin? "You have got to be kidding."

The creep's voice squeaks up a couple of octaves, his scarred-up head sags. He says, "Just trying to get over. This gonna be a rough winter."

It's always a rough winter at Fourteenth Street and Third Avenue. Rough for the blond junkie and his girlfriend. They told the people at the metha- done center on Second Avenue and Twelfth Street that they were going out of town. Back to Ohio to visit the chick's parents. The methadone people gave them a week's supply of bottles. It sounded like a good plan since the blond guy and his girlfriend weren't going nowhere except to Fourteenth Street to sell the extra shit. But they got into a pushing match with some of the Spanish guys drinking Night Train Express at the L train entrance. The methadone bottles fell down the stairs. A scuffle broke out, then the cops were there. One thing led to another, and soon the blond junkie and his girlfriend were back at the drug center trying to explain why they weren't in Ohio. Now they're on "permanent release," which means no more state-issue methadone. You can see the two of them out on the street, scratching and begging, looking for a taste, any taste.

A rough, cold winter. Some of the usual skells have taken off. Nobody in the Durkin, the creep joint with the tilted bar, has seen Joey the Eye for weeks. Joey the Eye was a mess—too fucked up to cop pills, never had a girl out on the street. But he could—and would—take his bloodshot eye- ball out of his head and hold it in the palm of his hand. He said if you didn't give him a cigarette, he'd tighten the grip, crushing his own eye- ball, which would make it all your fault: him having nothing but a dark pit where his eye should be. The Hung Man is also missing. He spent some of the summer leaning on a parking meter, stark naked. Valium pushers came over, slapped five, and said. "Man, you hung."

Beat Shit Green is gone, too. But no one in the pill-pusher ginmills on Second Avenue figures Beat Shit is soaking up rays in Miami Beach. Beat Shit is one of the worst scumbags ever to stand at Fourteenth Street and Third Avenue hustling "Ts and Vs" (Tuinals and Valium). He used to claim that he was the one who sold the white boy that fatal bunch of beat shit in Washington Square Park last year. Bragged about it. What did he care, he made his $2.50. Beat Shit has been known to sell methadone that was really Kool-Aid and aspirin. He'd suck the juice out of a Placidyl and sell the shell. But, they say, that kind of beat shit comes back on you. They say Beat Shit's not going to make the winter because he got thrown off a roof on East Thirteenth Street.

Rough. Cold. In one of the bars next to the cuchifrito stand, Willie ("call me Big W") is wondering if he'll see April. For a downer salesman, Willie is a pretty sweet dude. Sometimes if one of the barmaids in the Durkin is smooching it up with an off-duty cop, Willie will take a bar stool next to the chick and wait. Soon she'll curl her hand around her back and make a little cup. Willie will slip her a couple of Valiums. The barmaid will put her other hand in the cop's crotch and pull her face away—pretending to cough or something. While the cop is dealing with the barmaid's squeeze, she'll swallow the pills and go back to tonguing before the guy knows anything. Willie digs that kind of move. He says, "She's slick, huh?"

Recently, though, things haven't been going too good for Big W. Mostly he gets over selling pills to kids from Jersey. But, like they say, Willie is his own best customer. Talking to him gets you seasick; he's always listing from side to side. Tonight Big W is wearing his skullcap funny. It's not pulled down over his head; he's got it done up in a little crown. Willie says he don't want it skintight, it puts too much pressure on his stitches. Seems as Willie was in the Durkin a couple of weeks ago and got into an argument with a pimp. Willie thought the guy was just bullshitting until the iron rod came out. He forgets what happened next. Except that he woke up in Bellevue with a head that looks like a road map.

The stitches have made Willie mad. Mad enough to "get violent." The other night he decided he was "just gonna go mug myself somebody." He went around to the stage door of the Academy of Music. Aerosmith was playing. Willie picked out a kid who was completely destroyed on Tuinals. The kid was waiting for an autograph, but Willie figured anyone jive enough a wait for a fucking autograph has to be an asshole. It got better when the rock star came out the door, "got into his fucking limo, and didn't even give the sucker an autograph." So Willie made his move. The Jersey kid beat Willie into the sidewalk and "stole my Placidyls." At this rate, Willie figures he'll be lucky to live till spring.

I have always wanted to write a story called "The 10 Sleaziest Street Corners in New York." I mean, why did certain street corners—excluding obvious "ghetto"-area ones—become hangouts for pill-pushers, prostitutes, winos, bums, creeps, cripples, mental patients, mumblers, flimflam men, plastic-flower sellers, peepshow operators, head cases, panhandlers, and other socially unacceptable netherworld types. How did these corners get this way? How long had they been this way? What was their future? Which ones have McDonald's? Which ones have Burger King? Did this matter?

I compiled a fairly comprehensive list off the top of my head: Ninety-sixth Street and Broadway—the first subway stop down from Harlem; Seventy-second Street and Broadway—good old needle park; Fifty-third and Third—the Ramones sang about chicken hawking there; Twenty-eighth and Park Avenue South—the Bellmore Cafeteria cabdrivers bring the pross; Second Avenue and St. Mark's—the dregs of the burned-out hippies; Bowery and Houston—the cabbies will run over a bum before they let him wash their windshield; Sixth Avenue and Eighth Street—the aggressively plastic up-and-comer; Ninetieth Street and Roosevelt in Queens—home of the low-level Colombian coke dealer; and, of course, the granddaddy of them all; Forty-second Street and Eighth Avenue, the whole of Forty-Deuce Street actually.

Soon, however, it became apparent that it was crazy to "do" all the corners of crud in New York. How many burgers can one slip down his gullet? It would be better to home in on one singular slice of sleaze.

Fourteenth Street and Third Avenue was the natural choice. I live around there; it's my neighborhood sleazy street corner. The pross have seen me enough to know I don't wanna go out. But, also, Fourteenth Street and Third Avenue is a classic, time-honored choice. Fourteenth Street—the longest crosstown Street in Manhattan—has been on the skids, for the past 120 years.

Once, long ago, blue blood coursed through this stem. An 1853 edition of the *New York Herald* said of East Fourteenth Street, "Here, there are no stores—nothing but dwelling houses, which are substantial, highly finished, and first class." When stores did come, they were Tiffany's and FAO Schwarz. When the Academy of Music was built, in 1854, it was hailed as the city's center of classical music and opera. Europeans sang there. The Metropolitan Opera House was built uptown by smarmy nouveaux riches, like the Vanderbilts, who couldn't get boxes at the Academy.

It didn't last long. East Fourteenth Street did one of the quickest and earliest "there goes the neighborhoods" in New York history. By 1865, the *New York Times* was reporting that "all of the once-splendid row houses of the 14th Street-Union Square sector are now boarding houses." In 1868, Charles Dickens saw Fourteenth Street as a precursor of Levittown. He said: "There are 300 boarding houses exactly alike, with 300 young men exactly alike, sleeping in 300 hall bedrooms exactly alike, with 300 dress suits exactly alike. . . ."

Prostitution was firmly rooted on East Fourteenth Street by the turn of the century (a *Gentleman's Companion* of the time lists fifteen whorehouses in the area), and it aided some unlikely causes. Emma Goldman writes of doing a little flat-backing on Fourteenth Street to pick up revolutionary pocket money. Those days, there were plenty of Reds around. Socialists stood on soapboxes in Union Square Park. During the Sacco-Vanzetti trials, the cops mounted machine guns on top of the Guardian Life building. John Reed and Trotsky discussed eventualities in the Fourteenth Street cafeteria, which had a sign on the wall: A TRAYFUL FOR A TRIFLE.

Today the only vestige of leftist activity on Fourteenth Street is the sign from the sixties underground newspaper *Rat*, which had its offices next to the Metropolitan porno theater. It reads, HOT RATS WHILE YOU WAIT. Once-flourishing capitalists have also fallen on hard times. Macy's, Hearn's, Ohrbach's, and Klein's all were here. Now only Klein's on the Square remains as a massive, empty three-hundred-thousand-square-foot hulk. The square-rule logo makes the place look like a decrepit Masonic temple; except there's no "all-seeing eye."

The *East Village Other*, in one of its last issues, published a secret report predicting a deadly and monumental earthquake about to flatten half the city. The scientists (all Hitlerians, said *EVO*) were keeping the news from the public. The report said all the major fault lines ran right underneath Fourteenth Street. It was a totally believable story.

East Fourteenth Street should have settled into a typical cycle of urban decline and upshift. But the street has resisted, plotting instead a flatline course. Down and down. Most around here say it hasn't bottomed out yet.

Fourteenth Street at Third Avenue is more than a sleazy street corner, it's the epicenter of a mini-sleazopolis. In the blocks around the hub, several different creep scenes operate side by side, and almost independently. Occasionally a pimp hanging out in the Rio Piedras bodega, on Third Avenue near Eleventh Street, will go up to Fourteenth Street to sell some pills, but not often. The girls stay fucked up most of the time but don't sell. Pill-pushers don't even go to the same bars as the pross. It's a real division of labor. The thing that holds it all together is that it's all so low. *Low!* Ask anyone stumbling past the old Jefferson Theatre—they'll tell you: After Fourteenth Street, there ain't no more down.

Sure the pimps sit in the chairs of the barber college at Twelfth and Third pretending to get a swell $1.50 haircut like they're New Orleans patroons. But it is all front. Fakery and lies. These pimps have never gotten to check out the scene with a gangster lean from the front seat of an El D and they never will. They don't even have a fur hat to slouch about in. They're lucky to have one girl working, and you know she's going to be desperate. A working girl freezing skinny legs waiting for cars with Jersey plates turns two hundred dollars a week down here, when it's good. No chance of them taking their act to Lexington or even Eighth Avenue, either. They're on Fourteenth Street because the big pimps think the place is so funky they don't even care to organize it. The heartless say that Fourteenth Street is one step from the glue factory. A few weeks ago the cops picked up a fifty-seven-year-old pross outside the Contempora Apartments. It was believed to be some kind of record, age-wise.

Pill-pushers are no better. Most of them started turning up on Fourteenth Street back in the late sixties after two doctors, Vincent Dole and Marie Nyswarder—the father and mother of methadone maintenance—shook up the dope-fiend world by setting up a clinic at the Morris J. Bernstein Institute of Beth Israel Hospital. Methadone was touted as a wonder drug. Everyone said it would be the end of the heroin problem in the city. Junkies from all over the city were sent over to Bernstein (on Second Avenue and Seventeenth Street) and other nearby "model" clinics to drink little clear bottles and kick.

Some kicked. But most just got a short course in how to manipulate the Medicaid programs politicians loved to pour money into. Drugs led to drugs. It was easy to take your little methadone card and Medicaid slip over to a "scrip" doctor who would be willing to write you an Rx for a hundred Valiums if you told him you were "anxious, very anxious." This led to the famous junkie refrain: "I'd go to Doctor Zhivago if he'd write." Otherwise, you could write your own. The forms were usually lying around the program offices. A scribbled "X" might be good enough to get a pharmacist to fill the scrips. What you didn't use to get fucked up on, you could sell. Same thing with extra methadone.

Fourteenth Street and Third became the flea market. It was an Eco-101 example of supply and demand. The drug of choice among the dumbo suburban kids these days is downers: the Fourteenth Street stock and trade. Throughout Long Island and Jersey, blond-haired types driving their papas' Le Sabres know that Fourteenth Street is the place to go. Any night a useless boogie band is playing the Palladium (what they call the Academy of Music now), you can see the most mediocre minds of the next generation drag themselves through negro streets into the most desultory madness.

It is a game anyone can play. Go over to the emergency room at one of the hospitals in the area, tell them you're dying from a headache and want some Percodan. The intern there will be surprised and ask you, "Sure you don't want Valium?" Insist on Percodan and the intern will tell you, "Take the Valium. If you don't use them, sell them on Fourteenth Street. None of them have heard of Percodan."

There's no night (except for Sunday, when the Street is eerie and dead) when you can't walk from Fourth Avenue to Second Avenue on Fourteenth Street without at least half a dozen ballcap-wearing, pinpoint-eyed junkies asking you if you want downers. The price list fluctuates with supply: Placidyl usually go for $2.50; Valium, 75 cents; Tuinal, $3; Elavil, $2 on Fourteenth Street, with a 25 percent markup for rock show nights.

You'd figure that would add up. Especially with no overhead and Medicaid usually picking up the initial tab. But these guys ain't got no money. They're too spaced out. That's why they're on Fourteenth Street to begin with. They couldn't get over selling smack on 123rd Street. They couldn't even get over selling smack on Avenue B and Sixth Street. They don't got the concentration. Pusher wars don't happen. No one can remember where their turf is, or was. They are in trouble if you ask them for more than three Valiums. They pour the pills out into their hands and start counting. Then they recount. Order more than eight or nine and it can take an hour.

If you want to draw a map of the Fourteenth-and-Third sleazopolis, give the pill-pushers Fourteenth Street between Second and Fourth. That's the south side of the street; for some reason they're never on the north side. No one knows why, they sure aren't working on their tans. Scoring spots include the doorway of the Larry Richardson Dance Company at the corner of Fourth Avenue. Most of the guys up there are in business for themselves but there are also "steerers," creeps who will tell Jersey kids to come around the corner to Thirteenth Street. This is usually for "quantity" and sometimes for rip-off.

The rest of the scene, working from the west and down, goes like this: Union Square Park is bonkers these days, the sight of curving benches packed with leathery, saliva-streaked faces is truly impressive. The park isn't a major retail center for the pill-pusher, but many will come over for a little rural R and R. After a tough day of Placidyl pushing, you can lose your profits back playing craps or three-card monte. On the other side of the George Washington statue there are also several "loose joints" guys who got off the wrong subway stop on the way down to Washington Square.

The pross take Third Avenue. Their spiritual home is near Thirteenth Street, where there are two miserable excuses for peepshow joints as well as three porno theaters (that includes the Variety Fotoplays when it's not showing devil movies). The 'toots will also graze down to Fifth Street. The Regina Hotel on Third and Thirteenth (a featured backdrop in Scorsese's *Taxi Driver*) is no longer a big pross hole. The cops broke the manager's balls so now he's on the up-and-up, although you wonder why anyone would stay there if they weren't getting laid. The Bowery flops are the Ritz-Carlton compared to the Regina. Now most of the hotel tricking goes on at the Sahara, a little oasis on Fourteenth. The Sahara has a sign saying LOW WEEKLY RATES even though most guests spend less than a half hour at the Sahara. Seven dollars is the room tariff. A lot of the action, though, goes on in the parking lots along Third. The West Indian guy who used to work there charged two dollar a pop to get in the backseat of a parked car. Hope they didn't use yours.

The "he-shes" (also called "shims" or "he-haws") hang near Second Avenue and Twelfth Street and also congregate at Little Peters, a swish bar by St. Mark's Place. This is one of the biggest t.v. scenes in the city. Of the fourteen hundred pross arrests the cops made in the area during the past year or so, nearly half were men dressed up as women. Ask why he-shes are usually Puerto Rican, a working "girl" says, "Our people are so mean to us . . . besides, haven't you ever heard that Latins were made to love?" The he-shes are much classier looking than the straight pross. Johns claim you can't even tell until you get real close. And, even then . . . you can't. But, then again, most of the johns who cruise Fourteenth Street just don't care.

With this kind of scene it makes sense that many of the "legitimate" businesses that have stayed on East Fourteenth Street during the down-times fall into the seedy category. Up the stairs at the Gramercy Gym, where Cus D'Amato trained Patterson and Jose Torres, the fighters don't think too much about the sleazos below. Fighters figure they're on the fringe of the law themselves. They don't point fingers. But they keep distance. They know that Placidyls make it tough to run six miles in the morning.

At Jullian's Billiards, one of the great film-noir light-over-the-faded-green-cloth-Luther-Lassiter-played-here pool halls in New York, hardly anyone makes mention of the scene either. The old men who sit on the wood benches, watching the nine-ball games, don't have time to think about creeps. Nine-ball's got a big element of luck, true. But it's the money game up there, and anytime money's on the table you've got to concentrate. So just shoot pool, Fast Eddie. Who cares who pisses in the hallway?

Down the street, Paula Klaw has her private thoughts. She's been on East Fourteenth Street for better than thirty years. She remembers when the cuchifrito stand was a Rikers Coffee Shoppe. And when there were two Hungarian restaurants on this block. She is not, however, complaining. "Who am I to complain?" says Paula Klaw. Paula Klaw runs Movie Star News, a film-still and "nostalgia" store stuffed into the second floor of the building next to the Jefferson Theatre. It's the best place in the city to buy photos of Clive Brook and Irene Dunn. As Paula says, the street has a "strong movie pedigree." D. W. Griffith's original Biograph Studio, where Lilly and Dolly Gish made one-reelers, was on Fourteenth Street near Second Avenue. Buster Keaton became a star here.

Plenty of film was shot inside Movie Star News, too. As attested to by the half-soot-covered sign painted on the window, this used to be the studio of IRVING KLAW, THE PINUP KING. Irving, Paula's late brother, shot thousands of bondage pictures up here during the 1940s and '50s. Most of those pictures were of Bettie Page, the most famous bondage model of them all. Irving used his 8 x 10 camera to shoot Bettie for a variety of rags that had names like *Eyeful*, *Wink*, and *Black Nylons*. Most of the pics were distributed by mail order, which would lead to Irving running afoul of the bluenose Kefauver Hearings on "juvenile delinquency."

"They harassed my brother," Paula says now, adding that Irving always maintained "a tasteful relationship" with his famous model. When Howard Hughes once asked to meet Bettie Page after seeing some of the shots Irving took, Paula's brother advised Bettie to see the billionaire, but "only if he promises to be a total gentleman."

Paula was in charge of posing the pictures. She personally tied up Bettie Page "at least a hundred times," bound her to various chairs, gagged her on beds, and manacled her with leather. Bettie was always sweet about it, Paula said, never complained, except when the ropes were too tight. Paula sometimes helped Irving title the pictures, items like "Bettie Comes to New York and Gets in a Bind."

"It was wonderful those days," Paula says now. "We had politicians, judges, prime ministers coming here to buy our photos. They would park their limos right outside on Fourteenth Street." After a while, however, the court cases weighed everything down. Fighting back a tear, Paula says, "It was all that that killed Irving, I think. They said we sold porno. We did not sell porno." Today Paula sells a book called *The Irving Klaw Years, 1948–1963,* containing "more than two hundred out-of-print bondage photos." Paula calls it a "fitting remembrance to my brother." Paula, who has white hair, blue makeup, and wears Capri pants, doesn't have to come to Fourteenth Street every day. She lives in Sheepshead Bay and has "plenty of money." But she "just likes it . . . you know, this used to be quite a glamorous street." She says she hasn't washed the IRVING KLAW, PINUP KING window in twenty years. She does not intend to.

If Paula, Jullian's, and the Gramercy Gym fighters add aged seed to the surroundings, it's the cynical "businessmen" who give Fourteenth Street and Third Avenue its shiny veneer of plastic sleaze. Who could have been surprised when Burger King opened in the old Automat where John Reed, currently buried near Lenin in the Kremlin, once ate club rolls? Burger King knows its customers when it sees them. The burger boys probably have whole demographic departments to psyche out every sleaze scene in the galaxy. No doubt they felt they had to keep pace after McDonald's sewed up Ninety-sixth and Broadway.

Then there are the doughnuts. There are at least five doughnut joints in the immediate area of Fourteenth Street and Third Avenue. One even replaced Sam's Pizza, a lowlife landmark for years. Doughnuts are definitely the carbo-junkie wave of the future. In fact, if some doctor would publish a weight-losing diet of Placidyls and doughnuts, airline stewardesses would make Fourteenth Street another Club Med.

But, of course, the real merchants of Fourteenth Street and Third Avenue are the sleazos. They control the economy. And why not? No one else wanted to sell stuff on East Fourteenth Street. You have to figure that more Placidyls and pussy gets sold at Fourteenth and Third than the pizza joint sells pizza or the cuchifrito place sells pork rinds.

No wonder the sleazos were pissed the other day. The Third Avenue Merchants Association was having a fair. They closed off the avenue. Ladies in print dresses sold pottery. Bug-eyed kids stood by tables of brownies. A nice day in the sun for the well adjusted. But the fair halted abruptly at Fourteenth Street, even though Third Avenue continues downtown for several streets before it turns into the Bowery. The implication was clear, and the sleazos weren't missing it. A whole slew of the local losers stood on "their" side of Fourteenth Street, gaping at the fat-armed zeppoli men pulling dough and the little kids whizzing around in go-karts.

One Valium pusher looked up at the sign hung across the avenue and read it aloud. "T . . . A . . . M . . . A," he said. "What the fuck is a T.A.M.A.?"

The Third Avenue Merchants Association, he was informed. "Shit," he said, looking very put out. "Motherfucker, I'm a goddamned Third Avenue merchant."

So what if Fourteenth Street is low? Does every block have to look like SoHo or one of those tree-lined numbers in Queens? The other night I was helping my friend move. He had been living on Fifteenth Street and Third Avenue in a high-rise, but the money got tight. So he took a place on Twelfth between Second and Third. As we were carrying an enormous filing cabinet into the lobby of his new building, he said, "Well, this place is dumpy, but at least I won't have to pass the prostitutes every day on the way to work." A couple of seconds later we heard a noise on the staircase. A 'toot was slapping a solid on a guy who we swore had a turned-around collar. A *priest*! We almost dropped the cabinet, laughing.

Besides, where else but on East Fourteenth Street can you hear a blasted Spanish downer freak abusing a little Polish guy, saying, "*Que pasa? Que pasa? Que pasa?*" To which the Polish guy says, questioning, "Kielbasa? Kielbasa?"

Of course, there are those who do not find all this so amusing. Like Carvel Moore. Explaining why sleaze is essential to the big-city experience to her is a fruitless task. She is the "project coordinator" of Sweet 14, an organization dedicated to making Fourteenth Street "the Livingest Street in Town."

They are a cleanup group. The list of names who attended their kickoff meeting reads like a who's who among New York powermongers. Con Edison head Charles (Black-out) Luce, David Yunich, Mayor Beame, Percy Sutton, representatives of Citibank, the phone company, and Helmsley-Spear. They issued a joint statement saying that Fourteenth Street wasn't dead, it could "be turned around," and it was up to the businessmen and government to do it. Luce, chairman of the group, offered $50,000 of Con Edison money each year for three years to this end.

Carvel Moore, a prim lady who once headed a local planning board, said it was "dead wrong" to assume that Sweet 14 was a front group for Charles Luce, the phone company, or anyone else. Sweet 14 was an independent organization looking out for everyone's interests on East Fourteenth Street. She said that Luce's $50,000 was "just a small portion of the money" the group had to work with. Then she brought out a bunch of art-student line drawings showing me how "incredibly inefficient" the cavernous Fourteenth Street–Union Square subway station is. It is one of Sweet 14's major tasks to "help remodel the station," said Ms. Moore, pointing out how the station's "awkwardness" made it difficult for employees to get to work. The project will cost $800,000.

She also was very high on "Sweet Sounds in Union Square Park," a concert series sponsored by Sweet 14. Ms. Moore detailed how these musical events brought "working people on their lunch hour back into the park . . . and made the drunks and junkies feel uncomfortable." Drunks and junkies always feel uncomfortable when "normal" people are around, Ms. Moore said.

The most important task of Sweet 14, however, continued Ms. Moore, was "to break up the vicious drug trade and prostitution on Fourteenth Street near Third Avenue." What kind of business, Ms. Moore wanted to know, would want to move to this area with things the way they are now? Sweet 14, said Ms. Moore, was now working closely with the cops to take "special action" in the area. One of the main problems with local law enforcement,

Ms. Moore said, is that the yellow line down Fourteenth Street separates the jurisdictions of the Ninth and Thirteenth Precincts. Some of the more nimble-footed degenerates in the area know this and escape the cops, who are loath to chase bad guys into another precinct. Sweet 14, however, has been "instrumental" in getting Captain Precioso of the Ninth Precinct to set up a "Fourteenth Street Task Force" to deal with this situation. The organization has also "been active" in monitoring the OTB office at the corner of Second Avenue and Fourteenth Street. According to Ms. Moore, people have been known to loiter at the OTB, making it a "potential trouble spot."

I wanted to tell Ms. Moore that I often make bets at the Fourteenth Street OTB and then hang out there (admittedly not inhaling deeply), waiting to see how my nag ran. I considered this being a sportsman, not loitering. But I held it in. Instead, I wanted to know what, after Sweet 14 succeeded in making East Fourteenth Street safe for businessmen, she suggested doing with the several thousand nether-creatures now populating the street? She indicated that this was a "social problem" and not part of her job. All in all it was a somewhat depressing conversation. And I walked out feeling I would rather buy electricity from Beat Shit Green than a cleanup from Charles Luce.

More troubling was a talk I had with George and Susan Leelike. They are the leaders of "East Thirteenth Street Concerned Citizens Committee." The very name of the group brings up images of whistle-blowing at the sight of a black person and badgering tenants to get up money to plant a tree. But George and Susan Leelike are a little tough to high-hat. After all, they are from the block. They've lived on East Thirteenth Street for fifteen years. Raised a son there. And they came for cool reasons: Back in the late fifties and early sixties, the East Village was hip. Charlie Mingus and Slugs made it hip. The Leelikes related to that.

So, when these people tell you they don't think a pross and a priest in a hallway is funny, you've got to take them seriously. They do have a compelling case. George explains it all: he says the Lower East Side gets reamed because the neighborhood's major industry is "social service." Anytime a neighborhood is poor, "social service" expands. The Lower East Side is both poor and liberal. So, says George Leelike, it has a higher percentage of social work agencies than any other neighborhood in the city. He questions the validity of some of these projects, pointing out that one place, Project Contact, started in the sixties as a teenage runaway home, then went to alcohol treatment, then to drug rehab, and now is back to runaways. This is "grant-chasing," says Leelike. For the social workers to keep their jobs, the projects have to stay open. To stay open, they have to get grants. To get grants, they have to show they understand the "current" problems (read: whatever tabloid papers are screaming about this week) of the community and attract "clients." George Leelike says there are more "clients" on the Lower East Side than any other place in the world.

"Clients," the Leelikes say, are not the most stable neighbors. The worst are the methadone junkies. Beth Israel, says Leelike, has made "millions" from its methadone-maintenance programs that bring thousands of "clients" to the Lower East Side. So have the individual private doctors who run their own methadone clinics in the neighborhood. The Leelikes were a major force in a community drive that shut down one Dr. Triebel's clinic on Second Avenue and Thirteenth Street. Triebel pulled in more than seven hundred thousand dollars in one year, much of it in Medicaid payments.

This kind of activity brought still more sleazos to the neighborhood, the Leelikes said. They pulled out Xeroxed arrest reports from the Ninth and Thirteenth precincts, showing that the majority of the pill-pushers pinched on Fourteenth Street said they were on some kind of methadone program. They said it was a vicious cycle, that many of the people on methadone had no desire or intention of kicking. Most of the local meth freaks were here on "force" programs. The city told them, Sign up with a methadone clinic or no welfare.

These were frightening charges, not just because they were indisputably well thought out and apparently true, but because they went to the very core of the two most important issues in the city—race and class. Talking to George Leelike, you had to admire his rational approach to subjects that usually inspire mad, inflammatory outbursts. You also got a closer look at why Ed Koch will be the next mayor of New York City. Koch is the coming wave of politician in New York. His major policy thrust is to appeal to the get-the-creeps-out-of-my-neighborhood constituency. He takes the side of the harried, postliberal middle class against the nether class. It is, after all, a tremendously winning point of view. Even in New York we have to admit that we're so mad we're not going to take it anymore. I even feel like that myself. I'd be crazy not to.

It is chilling and inescapable. Tolerance levels have gone down. The Leelikes said the thing they hated most about the sleazos was that they're so snotty. In the old days, when Susan Leelike went to Cooper Union, junkies hung out in the Sagamore Cafeteria, near Astor Place. Dope fiends those days knew they were outcasts and acted accordingly. The Leelikes remembered these Burroughsian types with a touch of romanticism. Now, they said, methadone makes being a junkie legal. And the creeps have come out into the daylight, where it quickly becomes apparent that junkies aren't the nicest people you'd ever want to meet.

This hit home. A few weeks ago I was walking by Cooper Square. A guy in his mid-twenties was stretched out on the ground, twitching. He didn't look like a lowlife; he had French jeans on. A small crowd gathered around him. A cabbie stopped and put on his emergency blinker. The guy seemed to be having a seizure. Maybe he's an epileptic, said the cabby, pull his tongue out of his mouth. Two people went for the cops, another to call an ambulance. Finally an older man rolled up the guy's sleeve. The dude's arm looked like a Penn Central yard. The older guy threw the arm back on the sidewalk in disgust. "He's just a fucking junkie," the cabby said. "A fucking junkie." Half the people in crowd said, "Shit." And everyone just split. Me, too. I split. When the guy's an epileptic he's human; when he's a junkie, fuck him.

So I knew the Leelikes had the trend on their side. Also, it was clear— they are determined. They are willing to run the risk of being called redneck—Susan Leelike says, "I hate it when they call me the white lady"— to get rid of sleazos. And they don't flinch when you ask them where they propose the sleazos go. "It's just not our problem," they say.

Patrolmen Bob Woerner and Dennis Harrington are in an empty office above Glancy's Bar on East Fourteenth Street and Irving Place, hiding. Harrington and Woerner have been partners for six years. They used to work the smack detail on Avenues A, B, C, and D (called avenues X, Y, and Z in cop parlance). But pressure from Sweet 14 and local politicians on the department to "do something" about Fourteenth Street brought them here eleven months ago. Since then Woerner and Harrington, tough and smart cops, have been the most effective (in terms of arrests) of the twenty men on the Ninth Precinct's "Fourteenth Street Task Force."

Sometimes Woerner and Harrington walk down Fourteenth Street and ask buzz-brained cats, "Hey, man. What you doing?" It's a torture technique; they know that the toughest question in the world for a sleazo is "What are you doing?" Creeps' knees buckle under the weight of that one; they say, "I dunno, what *am* I doing?"

But what Woerner and Harrington really like to do is make busts. Which is why they are hiding in the empty room above Glancy's Bar with their binoculars trained on the action beneath the Palladium marquee.

Making busts on Fourteenth Street isn't tough. Sometimes guys will be so loaded they come right up and say, "Placidyl . . . Placidyl . . . oh, shee-it" before they realize they're talking to a uniformed policeman. It is tricky, however. First of all, the captain doesn't like cops to make too many arrests. He says busts take police off the street and put them in court. Primarily, though, when you're making "observation" busts on Fourteenth Street, you've got to see them good. Most of the sellers get their stuff from scrip doctors, which means their own name is on the bottle. It is not a crime to carry "controlled substances"—if the (not-forged) scrip is made out to you. Selling the stuff, however, is illegal. So, instead of just grabbing a single party, like a smack bust, cops have to get both the buyer and the seller as well as recover the stuff. They also have to see the deal go down perfectly—that is, if they're not into fudging evidence in court.

Woerner and Harrington say, Why fudge, on Fourteenth Street if you miss one sale, they'll soon be another. But still, it hurts when you've been freezing behind the Con Edison fence at Fourteenth and Third, waiting for just the right view. And then, right at the big moment, a bus goes by.

Tonight, however, it ain't gonna be no problem. Aerosmith is back in town at the Palladium and a dozen suburban kids are milling around in front of the theater, looking to get stupid. Woerner and Harrington are licking their lips. All they need is a seller. And from down the street, trudging slowly up from Third Avenue by the poolroom, here he comes. In unison the cops shout, "*All right, Ernest James . . . come on, Ernest James.*"

Ernest James, a gangly guy with a face and beard like Sonny Rollins, came on.

He walked into a crowd of leather-jacketed white kids. Got into a conversation with one. Took him off to the doorway of the fight gym. Then it couldn't have been clearer if Otto Preminger were directing. Out came the bottle. There went the pill. Across came the three dollars. And down the stairs went Woerner and Harrington.

Like nothing, Harrington was reading Ernest James his rights. Woerner had the buyer, a blond boy from Pelham Bay, up against the wall. Ernest James, the perfect degenerate, pulled out a slew of false IDs, a pack of Kools, and looked impassively at the sky. Against the wall another kid was screaming to the spread-eagled buyer, "Jeff, Jeff . . . give me your ticket for the show."

Ernest James was in big trouble. He had a goddamned drugstore on him. Ten bottles of pills in all: 26 big white tabs thought to be Quaaludes, 21 Tuinals, 15 Seconals, 40 unknown peach-colored pills, 34 unknown white pills, 23 ampicillins, 29 unknown yellow pills, and several dozen Placidyls. Most of the bottles were made out to Ernest James. Some to Ernest Jones. Others to A. Ramos. One was just to "Ernest," which prompted Woerner to wonder if Ernest James was on a first-name basis with his pharmacist. Also found were two Garcia y Vega humidors full of 5- and 10-mg Valium. Almost all the scrips were supposedly written by one Doctor Jacob Handler of West 103rd Street. Doctor Handler is a Fourteenth-Street favorite. Harrington keeps a little scorecard of doctors' names that appear on bottles. Doctor Handler is way up near the top of the list. But the cops say nothing will happen to him because "it's tough to bust a doctor."

Apparently to maximize his pill-gathering ability, Ernest James also had half a dozen different medical identification cards. Some were made out to the name William Summersall, others to A. Ramos and Ernest Jones. He also had a little notebook in which he has apparently been practicing different signatures. Most are Ernest Jones. But there is also a page on which Texas Slim is written a dozen times.

Under the fifteen-watt glare in the Ninth's arrest room, Harrington books Ernest James. This is nothing new—Harrington has arrested Ernest James before. In fact, Ernest has six busts for pills this year already. Too bad, figures Dennis Harrington: Ernest James is not a bad guy. In fact, Dennis thinks, most of the guys he busts aren't real bad. Just a bunch of losers. Ernest James had $84 on him, but that had to be his life savings. Most guys have about $30. "Sometimes it is that 'there but for fortune thing,'" says Dennis, who is haunted by the memory of his brother, who was "into junk." He also thinks about that same picture they always show of Karen Quinlan. Dennis wonders if she got her downs on Fourteenth Street.

Asked where he got all the pills, Ernest James is cool. "I'm qualified to have as many pills as I want," he says. Asked about all the different IDs, Ernest says, "I'm qualified to have as many names as I want."

While the cops count up the rest of Ernest's stash, I ask him if he thinks the businessmen and cops can clean up Fourteenth Street. He says, "I dunno 'bout no cleanup. All I know is I wanna get to St. Louis. I can do security over there. I can't sell these pills no more. But if I don't, I got bread and water. My philosophy is that if the city put the clean in the street, they put the dirt in the street, too. Goes both ways. There is one thing that's sure. Ain't no way to clean up this. Cops come fuck up with Fourteenth Street, people just gonna go somewheres else. If they want to get rid of the dirt, they gonna have to shoot those motherfuckers. Line up those motherfuckers and kill them. All of them. Dead."

Woe is Ernest James. He got caught in the cleanup. Usually Ernest winds up with one of those mumbo-jumbo raps like time served or adjournment contemplating dismissal. In other words, he gets off. Not bad, considering pill-pushing is a class-D felony worth up to seven years. This time, however, Ernest James is taking the fall. The D.A. is making an example of him. A special grand jury on soft drugs is indicting him. Instead of the usual weekend at Rikers, they're offering Ernest a year. And that's if he pleads.

Tough shit, Ernest James. Add insult to injury: When Ernest got picked up on September 30, he claimed it was his birthday. No one believed him. But it was true. *Happy birthday, Ernest James.*

Another thing Ernest James was right about: If you move a sleazo, he'll just go somewhere else. You got to kill the motherfuckers . . . dead. Down in Chinatown, they say that's what Mao did with the opium addicts. Hopheads can't drive tractors, so Mao's guys just put them up against the wall and blew their brains out. Bet there ain't no sleazy corners in Peking.

For a society stuck with half a million sleazoids (conservative metropolitan-area estimate), this could be an eminently modest proposal. Discussing this alternative with liberal city councilman Henry Stern, he says, "Of course, I'm not in favor of killing these people."

But Stern admits that he can't figure out what to do with them. "It's a dilemma," he says, "maybe it's one of the biggest dilemmas in the city today." Miriam Friedlander, another liberal councilperson who has been working closely with Sweet 14, also does not favor wholesale annihilation. She takes a more conventional tack, saying, "It's my primary function to break up that situation and get them out of the neighborhood."

In place of execution, the politicians offer "redevelopment." "Redevelopment" is a coming concept in the city-planning business. A modification of the pave-it-all-over-and-start-from-scratch school of urban studies, "redevelopment" essentially means taking over "depressed" areas and transforming them into middle-class shopping and residential areas. The best-known example of "redevelopment" is on Forty-second Street between Ninth and Tenth Avenues. A civic group came into possession of several "tax-arrears" buildings and redid them into boutiques. Henry Stern, Miriam Friedlander, Koch, and the rest feel that "redevelopment" is at least worth trying on Fourteenth Street and Third Avenue. And with economic biggies like Charlie Luce, Helmsley-Spear, Citibank, and Restaurant Associates around, you know the job will get done right. Oh, boy, will it.

Of course, "redevelopment" stops short of final solutions. So Ernest James's philosophy holds up. Due to the hard-nose police work by the "Fourteenth Street Task Force," the sleazos have begun a minor migration. Routed from parts of Fourteenth Street, they camped in Stuyvesant Park on Second

Avenue and Fifteenth Street. According to the locals, who say they pay extra rent to live near the park, the situation is becoming disgusting. Methadone addicts are leaving their bottles all over the place. Pill-pushers are dealing. The other day two of the he-shes got into a little mutual around-the-world.

The neighborhood forces rallied, led by one Jeanne Pryor, a right-minded lady who loves a firm grip on the bullhorn (who last week opened a cleanup storefront at Fourteenth and Third). They decided that the Thirteenth Precinct was not providing adequate protection from the sleazos. They demanded police guards in the park.

One night last month a protest march was organized. About 150 people showed up to carry signs saying things like OUR CHILDREN ONCE PLAYED FRISBEE IN THIS PARK. Others carried shopping bags full of empty scrip bottles they said were collected in the park. These were a present for Captain Joseph Neylan of the Thirteenth, who, Ms. Pryor kept shouting, "has been out to lunch for the past six months."

The march, accompanied by a man in a kilt playing a bagpipe, began at Fifteenth Street and headed up Third Avenue toward the precinct house on Twenty-first Street. Ms. Pryor had planted stories in the *Daily News*, so the local television stations sent out crews to cover. Arc lights flooded the streets as Ms. Pryor led the chant of "junkies out of the park."

As the march reached Seventeenth Street, it started to get interesting. A messed-up black guy bounded in front of the marchers and held up his hands like he was stopping a runaway team of horses.

"Stop!" he said, the TV lights glaring in his buzzed eyes. Stunned, Ms. Pryor halted in her tracks. The whole march bumped to a stop. There was a silence. Then the guy started chanting, "Junkies out of the park. Junkies out of the park." The marchers stepped back. The guy kept screaming, "Junkies out of the park. Junkies out of the park." Then he stopped and looked the bagpipe player right in the eye and said, "I'm a fucking junkie. I'm a fucking junkie. I'm a fucking junkie. Get me out of the park. Get me out of the park. Get me out of the park."

The mock turned to a plea.

It was then that Jeanne Pryor should have acted. She should have taken out a 12-gauge shotgun and blown the creep's head off.

9

Terror on the N Train

A strange adventure of youth, recalled. From the Village Voice, *1977.*

I spied my old fat friend Bart the other day. Like old times, he was sitting in a snot-green foreign car eating a brownie and swigging milk from the quart container in front of Cakemasters on Thirty-fourth Street. For eight years of no see, Big Bart could have looked worse. The car was an improvement. Big Bart used to drive a Corvair that had holes in the floorboards. He heard that Ralph Nader said Corvairs were killer machines, moving time bombs, that they could go off the road, smash right into a crowd of unsuspecting shoppers, with a single nudge of the wheel. So Big Bart went out and got one with no front alignment. He was that kind of guy.

Big Bart was one of those bald-spot-in-the-middle/long-greasy-hair-on-the-sides type of hippies. Now the bald spot has grown like a spreading Rorschach blot, but the grease remains the same. So did the chub. We had some info that Big Bart was married to a woman who had a snake tattoo on her tummy who put him on a yoga diet. You'd never be able to tell.

Back then, in 1969, when we shared a seventy-dollar-a-month pad on Hillside Avenue and Sutphin Boulevard in Queens, there was a saying that Big Bart either had the lowest-cut pants or the highest-cut ass in town.

The crack was always visible. Big Bart used to come out of his room naked. (The room was painted orange and black: Mr. Rotherstein, our landlord, railed, "You painted this wall psychodeckic. Psychodeckic is not in your lease." But we were the only whites in the building, so we got over.) He'd lay that hairy ass on me and my former wife. Moon over Miami, Big Bart called it. We hid under the covers hoping it would go away. But every time we peeked out it would still be there, shining on.

I was with Big Bart the last time I took acid.

Those days Big Bart played drums in bar bands on Long Island. If the joint was past Exit 51, Big Bart played it. For a sweating slob in a flannel shirt, Bart was immortal, in that Island rocker kind of way. He twirled his sticks better than Sal Mineo in *The Gene Krupa Story*. He knew the Young Rascals' greatest hits better than Dino Danelli. When Big Bart beat out "Can't Turn You Loose" on his meaty thighs, it could be magic.

On this particular night Big Bart was moving uptown. He had a gig in a church basement on Lexington Avenue and Twenty-second Street, borough of Manhattan. *The City!* Man, this was the big time. But the show wasn't until ten o'clock. We had eleven hours to kill and Big Bart had two yellow pills shaped like pumpkin seeds he said would do the trick. I had my doubts. I had just returned from California and was skeptical of what the potent combo of pumpkin seed acid and the Big Apple might foment in my increasingly pock-marked brain pan. Up in Tilden Park in Berkeley you could look at a tree for six hours, say "Oh, wow," and incur minimal permanent damage. New York was another story.

But after Bart dropped, there wasn't much choice. What was I gonna do, spend eleven hours watching him take acid? Everything was cool as long as the sun stayed up: we made faces at the gorilla in the Central Park zoo, acted unruly on Park Avenue, stared at the guy blowing smoke on the Times Square Camel ad, watched the buildings weave like in a Stan Van Der Beek underground movie. For a kick, we bought some Gypsy Rose, the cheapest rotgut available, and went looking for our buddy, George Washington Goldberg.

G.W.G., as he called himself, spent the majority of his time in Washington Square Park, where he had achieved a modicum of fame for once making his way up into an NYU biology lecture room. Pushing his way by the professor, George erased the diagrams on the blackboard and told the hundred students, "Okay, now G.W.G. is gonna tell you what biology is really all about." The Wackenhuts carried him out. A star, G.W.G. He'd see you from a distance, stand up, bow, and say, "Oh, finally, a better class of people . . . would you guys like a job, Sonny Liston is looking for sparring partners." This time, though, we blew G.W.G's mind, pulling out our bottle of Gypsy Rose from the brown paper bag and handing it to him, as a present.

"Unopened," George said, tears welling up in his eyes. "The seal not even cracked. No tooth marks. I'm overcome."

Later Big Bart and I went to Hong Fat on Mott Street to giggle over the bacon-wrapped shrimp with the rest of the hippies. Bart ordered his usual: curry beef, superhot extra sauce, five Seven-Ups. He ate the slop in sweaty spasms, banging his chest like a doctor gunning a pacemaker. And said, "Good!"

What a day we were having! Big Bart said there was only one hassle. For Big Bart, any time you had to do *anything,* it was a hassle. The hassle was that Bart had to call Ben the bassist to tell him where the gig was. Bart went off to find a working phone booth while I sat on the curb of Elizabeth Street staring at the streetlamp. It could have been the moon. Bart returned with a look of horror on his face. He was pasty white. Ben the bassist couldn't make it. He was sick. The only other bass player Bart knew was Lou, the crazed 650-Triumph freak who lived in Bensonhurst. There was something wrong with Lou's phone. We'd have to go out there.

Oh shit.

The N train, what the fuck do we know from the N train? We're from Queens. Brooklyn is a dark and scary thing. The subway map. Fuck. Some Puerto Rican wrote on it. In, like, *Spanish.*

Journey to the end of the Nightsville. Drunk on the subway, okay. Glue on the subway, ride it out. But acid on the subway, *yaaahhh.* Big Bart and I held on to each other. All we knew was: Bay Ridge Parkway, get off. The train is packed. Across the way a pizza-faced white guy in a pea coat is playing 45s on a portable turntable. Like life or death, Big Bart dives at the guy's leg and asks, "Do you have any Chuck Berry?" The kid pulls "No

Particular Place to Go" out of his pocket. Saved. Thank you, Lord! Saved again. The people on the train are going nuts. Half of them want the kid to turn it up, the rest want to kill him.

Somehow we found Lou, a husky weight-lifting type, communing with the television in his mother's living room. The mother, a Jewish-Italian widow lady, came to the door, took one look at our faces, and almost broke out crying. It was easy to see why. *Lou was taking acid too!* He was nearly catatonic. Big Bart and I breathed relief: Here, at last, was someone we could talk to.

Lou indicated, sure, he could play the gig. Only problem was he worked for Grand Union on Eighty-sixth Street and had to make his deliveries first. He said it would go faster if we came along. Eighty-sixth Street has an elevated train running over it. Lou shot that Dodge Tradesman between the subway pilings like an amphethamined slalom skier. Big Bart broke into a box of Oreos as we rolled around in the back of the van trying not to barf into the bags of groceries. How Lou had a nice smile for all those Italian ladies when he brought them their Ronzoni is an unsolved mystery. How we got to the gig is another event lost in the mists.

Talking in front of Cakemasters on Thirty-fourth Street, Big Bart and I agree that we can't remember much more of that day—except that the priest at the church smoked pot to show he was hip. Outside of that and a couple of questions about how our respective parents were, there wasn't all that much more to talk about, even if Bart did play "Can't Turn You Loose" on his leg for old times' sake. Bart has been in half a dozen bands since those days. Once he was supposed to go out on the road with Don Covay, author of *Chain of Fools*. But it fell through. Now playing in bands is just a job. Big Bart works in an auto parts store during the day. I remember when Big Bart slept all day. But what are you going to do when you're married and have three kids? Bart hasn't taken acid since that night either.

10

Re: Dead Letter Department, *Village Voice*

They shoot old bohemian newspapers, don't they? You know, when they can't dance anymore. A personalized NY media story of a wound that never heals. From New York *magazine, 2005.*

What a bittersweet little sojourn down memory lane it was, reaching into one of those nasty free boxes from which the *Village Voice* is dispensed these days to pick up a copy of the paper's fiftieth-anniversary issue. A big, fat thing it was, too, the big five-oh, sporting a reproduction of a *Voice* cover from each year of its existence, 1955 on to now. There were reprints of old stories, rekindlings of famous, long-vanished bylines. Up front was Mailer's, of course, the founding editor lambasting the paper's nonexistent copy department for so many "obvious mis-spellings,"in his essay "The Hip and the Square," and saying that he had no choice, given "the fairly sharp words—certain things said which can hardly be unsaid," but to resign his column.

Other hallowed names were invoked. There was Jane Jacobs, who stopped Robert Moses's Lower Manhattan Expressway, thereby making Soho safe for Prada. And Jack Newfield, who sent crooked judges and landlords to jail, ten at a time. Noted too were Jonas Mekas, Andrew Sarris (how much us budding Queens *auteur* theorists owed him!), the beatnik John Wilcock, Howard Smith, jill johnston (only lowercase for her), Lucian Truscott IV, Alexander Cockburn, Ellen Willis, and dozens more, with pictures by Fred McDarrah and cartoons by Feiffer, one more dance to the newsprint fungibility of it all.

The *Voice*: how to explain what it meant, in 1961, to plunk down a dime onto the counter of Union News on 188th Street and thumb through those mucky little pages—pages that opened a Cocteau-like portal to a whole other world. Here was the ticket from Mom's pot roast, from Queens civil service and the neat six-foot square of lawn in front of the corner house on Fifty-third Avenue. Simply to be seen with the *Voice* set you apart: you were one of *those* people—hair too long, mouth too smart, not likely to go to the prom. Growing up in Flushing, the dream felt good.

Later on, as a freshman at the University of Wisconsin, I had a subscription. The guys in the hall, all aggie majors and barely closeted Jew-haters (I assumed), looked at the picture of LeRoi Jones on the cover and asked, "What's this, a commie paper?" No, I tried to explain to these sons of McCarthy, it wasn't a commie paper, it had a lot of stuff in it: politics, jazz, stuff about movies. I tried to tell them I read the paper because I was from New York and to me the *Voice* embodied the legitimate, indigenous clarion of what mattered. Really, I read it because I was homesick and the *Voice* was my lifeline; it kept me sane, and warm, in the middle of fucking Wisconsin, where the temperature hadn't broken zero in weeks.

My dorm mates looked over the paper again. There were some naked hippies in there, I think, maybe some piece about some judge who took money. "This is a commie paper," they said again. "Yeah, right, it's a commie paper, you pig farmers," I said, slamming the dorm-room door.

The *Voice*: it was an attitude, back then.

This, and the fact that I would wind up writing for the paper during the seventies, made the fiftieth-anniversary issue a perfect nostalgia storm: Like, wow, look at that picture of Dustin Hoffman, I forgot he lived right next to that town house on Eleventh Street the Weather Underground blew themselves up in.

What a long, strange proverbial trip.

That was my frame of mind as I slipped past security at the current *Voice* office at 36 Cooper Square. I wanted to be there because it figured to be a special day, one that could only be conjured by the lords of irony that often hover over the paper. On this day, the same one that the fiftieth-anniversary issue hit the streets, the *Voice* management thought it would be an excellent idea to have the paper's new owner come by for the very first time. And there he was, blown in from the Barry Goldwater–whelped precincts of Phoenix, Arizona, one Mr. Michael Lacey, a tallish fifty-seven-year-old with spiky gray hair, watery pale-blue eyes, and spreading shanty-Irish honker.

In the fiftieth, there is a piece by Jarrett Murphy tracking the checkered history of *Voice* ownership. They are all in there, from Dan Wolf and Ed Fancher, who along with Mailer spent $10,000 to open the paper in a second-floor office at 22 Greenwich Avenue. Wolf sold it to Kennedy pal Carter Burden, who sold it to Clay Felker, the founder of *New York* magazine. Felker (one afternoon a disgruntled playwright who got a bad review burst into the office and screamed, "Clay Felker! Your days are numbered," prompting the entire staff to stand up and cheer) lost the place to Rupert Murdoch, the penultimate bigger fish who knew not to mess with a moneymaker no matter what anti-Republican swill it published. After that came Leonard Stern, the pet-food magnate, who paid an unthinkable $55 million in 1985. By 2000, Stern sold out to a consortium of faceless bankers and lawyers for $170 million. Now there was Lacey, almost certainly the only *Voice* owner to get his kicks from revving his mustard yellow Mustang Cobra past 100 while cruising the Navajo Reservation.

Actually, Lacey, who described himself as "this year's Visigoth, the new asshole in charge," his longtime partner, Jim Larkin, and their New Times Media corporation weren't exactly taking over completely. They were merging with Village Voice Media, which includes the *Voice* and five other "alternative" newspapers, most notably the *LA Weekly*. New Times was getting 62 percent of what was being called the "business combination," leaving VVM with the other 38 percent. Subject to Justice Department approval (more on this below), the merger will create a seventeen-entity mini-empire reputedly valued at $400 million. Together, the NT-VVM papers will reach as many as four million readers, dispensing "alt" staples like club listings, movie reviews, and reams of smudgy sex ads, along with local and a smattering of national reporting.

This was a long way away from 22 Greenwich Avenue and a dime at Union News. Still, as *Village Voice* management changes go, Lacey's visit to the paper's offices at 36 Cooper Square was far from notable. Nothing iconic happened as with the 1974 Felker takeover, when star writer Ron Rosenbaum ripped up his (meager) paycheck in the *New York* editor's face, saying there was "no amount of money" that could make him work for "the piece of shit" the *Voice* was certain to become. Rosenbaum then stormed out, a dramatic gesture, topped only by Felker's puzzled reaction: "Who was that?"

Later, in the great rebellion of 1977–78 that greeted the Murdoch regime, the *Voice* staff commandeered the office in support of editor Marianne Partridge. Partridge had been hired only two years before by the previously despised Felker, but in *Voice* land, dread of the future usurper always exceeds the virulent hatreds directed at the current one. Murdoch's choice for editor, David Schneiderman, was barred from the newsroom, forced to cool his muted jets for six months in an office on Fifth Avenue.

The great takeover of 2005 inspired no rampart-mounting. No one at the *Voice* seemed to know much about the impending merger, and when the announcement did come, staffers had to read about it in the *New York Times* and the *Washington Post*, the *Voice*'s once lively "Press Clips" column apparently not deemed worthy of a scoop. Few were even aware Lacey was in the building.

This was too bad, since Michael Lacey, Jim Larkin, and their New Times papers offer much potential fodder for traditionalist *Voice* fear and loathing. First off, there was the old Clear Channel saw, how the New Times–VVM merger would further inhibit the already highly constrained alt-media world, all but stamping out the woolly idiosyncrasy prized by what back in the Stone Age used to be called "the underground press." This owed to the troubling "cookie-cutter" nature of the New Times model, the fact that NT publications in such disparate locales as Broward County and Dallas tended to bear a strong resemblance to each other. Critics charge this is all part of NT's lean, mean business model orchestrated in no small part by its national-advertising arm, the Ruxton Media Group. Politically, the NT approach also raised hackles. Lacey detractor Bruce Brugmann, editor of the independent *San Francisco Bay Guardian*, summed up NT's stance to the current political landscape as "frat-boy libertarian, leering neo-conism. They don't endorse political candidates. To them it is one big, cynical joke."

Beyond this, despite a consensus that New Times often published excellent local investigative stories, there was the sense that Lacey and Larkin's papers were vicious corporate sharks. "These guys don't want to compete, they want to annihilate you, put you out of business," Brugmann said. This recklessness sometimes spilled over into the copy itself, such as in the recent Arthur Teele Jr. tragedy in Miami. The Miami *New Times* ran a story saying that Teele, a city commissioner indicted on corruption charges, had had numerous meetings with male prostitutes. The piece, called "Tales of Teele: Sleaze Stories," was based primarily on specious, unproven police reports. Many considered the story unnecessarily scurrilous, especially after Teele committed suicide the day it appeared.

Lacey acknowledges the Teele story as a disaster. "You can't publish unsubstantiated police reports. We were irresponsible." A month later, the Miami *New Times* editor of eighteen years, Jim Mullin, resigned.

But you rarely find Mike Lacey on the defensive. Born in Binghamton, New York, son of a construction worker, attendee of Essex County Catholic schools in Newark, which makes him by far the bluest-collared owner in *Voice* history, Lacey likes to mix it up. Verbally, physically, emotionally, it is all good to him. In response to Bruce Brugmann's attacks, Lacey published a many-thousand-word rejoinder in his Oakland-based *East Bay Express* titled "Brugmann's Brain Vomit." Warming up by comparing Brugmann to "a needy ferret blogging," Lacey called his fellow editor "a bull-goose loony" and wondered why he was even wasting his precious time "engaging a homeless paranoid in conversation about the contents of his shopping cart." For good measure, Lacey fingered one of Brugmann's backers as the late Donald Werby, who in 1989 was "indicted on 22 counts of having sex with underage prostitutes and paying for it with cocaine," the same Donald Werby who was "a friend and patron of Anton LaVey," who "underwrote LaVey's efforts in the Church of Satan (no, really)."

It was this spirit of healthy confrontation that left Lacey frustrated at not being able to set the record straight with the legendarily chippy *Voice* staff. As it was, all Lacey got to do was ride up in the elevator, discuss a few generalities with some *Voice* higher-ups behind closed doors in the office of current editor Don Forst, and "check out the urinals." Later on, Forst, the grizzled former daily-paper guy who has resided incongruously atop the *Voice* masthead for almost a decade, took Lacey on a small tour. They walked past Cooper Square, where in February of 1860 Abraham Lincoln delivered his most important antislavery addresses, to the true key juncture of the neighborhood, the Starbucks on Astor Place.

"Forst said this was where it was at," Lacey related, "because that's where NYU kids go, our supposed target audience."

It was all pretty tame, Lacey said in his deep-throat baritone. "I didn't get anything stuck between my shoulder blades. Someone could have at least told me to fuck off. What a letdown." But there was nothing to be done about it, as Lacey reminded, since John Ashcroft had forbidden further discussion, that is, the Justice Department had mandated that in media mergers of this size the new owner was barred from "engaging in major business practices," for a sixty-to-ninety-day review period. This included addressing the staff or even touring the building.

Not that Lacey was shy in explicating what he *would* have told the *Voice* staff should they have brought up any number of topics, like, say, that New Times papers are conservative. "Look," Lacey said, "just because I don't have eight reporters kneecapping George Bush doesn't make me conservative. One is enough; the other seven can be looking for dirt on local politicians. The idea is not to let politicians get away with shit. That's not liberal or conservative, and believe me *our papers have butt-violated every goddamn politician who ever came down the pike!* As a journalist, if you don't get up in the morning and say 'fuck you' to someone, why even do it?

"Look, a lot of people think I'm a prick," Lacey self-assessed. "But at least I'm a prick you can understand. I don't sneak up on you. You can see me coming from a long way away. Like the Russian winter."

It was quite a performance, aided by the fact we had just downed three bottles of Italian wine, at $120 per. But what about the *Village Voice*? Not to denigrate the fine towns where New Times operates its freebie papers, but this was New York City and we were talking about the *Village Voice*. *The Village fucking Voice*—not just one more property for Mike Lacey and Jim Larkin to insert into their strip-mall portfolio like a Kansas City *Pitch*, or a St. Louis *Riverfront Times*, or a Denver *Westword*.

"I'm sick of that crap," Lacey said with a snarl. "Like we're from Phoenix or some Wild West dung heap and we're hayseeds. Like we don't know what's up . . . of course I know we're talking about the *Village fucking Voice*!

"Listen," Lacey said, narrowing his eyes, "we started the Phoenix *New Times* back in 1970 at Arizona State University because the campus police said we couldn't lower the flag to half-mast after Kent State. We didn't want to burn down the ROTC building, we just wanted to lower the flag because it was the right thing to do. Somehow, we thought we needed to start a newspaper to get the nuances of that point across. And to have a little fun. Throw a little spirit of *Mad Magazine* into the debate.

"It wasn't easy. I was ready to sell blood to keep the thing going. We're successful because we're smart, we outwork everyone. Our papers have broken stories. We had the thing about sexual abuse of female cadets at the Air Force Academy. We had the story about mishandling nuclear waste in San Francisco. Not the *San Francisco Chronicle*, not the *Los Angeles Times*. Us. We've won more than seven hundred awards. But I never stopped thinking about the *Village Voice*. I know what it *was*. I know what it is now.

"I've got my own focus group in this town: twenty-year-olds, thirty-year-olds. They say, the *Village Voice*, no one reads that. I can't walk around town hearing nobody reads my paper. It wrecks my day. That's got to change. We're here to play, and anyone who likes to play like we play can play along."

Thanks for the phrase go to Cynthia Cotts, who used to write the *Voice* "Press Clips" column (she reported on New Times' failed 2000 attempt to buy the *Voice*, calling it a "hostile takeover"). "The *Village Voice*," she said. "It is the wound that never heals."

This I take to mean that once you are a *Voice* Person—no matter how many years go by or the number of jobs you do—you will always be a *Voice* Person. Even those without holes in their jeans, like Ken Auletta, who once wrote the *Voice*'s city-politics column, "Running Scared," back in the early seventies, agree.

"Yeah," Ken said. "It's like the blood on Lady Macbeth's hands.

You never know when your *Voice* personhood will crop up. A couple of years ago I was feeling extra crazy, so a friend gave me a shrink's name. I called, and this deep Donald Sutherland voice came on the line. Yes, he said, he had time, I should come by his office on Tuesday afternoon. "Eighty University Place," he said, sonorously. Sensing hesitation on my part, the shrink asked, "Do you have a problem with that?" No, I said. It was fine. The mere fact that I'd spent four years in the building working for the *Village Voice* wouldn't interfere with my therapy, would it? Yet when I arrived for the session to find the shrink's office on the fifth floor in the back, I had to demur. "Don't think this is going to work for me," I told the puzzled analyst.

"Fifth floor in the back, it was just too dense," I told David Schneiderman when I went to see him a couple of weeks ago. Schneiderman laughed. After all, Schneiderman, whose brother Stuart is a leading American authority on the French psychiatrist Jacques Lacan, was well familiar with the fifth-floor rear of 80 University Place, circa 1978. That was where the editor in chief's office was, the same glassed-in sector where I was hired by Marianne Partridge and, some years later, fired by David Schneiderman. (That should take care of any disclosure issues.)

In the days, and years, that followed I often heard myself referring to the rail-thin Schneiderman as the man who single-handedly did more than anyone to kill alternative journalism in the United States. Not that this was the time to act on old grudges. The firing was passed over as a regretful misunderstanding, a product of youth. Schneiderman was a good sport about the whole thing. He could afford to be, since he'd gone from staff-mandated exile, to editor, to publisher (under Stern), to CEO, and now stood to make a rumored half a million dollars for brokering the merger with New Times. He didn't even flinch when I told him I knew from the moment he walked in the door he was bad news, because if there was anything a 1978 Voice Person understood, it was, Don't hire anyone from the New York Times. Certainly not some deputy from the op-ed page—and never, ever, make him the editor in chief.

That's because back then a Voice Person didn't dream of working up to some swell job on the "Metro" section. The New York Times was the enemy. You knew it could send out its mirthless Maginot Line of Princetonians and it wouldn't matter. If you traveled light and right, you could still beat them to the spot. They could be had. Putting a Timesman, from Johns Hopkins, in charge of the Voice struck me as a sick Murdochian joke, a total capitulation.

But what did it matter now? Twenty-seven years later, Schneiderman was still there, still the boss. All those wild people, all those famous bylines, and he'd outlived almost every one of them. He was the dominant personality in the entire history of the institution.

He didn't look all that different, apart from the gray hair. He was still that same lantern-jawed, hingey-looking Ichabod Crane–Sephardim in a Brooks Brothers shirt. His status had changed, though. At 36 Cooper Square, he rode upstairs in what most people at the place referred to as "David's private elevator." Now the CEO of Village Voice Media, he'd become something of a ghost around the office. Longtime Voice people, including those he used to edit, said they saw him maybe once or twice a year, something like the principal of a large high school.

"I don't even know why you came over here," Schneiderman said, smiling. "Because you're going to write the same story everyone does, how the Village Voice isn't what it used to be anymore. But those people say they don't read the paper, so how would they know?" He could keep using that line to his uptown friends, but it wasn't going to work with me. Because I do read the Voice—every week, if only because there was stuff in there worth reading: my homey Hoberman's movie reviews, the great Ridgeway, Wayne Barrett, and Tom Robbins, still kicking municipal butt. Still, it was so, the paper wasn't what it used to be. But why was that?

We batted around the usual rationales: the end of the left (Schneiderman said it was "a dead movement"), the demise of bohemia, changes in the youth culture, and the decision, in 1996, to go free, that is, give the paper away, as all "alt" papers are. Told that many writers felt that the impact of their work had been diminished when the paper went free, Schneiderman scoffed, adding that there was no choice. "We were below 130,000 circulation, down from a top of 160,000. Now the circulation is 250,000 . . . wouldn't you rather be read by twice as many people?" Well, yeah, but I wondered where Schneiderman got this quarter-of-a-million number from.

"Returns," he said. "We've got only one percent returns. That's where the number comes from."

"You must be kidding. Are you counting those hundreds of papers that are thrown away because some dog pissed on them?" How could he claim 250,000 individual readers when most picked up the paper to see what time a movie began, threw it away, and got another one for the next movie?

"No one does that."

"I do."

"You're not typical."

No, Schneiderman said, it wasn't going free that hurt the paper. It *saved* the paper. Kept it going, making money. The true challenge was, as everyone knew, the Web. "Craigslist is the biggest single crisis the *Village Voice* has faced in its whole fifty years," he said with out-of-character vehemence. Schneiderman really had it in for "Craig," whom he said had cost the *Voice* more than a few million dollars in real-estate classifieds alone.

"That guy," Schneiderman said, "he puts himself on a pedestal, says what he's doing is for *the people*, but that's a lie. He's only in it for himself, like everyone else."

It was then, looking around Schneiderman's office, with its displays of the *Village Voice* Media holdings—covers of the Minneapolis-St. Paul *City Pages*, the *LA Weekly*, Orange County's *O.C. Weekly*, the *Seattle Weekly*, and the *Nashville Scene*—that it occurred to me how far we really were from the glassed-in office on 80 University Place. I was speaking to a fundamentally different person than the one who fired me twenty-five years before. Our particular visions of the *Village Voice* could no longer be the same. My paper was a chimera of longing and never-quite-requited obsession, an object to be held in the hand, sweaty ink on fingertips. Schneiderman's view, although indescribably deeper owing to his nigh three decades inside the beast through who-knew-how-much thick and thin, had a more abstract air. He was talking of the paper as a piece, albeit a big one, on an infinitely larger playing field.

Schneiderman grinned at this notion and said, even if he "woke up every morning thinking about how to protect the *Village Voice*," quite frankly, exactly what went into the paper had ceased to be his major concern long ago.

He said, "If Leonard Stern hadn't come here and made me a publisher, I think I would have been gone after five years. That's pretty much the burnout period for an editor at a place like this. Leonard helped make me into a numbers guy. Of course I'm still a word guy, but there's a longer shelf life to a numbers guy. That's been the real fun for me, flying around, looking after our papers, handling the business side."

Schneiderman didn't worry about what actually appeared in the *Voice* because, he said, he had trust in his editor, Don Forst. Indeed, the bantam, septuagenarian former head of New York *Newsday* has been *Voice* editor longer than anyone has ever held the job. Asked why he got the position, Forst, nothing if not blunt, said, "I'm a very good manager. I can handle a tough room. But really, I don't know. I needed a job."

It was clear from the start that Don Forst's paper was to be a wholly different animal. One of the first acts in the Forst era was the firing of Jules Feiffer, universally regarded as the paper's most visible and beloved symbol. "It wasn't just that they canned Jules," says one *Voice*r who, like almost everyone else, preferred to remain nameless. "It was well known that they thought he was making too much money, if you can call seventy-five thousand dollars too much for Jules Feiffer. They'd been after Karen Durbin, the last editor, to get rid of him. But she refused. She knew what Jules meant. What really blew people's minds was Forst's attitude after he pulled the plug. He said Feiffer was fired and that was that. There wasn't going to be any of the usual shit about it, none of that letters-from-the-outraged-staff stuff that has always gone on at the *Voice*. The staff tried to buy an ad to complain, but the ad department said they wouldn't run it. That's when we knew we'd entered a period of malign neglect at the *Village Voice*."

Once, for better or worse, the *Voice* was a "writer's paper," but the *I* word was soon banished from most *Voice* copy. "I am simply not interested in people's individual psychodramas," Don Forst said. Story length was restricted, with few features running longer than twenty-five hundred words. "Our younger demographic doesn't like to read long stories," said the seventy-three-year-old Forst. One day, Forst dropped a copy of *The Old Man and the Sea* on the desk of the late Julie Lobbia. "Your sentences are too long," he said. Most destructive, according to most, has been the redesign of the arts pages, allegedly at the behest of the ad department. In the old days, a lead *Voice* critic could address the week's fare in a free-ranging essay of about fourteen hundred words. Now it was decreed that they produce three separate "elements" on the page, each dealing with a separate film, play, or piece of music. The "big" piece runs eight hundred words.

"It is depressing," says one critic. "I thought if I stayed serious, I'd create a body of work that might win me a Pulitzer. At least I had the hope. Now what can I show, these little postage stamps?"

Meanwhile, management, always legendarily cheap (Schneiderman once declared that no *Voice* reporter was allowed to use 411; the policy was dropped after people started calling 1–718–555–1212, which was more expensive), kept downsizing. Gary Giddins, only the best jazz critic in the country, was pushed out after three decades. Sylvia Plachy, who along with James Hamilton had given the *Voice* a very distinctive photographic look, was laid off, apparently to save her $20,000 stipend. Her son, the actor Adrien Brody, an office regular back in his toddling days, often making copies of his face by pressing his nose to the glass of the Xerox machine, came to help her move.

"He had this baseball hat jammed down over his head, demanding to know who fired his mother," one observer recounts.

Hearing some of this, Michael Lacey frowns. He'd been ranting about how even though he'd come from a union household, and his brother, who helped build the World Trade Center, was the president of a midwestern boilermakers local ("which was no pussy union"), he had no use for organized labor. This didn't mean he expected any trouble from the *Voice* union. What he hoped would happen, Lacey said with confounding plutocrat noblesse oblige, was that the *Voice* employees would realize a union wasn't necessary, "because we take good care of our people."

Word of bad morale at the *Voice*, however, brought Lacey up short. Although no slouch with the downsize scythe himself (mass-firing tales are legend in the *New Times* canon), Lacey shook his head at stories of layoffs. "You don't get rid of good people just to save money. They're too hard to find. You don't discourage them. You want a lively newsroom, some action. *Sturm. Drang.* That place seemed dead."

He couldn't seem to get over David Schneiderman, his new partner, referring to himself as "a numbers guy." He liked Schneiderman and had learned not to underestimate him. But "a numbers guy? . . . Sounds like death. I can't even balance my checkbook. . . . It's so sick the way most of the business runs. The top editors don't edit. Never touch a piece of copy. What do they do all day, think beautiful thoughts? The way we do it, the editors have to write too. They should never forget how hard it is, *the fucking agony of it.* I make myself write and report. It kills me, but I do it."

Then, loud enough for the other diners to turn around, Lacey declared, "God help me, I'm in a business of weenies!"

The next day, I was talking on the phone to Robert Christgau, the *Voice*'s archetypically thorny "Dean of Rock Critics." He asked me what I thought of Michael Lacey. I said he'd probably turn out to be a nightmare, but so far I kind of liked him.

"What do you like about him?" Bob demanded.

"I don't know . . . he's got this bonkers sincerity about him. Who knows what he'll do, but I got the feeling he genuinely wants to make the paper better."

Christgau snorted. "I doubt if his conception of how to make the paper better conforms to mine."

Then he hung up. Conversations with Bob Christgau have a habit of being truncated without warning. Often voluminous on the page, verbally he retains a compelling gift of concision. After Nelson Rockefeller reputedly died after sex with the young Megan Marshack, Bob said, "If I knew it would kill him, I would have blown him myself." When John Lennon was shot, he bemoaned, "Why is it always Robert Kennedy and John Lennon, not Richard Nixon and Paul McCartney?" Personally, I've always treasured Christgau's assessment of my work. During the era of the Reggie Jackson Yankees, I wrote a not particularly friendly piece about the team. Christgau, a Yanks fan, came over to my desk.

"Read your piece," he said. "*Really sucked.*" Then he stomped away. I never even got a chance to thank him for his input.

Christgau's comment about Mike Lacey seemed likewise to the point, a perfect *Voice* Person reply. To wit: sure, Lacey and his crew could take over, as Leonard Stern, Clay Felker, and Murdoch had done before. They could fire everyone, turn the paper into a desert flatter than a Scottsdale Mall. They might temporarily own the paper's little red boxes, its famous name. But they would never control its soul, never truly silence the legitimate keepers of the VV logos.

Coming from Christgau, now sixty-three, more than half his life spent at the paper, it was a defiance you had to respect. This was especially so, since of all the supposed *Village Voice* "dinosaurs," those masthead survivors who never seem to go away, nobody comes in for as much sniping as Bob. Typical is the commentary of Russ Smith, the snarkish "Mugger" of the *New York Press*, the most recent bottom-feeder paper whose entire existence is bound up in the fact that it is not the *Voice*. Smith said the merger would certainly mean "sayonara to Robert Christgau, who could then be reached at either an upstate retirement community or the publicity department of a record company."

No doubt much of the ire directed at Christgau stems from his longrunning "Consumer Guide" feature, in which he hands out letter grades to discs each month, a practice that caused Lou Reed to once refer to Xgau as "an asshole" on a live record. The subtext: *School of Rock* might have been a hit, but "rock as school" will never be, and what's a sixty-three-year-old guy who has never burned a CD got to say about pop music in this day and age anyway?

The answer is quite a lot, if you care to listen. Present from the moment rock became "serious," Christgau, like other all-inclusive *Voice* critics J. Hoberman and Michael Feingold, knows everything from the beginning to now and continues to put it to the page, albeit a tad densely. Indeed, writers like Christgau—and this probably goes for Nat Hentoff, too, still batting away on his Selectric 3 and too busy to have me come by because "with the Constitution so endangered, it needs my total attention all the time"—could have existed only at the *Village Voice*.

This was the realm of the non-J-school, self-invented, pop-cultural autodidact, a place where the high tone met the vulgar and an Everyman could hawk his expertise. It is no coincidence that many of the older *Voice* writers come from working-class, outer-borough backgrounds (Christgau's father was a Queens fireman, Richard Goldstein's was a Bronx postal worker), people who threw in their lot with the egalitarian vision of the paper where they could write what they wanted. What's the term limit on that, even in a journo-world desperate to "get younger"? No doubt Christgau will go to his grave positive that the *Voice*, the true *Voice*, exists only as "a left-wing, intellectual, writer's paper," and believe me, he is not likely to go quietly.

"It might sound strange, but people my age are much more suited to working at the *Voice* the way the paper is these days," says Jarrett Murphy, a twenty-nine-year-old front-of-the-book reporter. "We came into this business knowing it was a potentially dying industry. I would have loved to have worked at the *Voice* when it was great. You just have to look at the fiftieth, see all those covers, and it gives you a chill. But you have to be realistic, deal with what is."

It made you wonder if it might have been better to have taken the paper out and shot it, like a used-up racehorse, before, say, the humiliation of going free.

"Don't think I would have liked that," said Richard Goldstein, who worked at the paper for thirty-eight years in an unparalleled career that comprised more or less inventing rock-and-roll criticism and establishing an above-ground media outlet for the gay community. This is not to mention uncounted hours of engaging in all intrapaper turf squabbles (in my day, the alleged macho "white boy" news writers at the front of the book were always at war with the whiny art-culture people in the back). Now sixty-one, Goldstein, raised in a Bronx housing project, is one more perfect *Voice* Person who started reading the paper early, sussing out that a trip on the Woodlawn-Jerome line to MacDougal Street could make even him a *bissel* cool. Present for every regime change in the history of the paper, Goldstein will not be around for the *New Times* era. He was fired in the summer of 2004, after an increasingly fractious relationship with Forst.

Goldstein contends that Forst has waged a long-running gay-baiting campaign against him. "He said things to me I hadn't heard since the playground in the Bronx. He just kept doing it. It was sick." In 1999, in accordance with *Voice* policy on verbal abuse, Goldstein wrote a letter of complaint. It was after that, he says, that Forst retaliated by "taking away my job. . . . I hired and edited Mark Schoofs, who won a Pulitzer Prize; I wrote 'Press Clips.' It wasn't like I was slipping. Then one day Forst comes in and tells me I won't be writing for the paper and I should just think of myself as a 'cobbler.' I don't want to be maudlin, but the *Voice* was such a big part of my life for so long, to have it disappear was incredible." Eventually, Goldstein wrote a letter to David Schneiderman, telling his side of the story.

"I trusted him. In my mind he still represented the *Voice* I knew. Then I got a call from the publisher, Judy Miszner, and she's telling me, 'So you've decided to resign.' I said, 'What?' Their attitude was, if I couldn't get along with Forst, I had to go. I couldn't believe it. This, at the *Village Voice*! Then they started giving me a hard time about my severance. I'm there thirty-eight years, and they're trying to stiff me."

"Richard broke the chain of command," says one *Voice* writer. "That was the unforgivable thing."

Finally, Goldstein filed a federal suit charging the *Voice* with, among other things, sexual harassment and age discrimination. "Even after all that, I didn't want to hurt the paper," he says.

Should you care to, you can go to TheSmokingGun.com, the Web site started by Bill Bastone, former *Voice* writer, to read the court documents in the case of *Richard Goldstein*, plaintiff, v. *Village Voice* Media, defendant.

In it, Goldstein accuses Forst of calling him "an ass-licker," "a slut boy," "a pussy boy," and saying he walked "like a ballerina." After years of hearing about dreary *Voice* p.c., the case makes surreal but grim reading.

Asked if the *Village Voice* was "the biggest basket case" of his acquisitions, Mike Lacey bugged his eyes like, "duh." "Without a doubt," Lacey said, but this only raised the stakes, because the *Voice*, and New York, was "such a big deal."

"This is it: unique, special, fucking exciting," Lacey said, walking through a driving rain on Ninth Avenue in the Thirties. He was spritzing, free-associating about what he might do with the *Village Voice*.

"I like the arts coverage. But we've got to work on the front of the book. We can't have stories cribbed from the Net. We have to get out of the office. Robbins seems good. He's a reporter. But I can't believe they don't have a front-of-the-book columnist, someone to give a sense of the fabric of what the streets are like. Come back, Jimmy Breslin!"

He was steaming now, talking louder, stomping across the avenue ."We could cover the courts. Have a reporter down there. We don't have to be *Time Out*." Did he feel he had a particular responsibility to the *Voice* staff, especially those writers long identified with the paper? "Of course, you want people who love the place, but this is a business that is based on performance. It isn't a legacy."

No doubt this was going to be hard, Lacey said. He was having some difficulty buying into David Schneiderman's circulation numbers. "Have to see about that," Lacey said, regretting that he wouldn't be able to move to New York to keep an eye on things. "No, I got this sixteen-year-old. He drove the car through the garage wall back in Phoenix. He requires surveillance."

Then Lacey said he had to rush. He was flying out in the morning to L.A., where he'd scheduled a meeting at the *LA Weekly*. It promised to be tense, after *New Times*'s typically vicious, ultimately losing attempt to start a rival paper to the *Weekly*. There'd be hard feelings, fences to mend, necks to snap back into joint. It was all a giant juggling act, Lacey said. With seventeen papers, you couldn't play favorites.

Meanwhile, the *Voice* threw a little party at Bowery Bar to celebrate the fiftieth-anniversary issue. The turnout was good, especially considering the announcement of the merger and how few whose work had been chronicled in the issue were invited or able to show up. (Newfield, Joel Oppenheimer, Joe Flaherty, Mary Nichols, Geoff Stokes, and Paul Cowan, among others, had a good excuse: they were dead. Many others just hated the paper.) A cake decorated with the famous *Voice* logo was served, and David Schneiderman, after laughingly introducing himself as "that mystery man," made a speech. Someone quoted Alexander Cockburn's famous line from a previous *Voice* takeover, how the change made him "dizzy with the prospect of a whole galaxy of new asses to kiss."

Then, with the dinner crowd arriving, the party was over. The *Voice* people walked out onto the Bowery. If you looked to the right you could see CBGB, where the drag queen Jayne (nee Wayne) County once knocked out Handsome Dick Manitoba of the Dictators with a mike stand. James Wolcott wrote a really cool story about it for the *Voice* sometime in 1975. Soon, they might close CBGB because Hilly Kristal won't pay higher rent. But that was the way it went. It was a new world out there, with new times to go with it.

11

Ground Zero/Grassy Knoll: 11 Bulletpoints About 9/11 Truth

The attack on the World Trade Center, with its attendant political and moral fallout, is without doubt the biggest story I ever covered. It doesn't stop. It is a rare day that goes by I don't think of the events of that nightmarish time. Along with almost every journalist in the City, I've written several pieces on the WTC and no doubt will continue to do so. For me, 9/11 time falls into several catagories. The first period is the event itself, the very day when "everything" supposed to have changed. I was there that day, at Ground Zero, arriving a couple hours after the towers fell. I was there when 7 World Trade Center collapsed. I'll know I've got the Alezheimer's when a day goes by and I don't think about what happened then. Another part of my version of 9/11 time involves the immediate political fallout, especially the exploitation of the event by the powers that be. The Republican Party's cynical decision to hold their 2004 nominating convention at Madison Square Garden was an affront to any real New Yorker. The notion that these creeps (fearmongering former Mayor Rudy Giuliani was one of the worst) could use the city as backdrop to push their increasingly disastrous post-9/11 agenda deserved nothing but a stiff middle finger, not the fawning, phony hospitality extended by Mayor Bloomberg. The strongarm policing job done by Commissioner Ray Kelly during the *convention, indiscriminately herding non-violent protesters into paddy wagons so people like Dick Cheney would hear nary a discouraging word, ranks as a low point in New York's long tradition of loud-mouthed democracy. New Yorkers showed what they thought of Bush's visit by giving him a big-time 16 percent of the vote in Manhattan, Brooklyn, and the Bronx.*

Past that is what I'd call the inevitable long-range psychology of 9/11, covered in the piece printed below. Conspiracy theory has a bad name these days, and this seems highly judgemental and unfair. It is only human to invent some sort of reason for the inexplicable. This said, if the pieces I've written about 9/11 reveal anything, it is that my feelings remain consistent: I experience as a New Yorker first, a citizen of the City. From New York magazine, 2006.

1. 11/22 and 9/11

They keep telling us 9/11 changed everything. But even in this photoshopped age of unreliable narrators, omniscient and otherwise, much remains the same. As with 9/11, the assassination of President John Kennedy in Dallas on 11/22/63, the Crime of the Century, occurred in plain sight, in front of thousands, yet no one can exactly be sure what happened. Like 9/11, an official explanation of the Kennedy assassination was produced. The Warren Commission confirmed early reports that Lee Harvey Oswald, a ne'er-do-well member of the Fair Play for Cuba Committee, shot Kennedy with a cheap Mannlicher-Carcano rifle from a sixth-floor window of the Texas Book Depository. The Commission said Oswald, who two days later would be shot dead by nightclub owner Jack Ruby, acted alone.

Yet, as with many major events, there is the sanctioned history and the the so-called secret history—actions and motives hidden from view, covered up, by the official historians. Many believe this was the case with the Kennedy assassination. Myriad theories have arisen about what really happened that day. Any number of culprits, from the Cuban government, to the Mafia and/or the CIA, have been deemed responsible. These ideas gained increasing traction in the popular mind-set.

The precise tipping point—the moment the Grassy Knoll supplanted the sixth-floor window—is not exactly clear, but four decades past Kennedy's murder it is difficult to find anyone who sincerely believes Lee Harvey Oswald was solely responsible. But if Oswald didn't kill the President, who did? No comprehensive, universally believed chronicle of events has emerged. 11/22 remains an open case, an open wound.

Now here we are again, contemplating the unthinkable of September 11. Again we confront an event that occurred on a bright clear day, with thousands of eyewitnesses, yet shrouded in mystery. The official explanation, offered first by the Bush administration and later confirmed, with some amendment, by the 9/11 Commission Report, has been released: the nation was attacked by the forces of radical Islam led by Osama bin Laden and his Al Qaeda jihadists.

Again, many Americans believe the official story. But not all.

2. WAR WITHOUT END

"We're just your average wild-eyed, foaming at the mouth, tin-foil hat wearing conspiracy nuts," said Father Frank Morales, a priest at the St. Mark's Church on the Lower East Side as he surveyed the two hundred or so graying beatniks and neighborhood anarchist punks sporting "Is It Fascism Yet" buttons who had arrived for the weekly Sunday night meeting of the New York 9/11Truth movement. They'd come to the church to hear a lecture by Webster Tarpley, author of the recent book, *9/11 Synthetic Terror: Made in the USA*.

Looking like a cross between a kindly medieval parson and Dick Cheney, whom he accuses of "high treason" in his book, the sixty-year-old Tarpley said he was in New York, "the scene of the crime, to debunk the myth . . . the absurd fairy tale" that tragic events of September 11, 2001, were the work of nineteen guys with boxcutters commanded to fly airplanes into buildings by a bearded cave-dwelling evildoer.

To this end, Tarpley displayed a slide titled "State-Sponsored False Flag

Terrorism," directing the audience's attention to a Venn diagram of three interconnected circles. Circle one was labeled "Patsies," denoted as "dupes," "useful idiots," "fanatics," "provocateurs," and "Oswalds." Included here were bin Laden and the alleged lead hijacker, Mohammad Atta. The second sphere, marked "Moles," contained "government officials loyal to the invisible government" such as Paul Wolfowitz, Tony Blair, Donald Rumsfeld, Cheney and, of course, George W. Bush. The third circle, "professional killers," encompassed "technicians, CIA and special forces, old boys"— the unnamed ones who did the dirty work and knew how to keep their mouths shut.

This was the true face of corporatized terror as practiced by the infinite octopus of the "secret government," said Tarpley, graduate of Flushing High School, class of 1962 (also Princeton). It was a terrain Tarpley knew well, as the author of an "unauthorized" biography of George Herbert Walker Bush, a tome that paints the Bush family patriarch, U.S. Senator Prescott Bush, as knowingly profiting from Hitler's Third Reich in his role as a director of the Union Banking Corporation.

According to Tarpley, this is how it went down, roughly, on September 11. Cheney, Rumsfeld, and the *Pet Goat*–engrossed president played their assigned roles enabling the strange events of that day, including the whole-scale malfunction of the multitrillion-dollar American air defense system. Cued by fellow mole Richard Clarke, the main players made sure the CIA-owned-and-operated Osama and his alleged seventy-two-virgin craving crew got the racist/religionist-fueled blame as Boeings were flown, likely aided by remote control, into the Trade Center towers, which collapsed not from the impact and resulting fire, as reported by the brainwashed mainstream media, but rather due to planted bombs and controlled demolition.

Laying out his scenario, Tarpley touched on many of the "unanswered questions" that make up the core of the 9/11 Truth critique of the so-called Official Story.

Like: How, if no steel-frame building had ever collapsed from fire, did three such edifices fall that day, including 7 World Trade Center, which was not hit by any airplane?

And why, if hydrocarbon-fueled fire maxes out at 1,800 degrees Fahrenheit and steel melts at 2,700 degrees, did the towers weaken sufficiently to fall in such a short time—only fifty-six minutes in the case of the South Tower?

And why, if the impact destroyed the planes' supposedly crash-proof flight-recorder black boxes, was the FBI able to find, in perfect condition, the passport of Satam al Suqami, one of the alleged American Airlines Flight 11 hijackers?

And how to explain the nonperformance of the FAA and NORAD? And why did the Defense Department choose to stage an extraordinary number of military exercises on 9/11—occupying matériel and spreading confusion about who was who on that day?

How could the U.S. government allow, an hour after the first World Trade Center crash, an obviously hostile plane to penetrate the world's most heavily protected air space and smash into the Pentagon, the headquarters of the entire military-industrial complex, for chrissakes?

And what about the short-selling spree on American and United airlines stock in the days before the attacks? Betting on the stocks to go down—was this real sicko Wall Street insider trading?

There were so many questions. But when it came to the big "why" of 9/11, there was only the classic conspiratorial query: "Who benefits?"

When it came to September 11, this was a virtual no-brainer. Here was a holocaust-as-ordered by the neocon cabal Project for the New American Century who in the mode of its shadowy mentor, Leo Strauss, understood the people of the U.S.A. to be nothing but robotized, meth-addled, postliterate, and postlogical lardasses, a race of "sheeple" who would never rise to mantle of world dominators without (as the PNAC said) "some catastrophic and catalyzing event—like a new Pearl Harbor." In other words, a new Pearl Harbor like the old Pearl Harbor, which Roosevelt was supposed to have known about weeks in advance and used as an excuse to get us into World War II.

Pearl Harbor, or Reichstag Fire, take your pick. What mattered was that the deed was done; three thousand human beings were dead in the worst single attack on American soil in history, freeing Manchurian Candidate Bush to decree his fraudulent War of Terror, a Social Darwinian/Hobbesian "with us or against us" struggle to corner the planet's dwindling bounty —a global conflict without end in which only the strong, the white, and the Republican would survive.

3. YOUR HOP LEVEL

In an April 2004 paper titled "What Is Your Hop Level," Nick Levis, who co-coordinates the NY911truth meetings with the aforementioned Father Frank Morales and Les Jamieson, categorizes the basic analytical responses to the events of September 11 "short of those who believe in divine or extraterrestrial intervention." Although offering a number of off-shoots, Levis's paper essentially boils down to four major choices.

A: The Official Story (called the Official Conspiracy Theory by 9/11truth activists). The received Bushian fantasy: Al Qaeda/Osama, nineteen guys with boxcutters, flight 93 made to crash in Shanksville, Pennsylvania, by heroic ("Let's Roll") passengers, etc., etc. As White House press secretary Ari Fleisher said in his initial response, there was "no warning."

B: The Incompetence Theory (a.k.a. the Stupidity, Arrogance, Dysfunctional, "Reno Wall" Theory): accepts the Official Story, yet allows for failure on the part of the White House/FBI /CIA/NSA to heed warnings of the plot brewing right under their taxpayer-funded noses. This line was partially advanced, with much butt-covering compensation, in the Kean 9/11 Commission Report.

C: LIHOP, or "Let It Happen on Purpose." Many variations here, but primarily: elements of the U.S. government and/or well-placed factions of the private sector were aware of specific details of the hijackers' plans and, recognizing that 9/11 suited their policy goals, did nothing to stop it.

D: MIHOP, or "Made It Happen on Purpose," that is, elements of the U.S. government and/or private forces actively planned and executed the attacks, including, quite possibly, using the airplane strikes as a cover to bring down the Trade Center buildings with secreted explosives.

"What are the alternatives to MIHOP?" asks Webster Tarpley, rhetorically, in the introduction of his book *Synthetic Terror,* dismissing the only other thinkable possibility, LIHOP, as being "increasingly at war with the masses of evidence."

Tarpley's "rouge network/invisible government MIHOP" is only one of the many MIHOPs floating around 9/11truth circles. Most popular are various configs of Cheney/Bush MIHOP, asserting that the vice president, who appeared to be charge on 9/11 (in violation of the constitutionally decreed chain of command), was the main actor in the plot. Also ambient is Peak Oil MIHOP, an ecodoomsday scenario stemming from the notion that the "peaking" of planetary petroleum reserves prompted the false provocation for the "oil war" in the Middle East.

Further afield are numerous versions of NWO MIHOP, or New World Order MIHOP, which Nick Levis characterizes as the concerted effort of "a global ruling elite seeking greater control of the world Zeitgeist" as a means to fomenting "a transition to open corporate feudalism." Many NWO MIHOPs take into account the long-standing influence of secret societies such as the Freemasons (if you don't believe it, just look at the pyramid-meeting-the-eye on the back every dollar in your pocket, fool!), the Illuminati, and their alleged modern-day standard-bearers like Yale's Skull and Bones Society (both Bushes bonesmen, John Kerry too), the Council on Foreign Relations, and blue-hat armies of the United Nations.

Less cited scenarios include a Sino MIHOP claiming the Chinese military was behind 9/11 as a first strike in the inevitable economic conflict between China and the West. And, in what cannot be considered a newsflash, Scientologists have suggested a Shrink MIHOP, claiming evil psychologists were a controlling force in the attack.

More controversial is Mossad MIHOP, the school of thought that Israeli intelligence played a crucial role in the disaster. This is based in part on the curious story of the "white van," that is, on the morning of September 11 five men, apparently filming the attack from Liberty State Park, were observed exchanging high fives as the planes hit the buildings. Later that day their moving-company van was pulled over by police on Route 3 by Giants Stadium. One of the men was found to have $4,700 in his sock. Extra passports were also recovered. "We are Israeli," the driver reputedly told cops. "We are not your problem. Your problems are your problems. The Palestinians are the problem." The men were taken to the Federal Detention Center in Sunset Park, Brooklyn, from where, sans further action, they were deported to Israel. Later an article in the Jewish *Forward* identified the company that owned the van, Urban Moving Systems, to be a Mossad front.

Much as been made of this and other such incidents among 9/11 truth sources, but this is clearly tricky terrain. As witnessed by the very first of so-called 9/11 conspiracies, the disproved but often repeated story that four thoudand Jewish WTC workers were warned to stay home that day, any Mossad MIHOP can easily morph to Zionist MIHOP and/or Jew MIHOP. In an odd revisionism of Art Spiegelman's *Maus*, well-known 9/11 truth researcher Eric Hufschmid (author of "Painful Questions") writes, "I see the Zionists as being analogous to an organization of cats who work together to catch thousands of stupid, unorganized mice. Why should I feel sorry for the mice? Why should I hate the cats?"

Despite laborious efforts to distinguish the difference between "Zionism" and "Judaism," this remains a difficult area for NY 9/11 truth advocates, many of whom are Jews. The specter of being too easily tarred with the anti-Semite brush by the Abe Foxmans of the world is a real danger. "Do I believe Israel has undue influence over U.S. foreign policy?" asks one local activist. "Absolutely. But there are people in this movement who are fucking Nazis. I think you have to draw the line at Holocaust denial."

But this aside, when it comes to 9/11, it is all MIHOP because as far as Truth activists are concerned, we are living in a MIHOP world.

4. MINUTEMEN OF HISTORY

"For me, MIHOP was inevitable, because in this, the more you know, the more you know," says Les Jamieson, a tall, friendly, eminently reasonable seeming forty-five-year-old guy from Brooklyn who serves as Northeast Program Coordinator of the nationwide 9/11truth.org. Like most 9/11truth people, Les remembers the moment when the scales of the Official Story media fog fell from his eyes.

"On September 11 my first reaction was like everyone else: shock, horror, rage. But then I kept coming across these items. One of the first was a story in *Newsweek*, which said these generals were told earlier that week not to fly. They said there was no warning, but obviously someone knew. I saw videos about the way the buildings fell, how they seemed to implode. My reaction was: 'holy shit.' That's what this process has been, one 'holy shit' after another."

Now, most Saturday afternoons, Les can often be found in front of the PATH station at Ground Zero holding up a banner proclaiming that 9/11 WAS AN INSIDE JOB. Reaction to this demonstration has been "mixed," Les reports. Last Memorial Day, when the Truth activists were "surrounded by these screaming sons of firemen," it was particularly rough. "It was like we were committing some kind of blasphemy," recalls Les, who vows to continue the vigils no matter what.

He says: "I truly believe that we, our 9/11truth movement, are sort of minutemen, trying to make the country aware of this terrible crime that has been committed. We're like prosecutors in the discovery phase, unearthing evidence for a trial that is sure to come."

Father Frank Morales agrees that "this is about history." Morales, who if not for his priest collar could easily be mistaken for an East Village hipster in his black stocking cap and quarter-inch beard vertically bifurcating his chin, is a longtime neighborhood hero. Raised in the Jacob Riis projects, ordained in 1976, Morales spent years as "a street priest walking in Jesus' path" in the then burning South Bronx before coming back to the Lower East Side to work with the squatter community. The day after 9/11 he got a call from the diocese asking him to go to Ground Zero to perform last rites for the victims.

"They said to be prepared because 'we're not talking bodies here, Frank, we're talking body parts,'" Morales recalls.

"It was a real test of faith, being down there, because I could feel myself getting madder and madder, not the way a priest is supposed to feel," says Father Frank, who recalls the ground being "rich and moist, enriched with the ground-up bodies of the dead." Sitting with a fireman who'd been "on the pile like forty-eight hours straight," Morales remembers cursing the hijackers, screaming that "I just wanna get those motherfuckers."

It was at this point, Morales says, that the fireman "put his hand on my shoulder and whispered, 'Hey, it's not about that. . . . You wanna know something? Bush and Bin Laden have the same banker.'"

It was everything that happened afterward, the Patriot Act, the Iraq War, that turned him into a 9/11truth activist, Morales said. Now, he's MIHOP too.

Activists like Nick Levis, Les Jamieson, and Frank Morales know that the sort of 9/11truth they seek is unlikely to meet the ontological standards of Saint Anselm. There are too many nuts around. After all, they've got people on their side like the "Web fairy" who runs a site supposedly proving the planes that hit the Trade Center were not planes at all but holograms, or "ghost planes." What can you say about a truth movement's relationship to the nature of truth when many of the entries about its main concerns in the Wikipedia bear the caveat "disputed"?

Yet for all this the 911truth movement retains one irrefutably puissant weapon in its struggle with the Official Story. As Frank Morales asks, "Would you believe anything George W. Bush told you?"

5. A FAST-MOVING MEME

Type "9/11 conspiracy" into the Google and the bytes bury you. The first truly great conspiracy theory of the Internet Age—imagine JFK assassinationology with the Web!—9/11truth is a fast traveling meme.

The thicket of "truth" sites seems endless. There is "911truth.org," "911truth.com," "911forthetruth.com," "911truthla.org," "nakedfor911truth .com," "911truthemergence.com," "911citizenswatch.com," "911inquiry

.org," "911research.net," "911–strike.com," "total911.info.com," "911blogger .com," "911review.com," "septembereleventh.com," "physics911.com," "psychics911.com," and dozens more.

There are radco guys too, like Alex Jones, proprietor of prisonplanet.com and infowars.com, an inveterate loudmouth who charges ahead with his smorgasbord New World Order MIHOP and video camera into the beating heart of old boy networks, accosting small potatoes like David Gergen outside the Bohemian Grove, supposed site of Bilderbergian Satanic rituals.

Such antics notwithstanding, it can be argued that a whole new kind of politics is being waged in the 9/11 truth assault, a kind of emerging pan-libertarianism that trashes not only the slack boundaries of the mainstream but also the supposed "Far" Left and Right. Apocalyptically minded sur-vivalists and extreme Bush-haters are equally attracted to the blanket *j'accuse* that the U.S. government has attacked its own people to prod them into a ceaseless, baseless terror crusade, a clash of civilizations to end all civilization. Be you a Starbucks window breaker or John Bircher, it ain't like you need a weatherman to tell you which way Thomas L. Friedman and his globalist windbaggery blows.

For a post-9/11 world, there is a post-9/11 flow of information. With-out the web, 9/11 truth does not exist. This is not a movement where people are taking their Nagra tape recorders to document the acoustics of Dealey Plaza, so as to better ascertain which bullet came from what angle. When 9/11 truth "researchers" refer to "the physical evidence," they often are re-ferring to pictures posted on various blog sites. They are stay-at-home in-terpreters of graphics, analyzers of webcasts. Paul Thompson, whose copiously detailed 9/11 timeline has become the undisputed gold standard of all Truth research, does all his work on the Net. If it's not online, it is not in the timeline.

"I don't have to be in any particular place to do this," says Thomp-son, who for a time moved to New Zealand so it would be easier for him to concentrate.

Yet it is difficult to deny the allure of this Web-based critique. The conspiracist has always relied on a degree of magical thinking. And, as Marshall McLuhan would doubtless assert if he wasn't dead, there has never been a tool more paranoia-ready than the Internet. It is an exhilarating serendipity that every surfer has felt: the way one link seems to lead miraculously to the next, each connection synchronistically handshaking to the one beyond, the notion of not knowing how exactly you wound up where you are but being sure, absolutely sure, that you have arrived at precisely the right place. Conclusions made by the aegis of such miraculous method cannot simply be random. For the moment, and maybe longer, it feels like Truth.

Spooky coincidences and clairvoyances abound. How does one accomodate the fact that in the months prior to September 11 parties unknown purchased the domain names "nycterrorstrike.com," "horrorinnewyork .com," "tradetowerstrike.com," "tradecenterbombs.com," and several others. Was this Mohammad Atta's idea of a cyber joke?

Consider Pammy Wynant, protagonist of the novel *Players* by Don De-Lillo (big surprise, that). Published in 1977, the book describes how Pammy, working for a firm called Grief Management Council, which has its offices in the World Trade Center, at first felt the WTC was "an unlikely head-quarters for an outfit such as this. But she changed her mind as time passed. Where else would you stack all this grief?" A few lines later, DeLillo writes, "To Pammy the towers didn't seem permanent. They remained concepts, no less transient for all their bulk than some routine distortion of light."

Even to dismiss the usual numerologic smut about how 9+1+1=11 and the fact that there are eleven letters in both George W. Bush and The Pentagon—for which ground was broken September 11, 1941, exactly 155 (1+5+5=11) years after the Masonic-dominated founding fathers opened the Constitutional Convention on September 11, 1786—not to mention that Kennedy was killed on 11/22 and, for CIA MIHOP fans, that Kissinger and the Langley boys chose September 11, 1973, to wipe out Chilean socialist president Salvatore Allende—it is fairly clear that we have entered a realm of the precognitively strange.

What, for instance, is to be made of the fact that the pilot for the conspiracy-themed *Lone Gunmen* (a short-lived Fox knock-off of the *X-Files*), which aired on March 4, 2001, tells the story of a secret U.S. government agency's plot to crash a remote-controlled 727 into the World Trade

Center as an excuse to raise the military budget and then blame the attack on foreign "tin-pot dictators" who were "begging to be smart-bombed."

And what, for instance, does it mean that if you fold a $20 bill just right it forms a likeness of the burning Pentagon on one side and the similarly enflamed Trade Center on the back? (see http://www.glennbeck.com/news/05172002.shtml).

No wonder Jungian shrinks are so crazy about 9/11. It's got so much archetype. I've got no less than three Jungian monographs on the Trade Towers in my possession at this moment. In examining 9/11 trauma, Dr. Ashok Bedi finds mythic resonance in the stories of Shiva, Parvati, and Kali. Dr. Sylvester Wojtkowski, who was kind enough to forward me his paper "Approaching the Unspeakable—Regarding 9/11," draws on the Medusa myth as an explainer. I should like someday to discuss with either of these learned men the significance of the curious arrangement of the smoke from the South Tower that appears to form the face of Lucifer. Put "Devil-face-9/11-smoke" into Google to check it out.

6. INSIDE THE TRUTH VACUUM

"No wonder these people come up with all this stuff about bombs and planes, shooting pods, and missiles. What are people supposed to think when the truth of what really happened is systematically suppressed?" This was how Monica Gabrielle felt four and half years after her husband, Richard, who worked on the seventy-eighth floor of the South Tower, was killed when the building collapsed. Monica, who describes herself as being "a completely normal, housewife paying my taxes, raising my children" before her husband's death and now lives on Long Island "with my dog, my alarm, and some plants," testified before the 9/11 Commission in late 2003. She ended her statement saying she hoped "this Commission understands the need to leave a legacy of truth, accountability and reform as a tribute to all of the innocent victims. . . . We now look to you for leadership."

Asked if she ever expected to get a "legacy of truth" she was looking for, Monica, a woman with an endearingly brassy New York manner, let out a loud, derisive laugh. "I must be an idiot because, yeah, I did. That was how I was brought up, to think the government did their job. But they didn't. We got screwed, that's what we got. A whitewash, a stonewall. I guess they didn't think three thousand people dead was enough to do the right thing. Maybe five thousand, or ten thousand would have been. When I read that report I felt like a sap, a sucker.

"They could have solved a lot of mysteries. They could have found out how the FAA screwed up. They could have figured out who was running the country when Bush was flying around in Air Force One. All they did was have people like Rumsfeld come in, make them promise to do better next time, and give them all medals. My husband was dead and nobody was at fault. They didn't point the finger at anyone. To me, that's a sin, something I can't forgive.

"One thing that bothers me is the realization that Rich's death wasn't just him dying. This was something that was going to be in the history books, stuff children might be learning about in school long after I was gone. And what are those history books going to say? Damn. A while ago the government came around giving out these ceremonial urns, a keepsake of the loved ones. I looked inside. It had beach sand. From Coney Island or somewhere. You figure they could have at least put some of the dust from the Trade Center in there. Something real."

Asked about 9/11truth, Monica laughed heartily. "Nutters? You want nutters? I'm a magnet for them. I keep getting these e-mails from this one woman. She has a lot of theories. She just wrote me that we all have to be careful because 'our thoughts, feelings, and bodily functions are being controlled 100,000 percent by secret electromagnetic waves.' How do you respond to something like that? Still, I write back. Everyone needs a friend, you know."

Hearing this, Laurie Van Auken laughs. "Yeah, I get those too," says Laurie, one of the original "Jersey Girls" whose now legendary persistence pushed the reluctant Bush administration to convene the 9/11 Committee in the first place. Her husband, Kenneth, a Cantor Fitzgerald employee working on the 105th floor of the North Tower, called her to say something hit the building and he wasn't sure if he was going to be able to get out. It wasn't until three days later, hearing that none of Cantor's employees survived, that she knew her husband was dead.

"Conspiracy theories," Laurie says, with a sigh. "That was one of reasons we demanded they have the Commission to begin with. To get to the bottom of things. So there wouldn't be any conspiracy theories."

Just talking about it was enough to get Laurie outraged all over again. "When I hear Philip Zelikow (the 9/11 commission "executive director," who oversaw the production of the report) wrote a book with Condi Rice or was seen with Karl Rove, it drives me crazy. I feel like I'm trapped in a truth vacuum."

One thing that has changed over Laurie's "career as a 9/11 widow." She's come to appreciate "these conspiracy nuts, or whatever you want to call them. . . . When we first started this process, we widows didn't want to seen with any of the conspiracy people. We thought they'd damage our case. But they kept showing up. They seemed to care a lot more than the people supposedly doing the investigating. If you ask me, they're just Americans. Americans looking for the truth, which is supposed to be our right."

7. WTC 7 FALLING DOWN

Talking to Monica Gabrielle and Laurie Van Auken reminded me of the last time I watched the Zapruder film, the most famous visual record of the Kennedy assassination. Shot by Russian-Jewish immigrant ladies garment manufacturer Abraham Zapruder, it is without doubt most highly scrutinized movie of all time. I wanted to see the driver of the limo shoot the President. Or rather, I wanted to see why anyone would ever come to such a conclusion. This stemmed from an interview I'd read with the Wu Tang Clan rap group. Several Wu Tang members (maybe RZA, GZA, or the Ghostface Killah) said their favorite book was Behold a Pale Horse, by one-time naval intelligence officer turned UFO researcher and bonker conspiracist, William Cooper.

It was Cooper's contention that the President was killed as part of vast intergalactic plot stemming from a botched deal between aliens from outer space and the Eisenhower administration. According to Cooper, the aliens wanted back their spaceship, the one that crashed near Roswell, New Mexico. They were willing to make a deal. They'd give the United States advanced, "black" technology (which would later go into "sleath" weapons like the B-2 bomber) in exchange for the return of the ship plus being given free reign to abduct a finite number of Americans on whom they performed numerous physiological tests. The problem was when the Kennedy boys got in, they wanted to renegotiate the bargain, which the aliens took as an unforgivable betrayal. Kennedy's fate was sealed. Says Cooper, the Secret Service driver of the president's limo that day in Dallas—the true murderer—was in the employ of the aliens, or perhaps even a shapeshifting alien himself. The Wu Tang, then residing communally in a Staten Island split-level they regarded as a Shoalin Temple, said they believed this. It was all in the Zapruder film, they said, look at it, you'd see.

Seemed worth a try, especially since now you can watch a frame-by-frame breakdown of famous film on the Web. But I saw nothing that resembled the driver turning with a gun in his hand. Maybe I wasn't stoned enough. That's what I thought. At least until I got to the frame where Kennedy's head explodes in a flash and shower of blood.

Forty years later, it was no less visceral—a frozen horrible, unchanging moment. One look and there I was, back in tenth-grade geometry class at Francis Lewis High School, the principal's voice on the loudspeaker saying that the President had been shot, that he was taken to the hospital, and that he was "dead."

Although less abrupt, that's what it was like talking to Monica and Laurie: a reconnection to the bitter emotion of the moment, a dose of the absolute truth (their husbands are never coming back), a note to self that 9/11 truth was more than a performance art mix-and-match of MIHOP-making. It was a fast-track teleportation back to the Day.

Actually this wasn't as much of a stretch as it sounds since I actually was there, at Ground Zero, on September 11.

I'd just walked right into what would come to be called Ground Zero. No one stopped me. I knew the towers had fallen, seen it on TV. Still, I didn't expect things that big to totally disappear, as if the ground had swallowed them up.

"Where are the towers?" I asked a fireman. "Under your foot" was the reply.

Late in the afternoon, I sat down beside another, impossibly weary firefighter. Completely covered with grayish dust that covered the area, he sat on a rock drinking a Poland Spring water. Half his squad was missing. They went into the South Tower and never came out. Then, almost as an non sequitor, the fireman looked up at the brickish-colored building in front of us, maybe three or four hundred yards away.

"That building is coming down," he said, with a drained casualness.

"Really?" I asked. At forty-seven stories, in most other cities the building would be a skyscraper, the high point on the horizon. But in New York, especially compared to the phantasmagoria of flattened towers, it merely seemed to be a nondescript box with fire coming out of a few windows. "When?"

"I don't know. Tonight. Maybe tomorrow morning."

This was around 5:15 or so in the afternoon. I know because five minutes later, at 5:20 P.M., the building, which turned out to be World Trade Center #7, did come down.

"Shit!" I screamed, unsure which way to run, not that it turned out I was in any danger, since #7 appeared to drop straight down. Far enough away, it was like watching a movie. I have revisited that moment many times, as often as not in dreams.

Now the 9/11 truth movement tells me that what I saw was something much, much more. According to Jim Hoffman, a mathematician and physicist who lives in Alameda, California, where he authors the site http://911research. wtc7.net, what I saw was a "classic controlled demolition," which means WTC7 was deliberately brought down by planted explosives. This is the reason, Hoffman contends and most 9/11 truth people believe, #7 fell so quickly (about 6.6 seconds, barely slower than the speed of an object free-falling in a vacuum), and so neatly, into its "own footprint."

For the building to have collapsed that quickly without explosives, Hoffman claimed, would mean "its 58 perimeter columns and 25 central columns of structural steel would have to have been shattered at almost the same instant, which is so unlikely as to be impossible."

The destruction of WTC7, hit by no plane, only marginally on fire, might just turn out to be the key to the entire mystery of what happened on September 11, the heart of the matter, Hoffman contended.

9/11truth advocates agree. The fact that Larry Silverstein Properties, the owner of WTC7, received $861 million dollars in insurance payouts for the building's collapse, a nifty $500 million profit over the original $386 million investment, is far too garden variety a motive to excite many activists. But the list of WTC7 tenants on September 11, 2001, sets conspiracy heads spinning.

To wit: the IRS, Department of Defense, and CIA kept offices on twenty-fifth floor. The Secret Service occupied 9 and 10, with the Securities and Exchange Commission (home to vast paper records of ongoing bank transactions, including still-pending fraud cases) on 11–13. On the twenty-third floor was Rudy Giuliani's oddly located Office of Emergency Management, from which the mayor planned to direct his troops during whatever crises that might befall the City. On 9/11 the office wasn't even available for Rudy to—as he would tell delegates at the 2004 Republican Convention—grab Police Commissioner Bernard Kerik's arm, and exclaim "Bernie, thank God George Bush is our president."

If this wasn't enough, as of October 2000, the mortgage of WTC 7 was taken over by the Blackstone Group, headed by Pete Petersen, chairman of the New World Order stalwart Council on Foreign Relations.

In the cosmology of 9/11truth, the destruction of World Trade Center 7 is akin to Jack Ruby shooting Lee Harvey Oswald. WTC7 was the home of secrets, a potential loose end. It had to go. Central in this is the comment made by Silverstein in a 2002 PBS documentary in which the realtor quotes himself as saying to the fire department, "We've had such a terrible loss of life, maybe the smartest thing to do is pull it."

"Pull it," as 9/11truth people never tire of repeating, is the term usually used for controlled demolition. Later Silverstein would later claim "pull it" meant get all the firemen out of the building. But they'd been out for hours.

These were vexing questions to be sure, especially in light of the fact that WTC7 is not even mentioned in the 9/11 Commission Report, nor is the building given much attention in "Final Report on the Collapse of WTC Towers" compiled by the National Institute of Standards and Technology (NIST).

And there I was, thinking all I saw was a building falling down.

8. THE MAGICIAN AND THE EXPERT

A few days after Webster Tarpley's lecture, I went to a Community Board #1 forum on Building Safety where the NIST report would be discussed. The meeting was held in the Woolworth Building, the world's tallest structure when it was completed in 1913. Since it was still standing, it seemed as good a place as any to talk about the only former world's tallest building(s) to fall down.

I was tagging along with William Rodriguez, who attends all NIST meetings and brings a video camera "so they know I'm watching them." There are people who believe their whole lives have been lived for a singular moment and purpose and William, a jovial forty-five-year-old with close-cropped black hair marked with a small streak of white "like a skunk," is one of these people.

Growing up shining shoes in a poor section of Bayamon, Puerto Rico, William was already dreaming of the day when he would be wrapped in a straitjacket and suspended upside down by a flaming rope. "That was going to be my trick, the one that would make me famous. It was my goal to become a magician, the youngest illusionist in the Caribbean basin," says William.

It was in P.R. that William met James Randi, a.k.a. the Amazing Randi. Once the magician on the children's show *Wonderama*, Randi is best known as a debunker of supernatural claims by psychics and the like, offering the One Million Dollar Paranormal Challenge to anyone able to demonstrate verifiable evidence of their powers. No one has yet taken him up on it.

"Randi became my mentor," William relates. "I admired him because he knew a lot of good tricks. But also because he never said they were nothing but tricks. He could separate the truth from what was fake."

In his early twenties William moved to New York, but his magic career never quite took off. He wound up working for a cleaning company in the World Trade Center. He'd stay there twenty years, the last few in charge of the stairwells in the North Tower. "I'd get there at eight, eat breakfast with my friends at Windows on the World, and then start mopping on the 110th floor. By the time I got to the lobby, it was time to go home."

On the morning of September 11, 2001, William arrived late, at around 8:30, a half hour that probably saved his life. This way, instead of being at the top of the building where everyone died, he was chatting with others from the maintenance crew on level B-1 of the WTC sub-basement. It was then that, he says, "I heard this massive explosion from down below. Somewhere in the subbasements, like level B-2 or B-3. I thought a generator blew up. But it was too big for that. The walls were cracking. Then I see this guy I worked with, the skin on his arms was peeled away, like . . . hanging. That was when we heard another explosion. This one from upstairs. Later I found out that was the first plane, hitting the building."

William's account of what happened next makes for harrowing listening. His first instinct was to try to save his friends, but as one of only five people in the building with the master key to all the offices, he soon found himself leading firefighters up the stairwells. "They were all carrying seventy pounds of equipment, the lights were off, and the sprinklers on. Huge chunks of the building were falling all around us. As we climbed the stairs I kept hearing these explosions. I was going on adrenaline. All I could think of was trying to save my friends . . . before it was over I helped twelve people out of the building.

"I don't know what happened to me once the Tower fell. I found myself under a firetruck, in a hole. It was hard to breathe. I told myself this is going to be a slow death, but I should make it last as long as I could. This is when my training as an escape artist helped me. It taught me how to be calm. But eventually they came and found me."

Acclaimed as "the last man pulled from the rubble," William became a hero of 9/11, touted in the Latin press all over the country. "They had me down to White House. I had my picture taken with Hillary Clinton. President Bush too."

Now, four and half years later, after repeatedly being rebuffed in his attempts to get this story on the record with both the 9/11 and NIST commissions about the explosions at the Trade Center, William is suing the United States government under the RICO statue, legislation originally drafted to prosecute Mafia families. The suit itself, filed by lawyer Philip Berg, reads like some Air America wet dream, with George Walker Bush, Richard Cheney, Donald H. Rumsfeld, Condoleezza Rice, John Ashcroft, George J. Tenet, Karl Rove, Thomas Kean, Paul Wolfowitz, and dozens of others listed as defendants.

"RICO stands for Racketeer Influenced and Corrupt Organizations," William says. "They say I'm a conspiracy theorist, I call them conspirators too. It is like the Amazing Randi told me. There's reality and there's illusion. Both are fine. But when you tell me the illusion is reality, we have a problem. September 11 is this gigantic illusion. I owe it to my two hundred dead friends to keep working to expose these lies. What can they do to me? I'm a national hero. Bush told me so himself."

"That's him, the NIST guy," William said, indicating Dr. S. Shyam Sunder, the agency's Deputy Director for Building and Fire Research and Lead Investigator for the Trade Center report.

A smallish, elegantly attired man in his fifties, Dr. Sunder, degree holder from the Indian Institute of Technology in Delhi and MIT, took his seat beside Carl Galioto, a partner at Skidmore, Owings and Merrill, architects of the brand-new, not-yet-occupied, fifty-two-story, $700 million replacement for WTC #7. Behind the men was a large slide of what the moderator called "the new downtown skyline" dominated by another Skidmore project, the planned "Freedom Tower," at an iconic 1,776 feet slated to be the next in the line of world's tallest buildings. Like the new WTC #7, which featured "a two-foot-thick vertical core encasing the elevators, utility infrastructure, and exit stairs," the Freedom Tower promised to be "among the safest buildings ever built," Galioto said. This was important, he said, because "constantly building and rebuilding" was what New York was really all about.

Dr. Sunder delivered his summary of the NIST findings (the plane impact and fire did it) with bureaucratic aplomb, after which the meeting was opened up for a brief question-and-answer period. A woman from

NY9/11truth stood up and with great emotion said that her best friend, an NYPD officer, had died at the Trade Center. "I cannot sleep at night," she said. She had hoped the NIST report, supposedly written by "scientists, not politicians," would settle some of the questions about what happened to her loved one. But this wasn't the case.

"I have here a report which contradicts much of what you say," the 9/11truth woman said, placing a paper by Steven E. Jones, a physics professor from Brigham Young University, in front of Dr. Sunder. Jones's paper makes the case for controlled demolition, claiming the persistence of "molten metal" at Ground Zero indicates the likely presence of "high-temperature cutter-charges . . . routinely used to melt/cut/demolish steel."

"I hope you read this; perhaps it will enable you to see things a different way," the woman said.

"Actually, I *have* read it," Dr. Sunder said with a sigh.

Later, asked if such outbursts were common, Dr. Sunder said, "Yes. I am sympathetic. But our report . . . it is extensive. We consulted eighty public-sector experts and 125 private-sector experts. It is a Who's Who of experts. People look for other solutions. As scientists, we can't worry about that. Facts are facts."

I asked Dr. Sunder about 7 WTC. Why was the fate of the building barely mentioned in the final report?

This was a matter of staffing and budget, Sunder said. He hoped to release something on 7 WTC by the end of the year.

NIST did have some "preliminary hypotheses" on 7 WTC, Dr. Sunder said. "We are studying the horizontal movement east to west, internal to the structure, on the fifth to seventh floors."

Then Dr. Sunder paused. "But truthfully, I don't really know. We've had trouble getting a handle on building No. 7."

9. CAN 49.3% OF THE PEOPLE BE CRAZY?

In the late summer of 2004, as Republicans gathered inside Madison Square Garden to nominate George Bush for a second term largely based on his touted strong leadership during 9/11, the Truth movement commissioned a Zogby poll, which asked whether people believed "some of our leaders knew in advance attacks were planned on or around September 11, 2001, and consciously failed to act."

A total of 49.3 percent of New York City residents (41 percent throughout the state) said yes.

A year and a half later the level of doubt had risen, at least according to my own informal canvassing. Basing the inquiry on Nick Levis's "Hop level" paper, I offered respondents four choices: A was the Official Story; B, the Official Story plus government incompetence; C, LIHOP; and D, MIHOP. Of the fifty-four respondents, twenty-seven said C, twenty-two picked B, with four (including two Muslim cab-drivers) opting for MIHOP.

Almost every white person said B. As much as many of these people hated the Bush administration, they couldn't bring themselves to believe that it would take part in the deaths of three thousand of its countrymen. An investment banker drinking at a downtown bar said, "I can see them wishing it would happen. I can see them being happy they lucked into their dream scenario. But doing it on purpose? Look at the way they've managed Iraq. They couldn't have pulled off 9/11 without getting caught. Not possible."

Uptown, the responses were different. "Yeah, they knew," said a man eating at Amy Ruth's Restaurant on 116th Street. A sixty-one-year-old retired transit worker, he was one of sixteen out of twenty black people questioned who picked C. Just the other night, he said, a friend told him that Marvin Bush, the president's youngest brother, was one of the heads of the company that did most of the security work for not only the Trade Center but also United Airlines and Dulles Airport, from where Flight 77 departed.

"That's true?"

Yeah, I said. The younger Bush was a significant stockholder in the Securacom company, later renamed Stratesec, which was reputedly backed by Kuwaiti money. According to several reports, he left the company on September 10, 2001.

"There anywhere Bush ain't got no brother?"

"His cousin worked there too, Wirt Walker III."

"*Wirt?* The third? You're shitting me."

This was pretty much the opinion above 110th Street. If Katrina proved Bush was willing to let people die, right there on TV, why should 9/11 been any different? Many attested that "Jadakiss had it right." This was a reference to the song "Why?" in which the rapper asks a long series of questions pertaining to the existential state of African-Americans, including the couplet, "Why do niggas push pounds and powder?/Why did Bush knock down the towers?" The line caused a good deal of controversy, Clear Channel bleeping the President's name like any other four-letter word.

In all my polling only one person picked A, the official story. This was a fireman, who was smoking a cigarette outside a downtown engine company. This isn't the kind of material you feel too comfortable asking firemen—this particular house had lost a number of men on 9/11—but I knew the guy's brother from high school.

"Not answering that," he said, warning me about going around querying other firefighters. This didn't mean that he'd ever seen anything as "corrupt, bullshit and sad as what happened down at the World Trade Center.

"They got their gold and shipped us to Fresh Kills," he said. Call it one more conspiracy theory, but it is not an uncommon opinion among uniformed firefighters: that the powers that be only cared about finding the massive gold reserves held in vaults beneath of the Trade Center (the $200 million in gold and silver from the Bank of Nova Scotia alone), not the bodies of fallen heroes. After the gold was secured, the fireman said, the body recovery detail was severely curtailed, leading to the massive protest in which firefighters duked it out with NYPD officers guarding the Ground Zero site.

It was clear, the firefighter blamed the city, primarily Rudy Giuliani, for the post-9/11 battle over finding human remains. "Giuliani, the great hero of 9/11," the fireman spat. "He's supposed to be a prosecutor? What kind of prosecutor goes along with taking evidence away from a crime scene?" It was the firefighter's belief that the effort to remove the debris around Ground Zero was nothing more than a "business decision," a heartless, premature attempt to jump-start downtown commerce.

It was just about "the money," the firefighter said. It was always about "the money." On the other hand, the fireman couldn't go along with any of the "crazy" theories about what might have happened on September 11. Sure he heard explosions, but "things blow up all the time in fires." He didn't believe "any of that shit about bombs in the Towers."

The truth was, he said, "the way they were built, you didn't need bombs to bring the WTC down. The Port Authority didn't have to follow City building codes, and they didn't." More steel than concrete, "those towers were made to fall down." That was "the real inside job" if you asked him, the fireman said, what made the WTC such a perfect target. Whoever did it knew airplanes would be enough.

All this said, the fireman said that if there was a gun to his head and he had to pick a letter in my poll, it would have to be A.

"That's the only choice I got," he said. "Osama fucking bin Laden, just like President Bush says. I have to think that, because of all those friends of mine who died that day. If I thought it wasn't Osama bin Laden, if I thought it was someone else, then I'd have to do something about it. And I don't want to think about what I'd do."

10. DISINFORMATION

It weighs on you, thinking about 9/11, the day and the unremitting aftermath. The wound remains unhealed, emotions close to the surface. Certainly there was an urgency as activists gathered at the Veselka restaurant after the Tarpley meeting.

With all the saber-rattling about Iran, this was no time to decrease vigilance, said Nick Levis, proposing a toast: "That in 2006, we will crack the Official Story so we can stop being 9/11–heads and return to normality." A classically hermetic New York conversation ensued, quickly moving from snickers about bin Laden's supposed CIA code name, "Tim Osmond . . . as in Donny and Marie," to speculation about the role of Jerry Hauer, Giuliani's former OEM guy, in the post-9/11 anthrax threats.

However, all conviviality fled as the conversation slipped into the matter of whether, on the morning of 9/11, the Pentagon was hit by American Airlines flight #77 or not. Sounds kind of crazy, debating if a 150-ton airplane slammed into the world's largest single building, but this is the way it is with the slippery discourse of 9/11 truth.

The matter was first broached by Thierry Meyssan in his 2002 book *L'Effroyable Imposture* (The Appalling Fraud), a #1 best seller in France, which said the damage at the Pentagon was caused not by Flight #77 as reported, but rather something else, most likely a cruise missile. This bold claim is based primarily on what Meyssan called "the physical evidence" gleaned from a series of photographs (see: "Hunt the Boeing," http://www.asile.org/citoyens/numero_13/pentagone/erreurs_en.htm) indicating, among other things, that the hole in the side of the building was no more than 15 to 18 feet wide, certainly not big enough to accommodate an airplane with a 125-foot wing span. Other pictures showed a decided lack of the debris one might expect at a plane crash site.

This theory, one of the first to challenge the Official Story, caused an early sensation among 9/11 truth people. But there are problems with the idea, such as the dozens of eyewitnesses that saw the 757 flying low near the Pentagon shortly before impact. Posting an item declaring "the Pentagon no 757 crash theory" to be a "booby trap for 9/11 skeptics," Jim Hoffman said, "this is just the sort of wackiness defenders of the Official Story harp on to show how gullible and incompetent we conspiracy theorists are supposed to be."

In other words, Meyssan and other believers in the no-plane idea were either flat wrong, unknowing dupes, or spreaders of disinformation, most likely the latter. And as is known to anyone present at the old Elgin Theatre nearly forty years ago when Kennedy assassination researcher Mae Brussel blew herself out of the water by asserting that the saintly I. F. Stone, who disagreed with her, was an obvious disinformer, to be tarred with the dreaded "d" word is no small thing in conspiracy circles. Things tend to get heated.

So it was at the Vesalka, where the question was floated that, if flight 77 did not crash into the Pentagon, what happened to the fifty-six people

listed as being on the plane. It was a query that did not sit well with Nico
Haupt, a tall, thin, black-clad man from Cologne, Germany, complier
of the extensive 9/11 Encyclopedia (http://911review.org/Sept11Wiki/
911Encyclopedia.shtml) and staunch no-plane advocate.

"Gassed," he hissed. "Have you ever heard of gassing? It is very easy.
You open the door of the plane, and it spreads."

"You think they gassed them?" Would even the Illuminati stoop to this
Auschwitz horror?

Haupt cast a withering look: how naive could anyone be? "That or some
other method of murder."

Someone said something about Cleveland, how the passengers might
have taken off in Cleveland. Another said she'd read flight 77 might
have crashed near the Kentucky border at that point to be replaced by a
missile.

These views seemed to support Haupt's no-plane stance, but did little
to calm the addled theorist. "Assholes," he sneered.

"Nico, Nico," said Webster Tarpley in a grandfatherly manner. "This
is only tactics. There's no reason to make an enormous moral issue out of
everything."

But Haupt was past consoling. "You are motherfuckers. Stupid motherfuckers." Slamming the tabletop, he gathered his things and stormed out.

"Nico is so emotional," said one NY9/11Truth activist, returning to her
plate of potato pirogues.

11. 250 GREENWICH STREET

After the meeting, on my way back to Brooklyn, I stopped off at Ground
Zero. My father used to take me down here, before they built the Trade
Towers, when the place was called Radio Row. We'd look over the reel-
to-reel tape recorders, buy some tubes, eat a hero sandwich and go home.
I always hated the WTC for that, taking away a place I used to go with my
father; it took me years to look at the big, ugly buildings without sneering.
In the weeks following 9/11 I came here several nights a week. It was hard

to get really close by then, the barricades up everywhere. But there were some spots, random vantage points, from which you could follow the arc of the great plume of water, shining in the vapor lamps, as it rained onto the smoking pit. It seemed the place to be, the thing to see. For more than a year later I couldn't cross the bridges or ride the elevated section of the F train without being able to trace a precise silhouette of the vanished towers, looming over the downtown skyline. Sometimes I'd just start crying.

Now my hold on the psychic geography has grown a bit shaky. We had someone from out of town in a few weeks ago. As we drove along the BQE, he asked where the Trade Towers had been.

"Ah, somewhere in there," I answered, vaguely.

Now I was back here again, standing before the not quite finished replacement for WTC #7, the building I saw fall down four and half years ago, a collapse Dr. Shyam Sunder and his experts "couldn't get a handle on."

A nice-looking building it is too, Larry Silverstein's new $700 million baby, a nifty parallelogram with a stainless steel finish reminiscent of a fancy Viking stove, way hipper than the old shit-colored WTC7. The place will provide 1,700,000 square feet of rentable space while still giving the impression of "airiness," according to the Web brochure. The brochure also repeated Carl Galioto's testimony as to the building's safety, attributing the old WTC7's demise as "probably" due to ignition of Con Edison diesel stored in the base of the building.

"To avoid this hazard in the new building, the diesel is stored under the new plaza across from the reopened Greenwich Street," the brochure said. Another change was the address. Silverstein was promoting the building's "alternative" address, 250 Greenwich Street, which brokers feel will play better in "the trendy TriBeCa neighborhood." Call it Real Estate MIHOP.

When the new building finally opens, sometime at the end of March, the 9/11 truth movement is planning a demonstration here, so "no one forgets what used to be here," says Father Frank, veteran of much street action. He is hoping for a large turnout, even better than the one last summer when three hundred people gathered outside the New York Times office to protest the mainstream media blackout of 9/11 Truth. Demonstrators screamed, "Ho, ho, hey, hey . . . bin Laden was trained by the CIA!" and "Truth! truth!" But few Timesmen looked out the window.

Now, however, it being late Sunday night, there wasn't anyone around, so I walked slipped past the construction barriers to get a closer look at the new building. The lights were on in the finished lobby, gleaming card-reading security gates already in place. A giant LCD screen, maybe a hundred feet long, hung across the empty lobby's back wall. They must have been testing it because it kept playing the full alphabet and numbers from 1 through 9 in various fonts. It just kept scrolling, hypnotically.

It was about then that a cop car came along. I figured they were checking me out, to see if I was the type who stole things from construction sites. They stopped a moment and stared at me before driving off. Obviously, they wanted me to move on. Cops always want you to "move on." But I had the right to be there. Larry Silverstein didn't own the sidewalk. And even if he did, fuck that. This is my city, born and bred. Knew it like the back of my hand. I had as much right to the site of the disaster as anyone.

But then the cops came around the corner again and I remember more factoid I'd heard tossed around the meetings of NY911truth. David Cohen, head officer of the CIA office at WTC7 on September 11, 2001, was the same guy hired by Ray Kelly as Deputy Commissioner for Intelligence; he instituted the subway bag search, one more of those chimeras of safety we're supposed to put up with in the forever-changed 9/11 world. Who knew what a guy like that might be up to? So I pushed off, got back in my car and left. It didn't pay not to be too careful nowadays.

ALL AROUND THE TOWN

12

Night Shifting for the Hip Fleet

This story served as the basis for the long-running TV show, Taxi. I didn't get rich, but Danny DeVito once bought me a sandwich while we talked about his character. Plus I didn't have to go back to cab driving, which is way harder than writing. The Dover garage is long gone now, of course. Also, as predicted, "leasing" did spell the end of the artist/writer cabby. You'll never find someone like me driving an NY taxi now. They're all from Lahore. From New York *magazine, 1975.*

It has been a year since I last drove a cab, but the old garage still looks the same. The generator is still clanging in the corner. The crashed cars, bent and windshieldless, still lie in the shop like harbingers of a really bad night. The weirdo maintenance guys continue to whistle Tony Bennett songs as they sweep the cigarette butts off the cement floor. The friendly old YOU ARE RESPONSIBLE FOR ALL FRONT-END ACCIDENTS is as comforting as ever. The dispatcher hasn't lost any weight. And all the working stiffs are still standing around, grimy and gummy, sweating and regretting, waiting for a cab at shape-up.

Shape-up time at Dover Taxi Garage #2 still happens every afternoon, rain or shine, winter or summer, from two to six. That's when the nightline drivers stumble into the red-brick garage on Hudson Street in Greenwich

Village and wait for the day-liners, old-timers with backsides contoured to the crease in the front seat of a Dodge Coronet, to bring in the taxis. The day guys are supposed to have the cabs in by four, but if the streets are hopping they cheat a little bit, maybe by two hours. That gives the night-liners plenty of time to stand around in the puddles on the floor, inhale the carbon monoxide, and listen to the cab stories.

Cab stories are tales of survived disasters. They are the major source of conversation during shape-up. The flat-tire-with-no-spare-on-Eighth-Avenue-and-135th-Street is a good cab story. The no-brakes-on-the-park-transverse-at-fifty-miles-an-hour is a good cab story. The stopped-for-a-red-light-with-teenagers-crawling-on-the-windshield is not bad. They're all good cab stories if you live to tell about them. A year later the cab stories at Dover sound a little bit more foreboding, not so funny. Sometimes they don't even have happy endings. A year later the mood at shape-up is just a little bit more desperate. The gray faces and burnt-out eyes look just a little bit more worried. And the most popular cab story at Dover these days is the what-the-hell-am-I-doing-here story.

Dover has been called the "hippie garage" ever since the New York freaks who couldn't get it together to split for the Coast decided that barreling through the boogie-woogie on the East River Drive was the closest thing to riding the range. The word got around that the people at Dover weren't as mean or as stodgy as at Ann Service, so Dover became "the place" to drive. Now, most of the hippies have either ridden into the sunset or gotten hepatitis, but Dover still attracts a specialized personnel. Hanging around at shape-up today are a college professor, a couple of Ph.D. candidates, a former priest, a calligrapher, a guy who drives to pay his family's land taxes in Vermont, a Romanian discotheque DJ, plenty of M.A.s, a slew of social workers, trombone players, a guy who makes three-hundred-pound sculptures out of solid rock, the inventor of the electric harp, professional photographers, and the usual gang of starving artists, actors, and writers.

It's Hooverville, honey, and there isn't much money around for elephant-sized sculptures, so anyone outside the military-industrial complex is likely to turn up on Dover's night line. Especially those who believed their mother when she said to get a good education so you won't have to shlep around in a taxicab all your life like your uncle Moe. A college education is not required to drive for Dover—all you have to do is pass a multiple choice test on which the hardest question is "Yankee Stadium is in A) Brooklyn B) New Jersey C) The Bronx—but almost everyone on the night line has at least a B.A.

Shape-up lasts forever. The day-liners trickle in, hand over their crumpled dollars, and talk about the great U-turns they made on Fifty-seventh Street. There are about fifty people waiting to go out. Everyone is hoping for good car karma. It can be a real drag to wait three hours (cabs are first-come, first-served) and get stuck with #99 or some other dog in the Dover fleet. Over by the generator, a guy with long hair who used to be the lead singer in a band called Leon and the Buicks is hollering about the state the city's in.

"The National Guard," he says, "that's what's gonna happen. The National Guard is gonna be in the streets, then the screws will come down." No one even looks up. The guy who says that his family owns half of Vermont is diagnosing the world situation. "Food and oil," he says, "they're the two trump cards in global economics today . . . we have the food, they have the oil, but Iran's money is useless without food; you can't eat money." He is running his finger down the columns of the *Wall Street Journal*, explaining to a couple of chess-playing method actors what to buy and what to sell. A lot of Dover drivers read the *Wall Street Journal*. The rest read the *Times*. Only the mechanics, who make considerably more money, read the *Daily News*.

Leaning up against the pay telephone, a guy wearing a baseball hat and an American-flag pin is talking about the Pelagian Heresies and complaining about Saint Thomas Aquinas's bad press. His cronies are laughing as if they know what the Pelagian Heresies are. A skinny guy with glasses who has driven the past fourteen nights in a row is interviewing a chubby day-liner for *Think Slim*, a dieters' magazine he tries to publish in his spare time. The Romanian discotheque DJ is telling people how he plans to import movies of soccer games and sell them for a thousand dollars apiece.

He had already counted a half million in profits and gotten himself set up in a Swiss villa by the time the dispatcher calls his number and he piles into #99 to hit the streets for twelve hours.

Some of the old favorites are missing. I don't see the guy with the ski tours. He was an actor who couldn't pay his Lee Strasberg bills and was always trying to sign up the drivers for fun-filled weekends in Stowe. Someone says he hasn't seen the guy for a few months. Maybe he "liberated" himself and finally got to the mountains after all. Maybe he's in a chalet by a brook right now waiting for the first snowfall instead of sweating and regretting at shape-up. Dover won't miss him. Plenty of people have come to take his place.

"I don't look like a cabdriver, do I?" Suzanne Gagne says with a hopeful smile. Not yet. Her eyes still gleam—they aren't fried from too many confrontations with the oncoming brights on the Queensboro Bridge. Suzanne, a tall woman of twenty-nine with patched blue jeans, is a country girl from the rural part of Connecticut. Her father gave her a car every time she graduated from somewhere, so she has three different art degrees. When school got tiresome, she came to New York to sell her "assemblages" ("I don't care for the word *collage*") in the SoHo galleries. There weren't many immediate takers, rent was high, Dad and his bankbook had split for Europe with his mistress, so now Suzanne drives for Dover several nights a week.

A year ago or so, any woman hanging out at shape-up was either waiting to report a driver for stealing her pocketbook, a Dover stiff's girlfriend, or some sort of crazy cabdriver groupie. In those days the two or three women who were driving were banned from the night line, which is notably unfair because you can make a lot more money with a lot less traffic driving at night. Claire, a longtime Dover driver, challenged the rule and won; now fifteen women drive for Dover, most on the night line. There are a lot of reasons why. "I'm not pushing papers anymore," says Sharon, a calligrapher and former social worker who drove for Dover until recently. "I can't hack advertising."

Sharon says many more women will be driving soon because women artists need the same kind of loose schedule that has always attracted their male counterparts to cabdriving. At Dover you can show up whenever you want and work as many days as you can stand. Besides, she says, receptionist and typist positions, the traditional women's subsistence jobs, are drying up along with the rest of the economy. The women at Dover try not to think about the horrors of the New York night. "You just have to be as tough as everyone else," Sharon says. But since Suzanne started driving, the artwork she used to do in two or three days is taking weeks.

"I'm tired a lot," she says, "but I guess I'm driving a cab because I just can't think of anything else to do."

Neither can Don Goodwin. Until a while ago he was president of the Mattachine Society, one of the oldest and most respected of the gay-liberationist groups. He went around the country making speeches at places like Rikers Island. But now he twirls the ends of his handlebar mustache and says, "There's not too much money for movements, movements are *ga-stunk*."

Don sometimes daydreams in his cab. He thinks about how he used to dress windows for Ohrbach's and how he loved that job. But his salary got too high so they fired him. Don offered to take a cut in pay but "in the window-dressing business they don't like you to get paid less than you got paid before, even if you ask for it. Isn't that odd?" Now Don's driving seven days a week because "after window-dressing and movements, I'm really not skilled to do anything else."

A driver I know named David is worried. David and I used to moan cab stories to each other when I was on the night line. Now he keeps asking me when I'm coming to work. After four years of driving a cab, he can't believe interviewing people is work. David is only a dissertation away from a Ph.D. in philosophy, which makes him intelligent enough to figure out that job openings for philosophers are zilch this year. The only position his prodigious education has been able to land him was a twenty-five-dollar-a-night, one-night-a-week gig teaching ethics to rookie cops. David worked his way through college driving a cab. It was a good job for that, easy to arrange around things that were important. Now he has quit school in disgust and arranges the rest of his life around cabdriving. He has been offered a job in a warehouse for which he'd make $225 a week and never have to pick up another person who has a crowbar stuffed into his pants, but he's not going to take it. When you're zooming around the city, there's an illusion of mobility.

The turnover at the garage (Dover has over five hundred employees for the 105 taxis; it hires between five and ten new people a week) makes it easy to convince yourself this is only temporary. Working in a factory is like surrender, like defeat, like death; drudging nine to five doesn't fit in with a self-conception molded on marches to Washington. Now David's been at Dover for the past two years and he's beginning to think cab freedom is just another myth.

"I'll tell you when I really started to get scared," David says. "I'm driving down Flatbush and I see a lady hailing, so I did what I normally do, cut across three lanes of traffic and slam on the brakes right in front of her. I wait for her to get in, and she looks at me like I'm crazy. It was only then I realized I was driving my own car, not the cab."

David has the Big Fear. It doesn't take a cabdriver too long to realize that once you leave the joy of shape-up and start uptown on Hudson Street, you're fair game. You're at the mercy of the Fear Variables, which are (not necessarily in order): the traffic, which will be in your way; the other cabdrivers, who want to take your business; the police, who want to give you tickets; the people in your cab, lunatics who will peck you with nudges and dent you with knives; and your car, which is capable of killing you at any time. Throw in your bosses and the hack inspectors and you begin to realize that a good night is not when you make a living wage. That's a great night. A good night is when you survive to tell your stories at tomorrow's shape-up.

But all the Fear Variables pall before the Big Fear.

The Big Fear is that times will get so hard that you'll have to drive five or six nights a week instead of three. The Big Fear is that your play, the one that's only one draft away from a possible showcase, will stay in your drawer. The Big Fear is thinking about all the poor stiff civil servants who have been sorting letters at the post office ever since the last Depression and all the great plays they could have produced. The Big Fear is that, after twenty years of schooling, they'll put you on the day shift. The Big Fear is, you're becoming a cabdriver.

The typical Big Fear cabdriver is not to be confused with the archetypal Cabby. At least in the movies, the Cabby is a genuine New York City romantic hero. He's what every out-of-towner who's never been to New

York thinks every Big Apple driver is like. The Cabby "owns his own," which means the car he drives is his, not owned by some garage boss (58 percent of New York's 11,787 taxis are owned by "fleets" like Dover, which employ the stiffs and the slobs of the industry; the rest are operated by "owner-drivers"). The Cabby hated Lindsay even before the snowfalls, has dreams about blowing up gypsy cabs, knows where all the hookers are (even in Brooklyn), slurps coffee and downs Danish at the Bellmore Cafeteria, tells his life story to everyone who gets into the cab, and makes a ferocious amount of money. Sometimes he might even, accidentally on purpose, take an unsuspecting passenger to the Bronx by way of Staten Island (leading one such driver to say, "One day they'll put my picture on TV and every little old lady in New York will shout: *That's him!*) But for the most part, the Cabby is the genuine article, a Big City staple. As much as he complains, he really loves his work.

The Dover driver doesn't fit this mold. He probably would have voted for Lindsay twice if he had had the chance. He doesn't care about gypsy cabs; if they want the Bronx, let them have it. He knows only about the hookers on Lexington Avenue. He has been to the Bellmore maybe once and had a stomachache the rest of the night. He speaks as little as possible and barely makes enough to get by. He also hates his work.

The first fare I ever had was an old bum who threw up in the backseat. I had to drive around for hours in miserable weather with the windows open trying to get the smell out. That started my career of cabbing and crabbing. In the beginning, before I became acquainted with the Big Fear and all its attendant anxieties, the idea was to drive three days a week, write three, and party one. That began to change when I realized I was only clearing about twenty-seven dollars a ten-hour shift.

There are remedies. The nine-hour shift stretches to twelve and fourteen hours. You start ignoring red lights and stop signs to get fares, risking collisions. You jump into cab lines when you think the other cabbies aren't looking, risking a punch in the nose. You're amazed at what you'll do for a dollar. But mostly you steal.

If you don't look like H. R. Haldeman and take taxis often, you've probably been asked by a cabdriver if it's "okay to make it for myself."

The passenger says yes, the driver sets a fee, doesn't turn on the meter, gets the whole fare for himself, and that's stealing. Stealing ups your Fear Variables immeasurably. You imagine hack inspectors and company-hired "rats" all around you. Every Chevy with blackwall tires becomes terror on wheels. The fine for being caught is $25, but that's nothing—most likely you will be fired from your garage and no one will hire you except those places in Brooklyn with cars that have fenders held on with hangers and brake pedals that flap. But you know that if you can steal, say $12 a night, you'll have to drive only three nights this week instead of four and maybe you'll be able to finish that play, which some producer will love to death and this will lead to that, and you'll be hobnobbing at the Public Theatre in no time.

Well, you can dream, as long as you don't start dreaming in the middle of traffic on the BQE. What you want to avoid are the premonitions. Nothing is as bad as a cabdriver premonition. Sometimes a driver would not show up at Dover shape-up for a couple of days and when he came in he'd say, "I didn't drive because I had a premonition." A premonition is knowing that the Manhattan Bridge is going to fall in the next time you drive over it and thinking about whether it would be better to hit the river with the windows rolled up or down.

On a job where there are so many different ways to die, premonitions are not to be discounted. Of course, a smile would lighten everything, but since the installation of the partition that's supposed to protect you and your money from a nuclear attack, cabdriving has become a morose job. The partition locks you in the front seat with all the Fears. You know the only reason the thing is there is because you have to be suspicious of every-one on the other side of it. It also makes it hard to hear what people are saying to you, so it cuts down on the wisecracking. The partition has killed the lippy cabby. Then again, you can always talk to yourself, and most Dover drivers do.

When I first started driving, cabbies who wanted to put a little kink into their evening would line up at a juice bar where they gave Seconals along with the Tropicana. The hope was that some Queens cutie would be just messed up enough to make "the trade." But the girl usually wound up passing out somewhere around Francis Lewis Boulevard, and the driver would have to wake her parents up to get the fare. Right now the hot line is at the Eagle's Nest underneath the West Side Highway. The Nest and other nearby bars like Spike's and the Nine Plus Club are the hub of New York's flourishing leather scene. On a good night, dozens of men dressed from hat to boots in black leather and rivets walk up and down the two-block strip and come tumbling out of the "Tunnels," holes in the highway embankment, with their belts off. Cabdrivers with M.A.s in history will note a resemblance to the Weimar Republic, another well-known Depression society.

Dover drivers meet in the Eagle's Nest line after 2 A.M. almost every night. The Nest gives free coffee, and many of the leather boys live on the Upper East Side or in Jersey, both good fares, so why not? After the South Bronx, this stuff seems tame. Besides, it's fun to meet the other stiffs. Who else can you explain the insanity of the past nine hours of your life to? It cuts away some of the layers of alienation that have been accumulating all night.

Big Fear cabdrivers try to treat each other tenderly. It's a rare moment of cab compassion when you're deadheading it back from Avenue R and you hear someone from the garage shouting "Do-ver! Do-ver!" as he limps out to Coney Island. It's nice, because you know he's probably another out-of-work actor-writer stiff like you, lost in the dregs.

So it figures that there is a strong feeling of "solidarity forever" in the air at Dover. The Taxi Rank and File Coalition, the "alternative" cab union in town (alternative to Harry Van Arsdale's all-powerful and generally despised Local 3036), has been trying to organize the Dover drivers. Ever since I started cabbing, Rank and Filers have been snickered at by most drivers as Commies, crazy radical hippies, and worse. A lot of this was brought on by the Rank and File people themselves, who used to go around accusing old-timers of being part of the capitalist plot to starve babies in Vietnam. This type of talk does not go over too big at the Bellmore.

Now Rank and File has toned down its shrill and is talking about more tangible things like the plight of drivers in the face of the coming Depression. Dover, naturally, is their stronghold; Van Arsdale's people have just about given the garage up for lost. Suzanne Gagnes wears a Rank and File button. Suzanne says, "It's not that I'm a left-wing radical or anything. I just think it's good that we stick together in a situation like this."

Last winter a bitter dispute arose over an incident in which a Dover driver returned a lost camera and the garage allegedly pocketed the forthcoming reward money. The Rank and File leaders put pressure on the company to admit thievery. The garage replied by firing the shop chairman, Tom Robbins, and threatening the rest of the committee. Tempers grew very hot; petitions to "Save the Dover 6" were circulated. Robbins appealed to the National Labor Relations Board, but no action was taken. There was much talk of a general strike, but Rank and File, surveying the strength of their hardcore membership, decided against it. Now they have another NLRB suit against Dover and the Van Arsdale union for what they claim is a blacklist against Robbins, who has been turned down in attempts to get a job at twenty different garages in the city.

Gerry Cunningham, who is the boss at Dover, says Rank and File doesn't bother him. "You'd figure there would be a lot of those types here, the way I see it. Big unions represent the median sort of guy, so you'd figure that with the general type of driver we have here, there would be a lot of Rank and File. Look, though, I'm not particularly interested in someone's religion as long as he produces a day's work. If the drivers feel a little togetherness, that's fine with me."

Gerry, a well-groomed guy with a big Irish face, is sifting through a pile of accident reports and insurance claims in his trailer-office facing Hudson Street. It seems like all cab offices are in trailers or temporary buildings; it's a transient business. This is the first time, after a year of driving for Dover, that I've ever seen Gerry Cunningham. I used to cash the checks too fast to notice that he signed them. Cunningham smiles when he hears the term "hippie garage."

"Oh, I don't mind that," he says. "We have very conscientious drivers here. We have more college graduates here than any other group. . . . I assume they're having trouble finding other work." Gerry is used to all the actors and writers pushing around Dover hacks and thinks some of them make good drivers and some don't. "But I'll tell you," he says, "of all the actors we've ever had here, I really can't think of one who ever made it."

Well, thanks for the support, Gerry, baby! Not that Cunningham should care. He says he's got his own problems. "Owning taxis used to be a great business," he says. "But now we're getting devoured. In January of 1973, I was paying thirty-one cents for gas, now I'm paying sixty. *Sixty cents!* I'm barely breaking even here. It costs me twelve dollars and fifty cents just to keep a car on the streets for twenty-four hours. Gas is costing almost as much as it costs to pay the drivers."

Fleets like Dover are in trouble. They were the ones who pressed for the 17.5 percent fare rise and still say it's not enough to offset spiraling gas costs, car depreciation, and corporate taxes. Some big fleets like Scull's Angels and Ike-Stan, which employ hundreds of drivers, are selling out; many more are expected to follow. There is a lot of pressure for change. The *New York Times* has run editorials advocating a major reshaping of the industry, possibly with all cabs being individually owned.

According to Cunningham, president of the MTBOT (the Metropolitan Taxicab Board of Trade, which represents the fleets), the future is "leasing," a practice the gypsy cab companies have always used. "Leasing means," Cunningham says, "I lease my cars out to drivers for about two hundred dollars a week. That way only one man drives the car instead of the six or seven, the car lasts much longer, and you cut away a good deal of the maintenance and things like that."

One thing that Cunningham does not mention is while "leasing" will be great for the owners, who will be pocketing their $200 up front (and leaving all the financial risk to the drivers), it will spell disaster for the bohemian cabdriver. Cunningham says the "part-time driver" can always "sublet" taxis if they can't come up with the $200.

Every driver who ever had the Big Fear knows the lie in that. The Dover-style drivers, people who don't work when the painting is going well or a premonition sets in, are not going to sublet. Subletting an apartment is commitment enough. The whole idea of driving for places like Dover, driving a cab at all, is the flex, the shiftlessness option. The topic is much in the air, and a couple days later some drivers who are really actors and musicians are talking about leasing while waiting in line at the La Guardia lot.

"What a drag leasing would be," says an actor who has only twelve dollars on the meter after four hours out of the garage. "If that happens, I don't know, I'll try to get a waiter's job, I guess."

"Yeah man, that'll be a bitch all right," says the musician. "I hate this goddamn job. Hey, I'd rather be playing, but right now I'm making a living in this cab. I won't dig it if they take it away from me. Damn, if the city had any jobs I'd be taking the civil service test." He sits there a moment amid the garage clatter and shouts, "Then I can be a sanitation guy like my dad. And how great will that be?"

13

The Last Irish Cowboy

The annals of crime and rascality are never-ending in the Big City. Every neighborhood has their Robin Hoods who take from the rich and the poor alike, and keep everything for themselves. Here's one case that never made it to Law and Order. *From the* Village Voice, *1978.*

In the bars of Sunnyside, Queens, the remaining white men drink fifty-cent drafts and grouse about how when the jukebox guy came in, all he had were Spanish records.

"Who listens to that Puerto Rican shit?" they bitch.

They also grumble about how the Jews don't run the newspaper stands anymore. Now it's Indians. From India. And what happened to the Italians at the fruit stands? What's a Korean know about an eggplant? Nowadays, you look at the mailboxes in the apartment lobbies on Queens Boulevard and its only the old, flattened-down name tags that say Doyle and O'Sullivan. The shiny new ones say Ramirez and Wong. It's the United Nations in Sunnyside these days, for chrissakes.

The complaints stop when you bring out mug shots of Patty Huston. In the bars on Queens Boulevard and Forty-eighth Avenue, they know Patty Huston. They know his big bellow after he hits the double at the trotters. They know the way he slams C-notes on the bar and puts up drinks for everyone. So what if he robbed a few banks? Everyone's got to make a living. Fine fella, that Patty. He's top mutt in Sunnyside—Woodside too—a 225-pound lug of a gunman.

"He's the Last Irish Cowboy, he is," says a big-chinned man clutching a tiny shot glass, "the Last Irish Cowboy from Sunnyside."

When you ask for specifics, everyone clams up. After all, Patty's on the lam. It's like half the precincts in Queens got nothing to do but look for him. The FBI just made him a Top-10 crook. Top-10 crook from the neighborhood, not bad! That's as much as anyone says. Loose lips sink ships. No one around here is going to let on anything to get the Last Irish Cowboy caught.

Not that it's hard to get a look at Patty Huston. Just go to the bank—pretty much any bank—and glance at the New York Clearing House WANTED poster. It features images of alleged felons, some furtive, some tough and defiant, many pictured in the act of robbing a bank. Many of the photos are obscured by pieces of red and white tape pasted across the supposed bad man's face. The tape says APPREHENDED. This supposed to make the federally insured depositor feel secure, to let you know Dick Tracy is out there, rounding the vermin who take things that don't belong to them.

Patty Huston, however, is never APPREHENDED. Month after month, as other wiseguys get pinched, Patty's thick-necked, beady-eyed mug stares from the upper left-hand corner of the poster, balefully UNAPPREHENDED.

After a year of so of standing in line at the Chemical Bank looking at his merciless mug, you begin to wonder about Patrick James Huston, who, says the poster, robbed a bank at 95–46 Roosevelt Avenue, Queens, on September 6, 1974, at 9:14 in the morning. You begin to think, this is one scary-looking guy. Maybe that's why he's never APPREHENDED—the cops just don't want to catch him. Call up the FBI, which has jurisdiction over all federal bank robbery cases, and say you're interested in Patty Huston and the agent on the line, momentarily dropping Bureau decorum, says, "He's a goddamn legend in his own time."

Agents will tell you that Patty is "one of the most vicious men in America" and a "real menace." But even if Patty's poster has some juicy tidbits like: "tattoo: 'In memory of Mom,' upper right arm," it doesn't begin to tell the story of how the Last Irish Cowboy became a "goddamn legend in his own time" and made the Top 10.

When Patty was growing up in the Woodside-Sunnyside area the place was called Irishtown. Much of it looked the way it does today: red-brick apartment buildings, colorful bedspreads on the clotheslines, young girls in plaid skirts getting off the bus from St. Mary's. From the start, however, Patty Huston stood out from the civil-servant-to-be crowd. After his first bust—in 1946, at age sixteen—a police psychiatrist (according to the feds) diagnosed Patty as the "hardened-criminal type, the kind of individual who will likely spend at least half his life in prison." The shrink was on the money, with change. With a record of thirty arrests in thirty years, Patty, now forty-seven, has already logged twenty-five years in stir.

He made his first newspaper splash back in 1953. That was when, according to the July 30 edition of the *Daily News*, Patty was nabbed as a member of the notorious "3-D Mob." The gang got its name, says the musty clipping, due to their "penchant for robbing movie theatres showing three-dimensional films." Patty's guys knocked over the Sunnyside Theatre, the Bliss Theatre, and the Fortway Theatre within a span of fifteen days, the *News* reporting that "the gang used the fact that everyone was wearing 3-D glasses to cover their brazen actions." The spree, however, came to an end as the cops, acting on a tip, staked out the Dover Theatre in Brooklyn, which was then showing the Vincent Price 3-D classic, *The House of Wax*. Nabbed by the popcorn counter, Patty got sent up for a few years.

He came back big during the early '60s as a member of the Long Island City–based "Dummy Brain" Taylor gang. "Dummy Brain," a seventy-three-year-old vet of the crimeways, got the "Brain" half of his nickname for his intricately planned bank and payroll jobs. The "Dummy" part referred to how, whenever the coppers pinched him, he would always say, "I don't know nuthin', I'm a dummy."

In November of 1962, Dummy Brain focused his talents on the Franklin Simon warehouse at 560 Washington Street in Greenwich Village. It figured to be a big score, but there were problems. According to classic crime reporter Mike Pearl, writing in the *New York Mirror*,

Patty, "growing impatient and demanding to know when the job would come off," thought the Dummy Brain was slipping. Spreading dissension in the gang, Patty turned Dummy Brain's own son and grandson against the old man.

Unbeknownst to the Dummy Brainers, however, when they arrived at the payroll office disguised as window washers in their 1950 black sedan, the NYPD Safe and Loft detail were waiting. The gangsters broke into the office as planned and grabbed the payroll. But when they left the building they were looking down the barrels of a dozen police .38s. Patty, according to a *New York Times* report, opened fire with a shotgun. A siege ensued. Police estimated that at least forty shots were fired, twenty of which lodged in the getaway car.

"Hundreds of persons in the area, drivers and workmen on the loading platforms, fell flat to escape the bullets," said the newspaper story. In the murderous crossfire, both Dummy Brain's son and grandson were killed. Patty "was wounded early in the battle, but managed to drag himself through the police bullets across the intersection of West Houston and Washington streets, more than 100 yards away, where he finally slumped in the gutter."

They took Patty to St. Vincent's, where he had seven shells dug out of him. That must have hurt but probably not as much as the fact that the payroll consisted, according to the *Times*, "of $54,000 in non-negotiable checks and 34 cents in nickels, dimes, and pennies." Dummy Brain, who said he didn't make the job because he "had a cold," took the news of his son's and grandson's deaths in stride. He refused to talk, a dummy to the end.

Patty had a few more years in the slams to mull that one over. But he was far from finished. If the payroll caper proved Patty was no common criminal, the Roosevelt Avenue bank job (the one that got his picture around) showed exactly how uncommon he is. Events started sanely enough. Patty and two guys from the Bronx broke into the First National Bank branch brandishing submachine guns, swiping $31,000. But then, driving off, the three decided to change cars. Waving his gun as persuasion, Patty commandeered the first automobile he saw. It was a late-model station wagon. The problem was the wagon was owned by Patrick Deignan, who happened to be running for Democratic district leader in Jackson Heights. The car was plastered with PATRICK DEIGNAN FOR DISTRICT LEADER posters. This made the getaway vehicle somewhat easy to spot as the cops chased Patty and his buddies across the Fifty-ninth Street Bridge to Manhattan. Patty and the boys led the cops on a high-speed chase before the would-be district leader's car ran out of gas in the middle of Times Square.

A recent visit to the First National Bank in question, now a Citibank, reveals that Patty Huston is well remembered. Asked about the robbery, Mr. Garcia, the dapper bank manager, shrugged and said, "I don't know, this bank get robbed many times." But shown a picture of Patty Huston, Garcia's eyes widened. "Oh . . . *him*. He's the reason we have this," he says. And points to the bulletproof glass between the tellers and the customers.

By rights, the bank bust should have been all she wrote for Patty. But not quite. Patty soon jumped four flights out of an open window at the Old West Detention House near Sheridan Square. He broke his ankle in the fall, yet still he managed to escape, on St. Paddy's Day, no less. This was in 1975 and he hasn't been seen or heard from by the blueshirts since.

Nowadays, the FBI has at least one agent in each of its fifty-nine regional office trying to nail Patty Huston, who's stayed in the Top 10 of escaped federal prisoners for twenty-four straight months. The feds have chased leads to Texas, Florida, Canada, and even Ireland. This pisses the FBI off because as most agents will tell you, the Top 10 list doesn't necessarily about how dangerous a person is, but rather how famous he is—or how hard he, or she, is to catch. In other words, the fugitive's capacity to embarrass the bureau by staying at large.

The maddening part for the feds is that they're convinced Patty is right under their noses. Somewhere right there in the old neighborhood. "He's close, I know it, right there in Sunnyside," said Agent Joe Martinolish, a polite FBI agent who's been in charge of the Patty Huston case for two years. "This is one of the most frustrating things I've ever done. We've talked to literally dozens of people who know Patty or have known Patty. We've been over to those bars in Queens. But we just can't get anyone to say anything about him. They're completely uncooperative. I tell them about the ten-thousand-dollar reward for information leading to Patty's capture. Nothing doing. I think the lack of informants is the most significant thing about this case. I just can't understand it."

A couple of days later, I stopped by the 108th Precinct on Fiftieth Avenue in Long Island City to ask about Patty. "Sure, Patty Huston. I arrested his son the other day," said a young detective. "Jumped a turnstile. He had a warrant out for him." I said I wasn't aware Patty had a son. The FBI said he had never been married. The cop shook his head. What are the feds supposed to know about Sunnyside? He's got a wife too, here's the address. It was about six blocks from where we were, off Queens Boulevard.

A half hour later, I rang the bell. A thin woman about forty came to the door in a pink bathrobe. She had a green towel around her head, like she just got out of the shower. She was smoking a cigarette.

"Mrs. Huston?" I asked.

"Yeah?" Her voice was sweeter than you'd figure. She wasn't very tall and over her shoulder you could look into the living room. There was an exercise bicycle and a La-Z-Boy recliner.

"I'd like to ask you about your husband, Patty."

"Who are you?" She was waiting to see a badge of some sort, as if my visit was part of a ritual, a weekly event. Hearing I wasn't a cop but rather a reporter from the *Village Voice*, she let out a laugh.

"The Village what? . . . Look, my husband Patrick is dead to me. There's nothing between us. I wouldn't tell you anything anyhow." Then she closed the door in my face.

There was nothing else left to do but go back to the bar, where they said if Patty gets caught it'll be because of the Puerto Ricans. Apparently, after all that jail time, Patty buddied up with a lot of PRs. He even learned to speak Spanish. People even spoke of him taking a car service over to Corona to eat "that Puerto Rican food."

"He likes that big-ass PR tail," said one of the local drinkers. This, everyone said, would be Patty's real downfall, because Puerto Ricans, they're not stand-up. If you ain't one of them, they'll rat you out in a second. It wasn't anything anyone would have expected from Patty Huston, trusting people from outside the neighborhood. Inevitably the cops would catch Patty again, everyone said. But until then, no one wanted to say nothing else. When it came to Patty Huston, the last Irish Cowboy from Sunnyside, they were dummies.

14

The Ear of Sheepshead Bay

I am an easy laugh. But the jokes have to be funny. If they are not funny, I get depressed because there is nothing more depressing than someone try-ing to be funny and not being funny. George Schultz, of the Sheepshead Schultzs, knew this better than most. Arbiter of the funny, he retained sym-pathy for the unfunny. Up to a point. As they say, comedy is a very, very serious business. A story of high stakes in a small venue. From the Vil-lage Voice, *1978.*

Half my family (my mother's side) is from Sheepshead Bay. They lived on Avenue Z until Robert Moses routed the Belt Parkway through their kitchen. Then they moved to East Nineteenth Street and Avenue X. My mother never could figure if living on Avenue X or Avenue Z carried a bigger psychological stigma.

For years we used to come the Bay, to visit the remaining family mem-bers. It was always fun, walking by the mucky water, hearing captains of the fishing boats like *The Brooklyn Five* bark like carnies, "Bluefish! The big boat for the blues!" Sometimes we'd eat dinner at Lundy's, "the world's largest restaurant" (it said so in the *Guinness Book of World Records*), which was big enough to have seventy-four illegal aliens picked up by the Immi-gration Department on a single shift. Now most of the relatives, includ-ing my beloved uncle Jack who always got plastered at the bar mitzvahs, have either died or moved to New Jersey.

But I still come to the Bay, to see my old friend George Schultz, who runs a little comedy club on Emmons Avenue called Pip's. George lives above the club in a two-bedroom apartment he shares with his two sons, Marty and Seth. The boys, both in their late teens, are a fine-looking pair, George doesn't mind telling you.

"They're my two Jewish Warren Beattys, *yiddisha* hunks." In deference to Seth and Marty's Hebrew handsomeness, George never lets his sons see him nude. "It's the old ass," says George, in the midst of complaining about his various ailments, real and imagined, which include insomnia, diabetes, emphysema, imminent heart attack, collapsed lungs, and the terrible desire to throw himself into the bay that overcomes him at any time of the day or night.

"I can't let them see the old ass," George says. "They're young, they're beautiful, let them live a little, the inevitable will come soon enough."

There was a time George did not have an old ass. He had a pompadour instead. That was back in the early 1950s when he called himself Georgie Starr, master of mimicry and dean of satire. Around East Fifth Street and Avenue N, where George grew up, masters of mimicry and deans of satire were a dime a dozen. Georgie Starr knew them all. His best friend was Jack Roy, the once Jacob Cohen and future Rodney Dangerfield. They hung out all the time, mostly trying, and failing, to pick up girls at Brighton Beach.

It was on one all-to-typical night on the Brighton boardwalk that George went off on one of his gangster *spritzes*. "I was inspired because we had gone over to Coney Island and walked by the Half Moon Hotel where they threw Abe "Kid Twist" Reles out the window. The guy is guarded by six detectives and somehow he falls four stories. He tripped, they said. . . . Anyway, I'm doing my bit, in between eating a Nathan's hot dog, in my gangster voice, saying 'There's no respect for a guy like me. . . . I kill seventeen guys and still there's no respect.'

"Now Rodney, he's barely paying attention, maybe hoping some asshole is gonna fall off the Parachute Jump, and all of a sudden he says, 'No respect' . . . 'I like that *no respect*.' Now when a comic—and we weren't really even comics then—says he likes something that usually means, 'Can I have that?'

I'm thinking, sure, what do I care, it's yours. That's how Rodney got the 'I don't get no respect' thing, which made him, and I've always thought that was swell because he kind of *developed* the concept, if you know what I mean. Plus, he used to take me to Vegas with him, all expenses paid, back when I still could get a hard-on."

George had other friends in the Avenue N days. There was Buddy Hackett, whom George calls "a top prick, even then." There was Joe Ancis, the funniest of them all, too anxiety-ridden to ever tell a joke for money but famous for his phobias, like always carrying his own roll of paper so his bare *tukhis* never touched a public toilet seat. There was Lenny Schneider, who changed his last name to Bruce.

George has plenty of Lenny stories. He remembers the first time they met at the Bali Club, a little dive off Ocean Avenue. "Lenny came in with his mother. He was wearing a navy uniform. He was young. Nice. Funny. We became friends and he moved into the apartment I shared with Rodney on Avenue N. Just the three of us. There wasn't a stove. But didn't matter. We weren't the cooking types. Lenny's mother used to bring by food, stand there while we ate it. A lot of pot roast, it was, with those little overcooked Jewish peas."

Nearly twenty years later George would see Lenny one last time, shortly before Bruce overdosed. Bruce was staying in a West Eighth Street hotel room, with bloody towels in the bathroom.

Those days all the Brooklyn neighborhoods had comic clubs. Besides the Bali, there was the Pink Elephant in Brighton and Jinks in Coney. Even Bay Ridge, full of Italians, had joints. The patter was thick, a real Jewish cutting contest, like the ones black piano players used to wage up in Harlem. Remembering the old act, George starts twitching, his rheumy eyes blinking like hazard lights.

"Forget about it," he says. "I did stupid stuff. Bad. Shithouse song parodies, *facockta* impressions of John Garfield dying at Guadalcanal. Everyone wanted to get on *The Ed Sullivan Show*. I never even watched *The Ed Sullivan Show*. For me it was beautiful *shiksas*. Kissing them. Screwing them. Marrying them. Divorcing them. I guess I never had the lunatic ego it took to make it."

So Georgie Starr gave up stand-up. He got married and moved to Little Neck, in Queens, where he sold storm windows and cemetery plots ("You'll *plotz* for our plots!!"). A decade it was, schlepping in the middle class. The only good thing was the new Chevy the electrical appliance company gave him. But he never could get away from the jokes.

"It's inside," George says, grabbing at his ample chest. "Jews tell jokes."

So in 1962 George came back to Brooklyn. The Bali and the rest of the decent clubs were long gone. Sheepshead Bay was one the few neighborhoods where the survival rate for a ten-minute walk after dark was over 50 percent. He and his then-wife, Rita, rented a long-vacant Emmons Avenue storefront beside the calamari stands and called it Pip's, referencing Dickens's *Great Expectations*, "like it was going to be something." Opened before Manhattan clubs like the Improv and Catch a Rising Star, and set up like a beatnik coffee shop where dewy-eyed romantics from Brooklyn College could strum songs about John Henry and pretend to be Parisian expatriates, George envisioned Pip's as "a university of comedy, a place to come learn how to be funny."

This was prescient since over the next decade or so almost every working comic in the New York area—Joan Rivers, Andy Kaufman, George Carlin, Robert Klein, David Brenner, Woody Allen, Billy Crystal, Jay Leno, Gabe Kaplan, Ed Bluestone, David Steinberg, Elaine Boosler, and Rodney among them—have played Pip's, pocketing the fabulous $6.90 Schultz pays for a half-hour set.

In the beginning George would introduce the acts, do a little patter. But this was a waste of his true talent. They call George "the ear," that is, it takes George about thirty seconds to tell whether someone's funny or not. Give him another ten seconds and he'll tell you if the comic will *ever* be funny. In this, George is never, ever, wrong.

Like the other night this little sawed-off guy came in off Emmons Avenue wearing a caftan. Calling himself Kid Brooklyn, he claimed to be the funniest fucker this side of Kings Highway.

"If you're so funny, how come I haven't seen you," George asked Kid Brooklyn. That's because he'd been in Cleveland, The Kid said, going to Case Reserve University. That so, George reposited, adding that he'd gone to college in Cleveland, too. "Cleveland Rabbinical." Really, Kid Brooklyn said, with clueless lack of uptake. "Haven't heard of it. Is it a good school?"

"Need I say more?" George asked, rolling his eyes as he related the incident. "Listen, if someone is nice-looking, well-adjusted, swell parents, good teeth—the kid is not goint to be funny." Maybe two years from now he's the head writer of Mary Tyler Moore or some other goyim show, but no, not funny. If he comes in looking like shit, depressed, bleeding gums, lives in a furnished room—then there's a chance."

Mostly "the ear" provides his special talent free of charge to comics he likes. Richard Lewis tells the story of a usual session with George.

"I don't have a car. So I got to take the damn train out there. The IND to the end of the line. It's like a bad neighborhood on wheels. You get there alive, you're already ahead of the game. One time I show up, and it's the middle of the afternoon. Like fifty below zero, wind off the ocean, these Italian clam-opener guys standing around like they're gonna tear your heart out and eat it. I knock on the door and George comes down in this green terry-cloth bathrobe. He squints out at the light, like he's some kind of mole. Then sits down. Okay, he goes. That means you start doing your act. You do your bits, he sits there, doesn't move a muscle, not a single facial expression.

"You finish a hunk and he says, 'Funny.' That's it. Just 'funny.' No explanation, no commentary. Nothing. Just 'funny.' You do another bit. He listens. Again, no clue, a total stone face. 'Not funny,' he says. 'What do you mean,' I'm yelling, 'not funny? I love this bit. It's a fucking riot. He looks at me like I'm a bug. 'Look,' he says, 'I ain't here to suck your dick. I'm here to tell you what you came to find out.'"

After Lewis thought about it awhile he concluded, as almost every comic who comes to see "the ear" eventually does, "That George was right."

Comics for whom George offers "the ear" know what they're getting. Every so often, the big names like Robert Klein and David Brenner, who make as much as $30,000 a week in Vegas, come by to do sets for the traditional $6.90 plus subway fare pay. The place is packed, everyone's drunk, and George gets the money to stay in business another season.

Back in the day, George used to listen to all the comics who came into Pip's. It didn't matter if they were good or bad. "There was something about the process that thrilled me. Call it what you want but being a comic is an existential act. It takes risk. Like, if you get some kid up here and he's a singer and he's fucking awful people will say, Wow, that kid can't sing at all. If a comic gets up and he's rotten, the response is going to be, 'What an asshole, I hate that *mocky* bastard.' They want to murder you. . . . Comedy is personal that way. The stakes are high. If you do good you say you killed. If you do bad, you say you died. Kill or be killed. Simple as that."

Now, though, George says, the drama has gone out of the laughing game. "Probably it's TV but everyone more or less knows what a comic sounds like. They know how to pace their act, how to defuse hecklers. They have a safety net. That's the way it is with everything now. You see a stock broker on TV, then at least you know how to talk like a stock broker. The gangsters watch the *Godfather* to learn how to talk like a gangster. Once I'd come down and didn't know what the hell I was going to hear. It could be really terrible, just the worst shit you ever heard. Or it could be something totally new. Flat-out brilliant. Either way it would be *interesting*. Now hardly anyone is really bad, but hardly anyone is really good. I'd rather stay upstairs and jack off."

This doesn't mean strange nights don't come up. "I get a lot of wannabes in here, you know," George says. "There was this one guy, he's like a candy salesman from Buffalo or somewhere. He comes to the City a couple times a year. Always calls me. 'George! Let me stand-up! I got stuff that's great. You'll piss in your pants.'

"I always put him off. One time I guess I'm feeling kindly, or stupid, so I say, 'Yeah, if you want to come in early do a few minutes.' But I forgot that was the night my friend who teaches these adult slow learners is bringing his class in. I didn't know what to tell the guy, so I just kept my mouth shut. He comes in, with this idiot Frank Fontaine hat on and squirting flower on his lapel, I kid you not. He does his five minutes or so, these terrible old jokes. But the slow learners—they love it. They're cracking up every time he opens his mouth. They'll laugh at anything. The guy gets off stage and he's completely blitzed. 'Did you hear them,' he's shouting. 'They loved me. *I killed!*' He goes back to Buffalo thinking he gets more laughs than Jack Benny. Now he keeps calling me. 'George,

I'm gonna be in. My shit's *even better now*.' I'm ducking him. I don't have the heart to tell him: 'You made retards laugh. That's what you did, you fucking idiot.'"

These days with his sons taking over a lot of business of the club, George finds himself with more time to do a little fishing in the Bay, if you want to call reeling in a mutant eel fishing. Sometimes he'll stroll around the now shuttered Lundy's where the last reclusive Lundy brother used to live in the attic surrounded by a dozen Doberman pinchers he used to sic on bill collectors.

"Mostly I just walk around and blink," George says. "The blinking, I don't know where it came from. It starts like a twitch in my forehead, moves down to my eyes. It comes in patterns. Like blink, then blink, blink. I think maybe I'm sending Morse code only I don't know to who. I could be sending out Paul Revere one-if-by-land-two-if-by-sea signals to aliens in flying saucers waiting for a sign to take over earth."

George figures he'll keep Pip's until he croaks. Recently, in an attempt at upgrade, he put in a brunch menu. "It's the only place in Brooklyn you can get brunch, whatever the hell that is."

Just then a mah-jongg lady who said she'd been living in Sheepshead Bay since before Lundy's walked by.

She said, "You had David Brenner, I hear."

George said, "Yes, David Brenner."

She said, "David Brenner, very good. David Brenner."

George said, "David Brenner."

She said, "David Brenner, I like him. On the TV, very funny."

"David Brenner. He's good." Then the mah-jongg lady looked at George's window where Marty had stenciled SUNDAY BRUNCH, SALADS QUICHES. And said, "So what's a quitch?"

To which George said, "Quiche. Quiche."

To which the lady said, "Quitch. I don't know from this quitch."

To which George turned and looked across Sheepshead Bay and blinked rapidly.

15

Wynton's Game

Next to Bill Clinton, trumpeter Wynton Marsalis is about the most charming man you'll ever meet. No matter how busy he appears to be, he has all the time in the world to talk to you. His recall for small pleasantries, like remembering your birthday or the names of your children, is hard to beat. He also can play better than Clinton. For sure no jazzman, not Charlie Parker, not Duke Ellington, ever raised $130 million. The story of a modern Balanchine in full, but cool, glad-hand mode. From New York magazine, 2001.

"Let the ass-whipping begin," Wynton remarked, a bit of opening commentary as he walked onto the courts behind the Sixty-fifth Street projects. Nothing personal, the musician said; with him, ass-whipping need not be adversarial. It can be more a statement of loving engagement with the material at hand, be it Mahler, another take on "East St. Louis Toodle-oo," or a supposedly friendly game of one-on-one.

Still, it was probably a mistake, snickering when the trumpet player started in about his jumper, how sweet it was. Somehow it seemed unlikely, unfair, creepy even, that Wynton Marsalis—only forty but already into his second decade as the semi-officially anointed "most important musician of his generation," the only jazzman ever to get a Pulitzer Prize (for his symphonic-size *Blood on the Fields*), winner of both jazz and classical Grammys on the same night, one of *Time* magazine's "25 most influential Americans"—might be good at basketball too.

But here they came, the jumpers raining down. "Money in the bank," Marsalis gloated, canning his seventh in a row, which is a bitch when you're playing winner's out, which is the way Win-tone, as he is sometimes known, always plays. There was nothing to do but watch the perfect ball rotation and flawless follow-through, all that immaculate, Apollonian form. After all, a lot of things, nasty and nice, have been said about Wynton Marsalis since he arrived on the scene with his brother Branford back in the late seventies, a Jazz Messenger with an unbeatable New Orleans pedigree, formidable upper register, and decided lack of shyness in matters of cultural-aesthetic polemicizing. No one, however, has ever knocked Marsalis's technique.

Except now our contest had taken a critical, potentially calamitous turn. You see: When Wynton's got that J going, you've got to play him close. In such proximity, a defender's elbow might—inadvertently of course—come in contact with the jazzman's wry, moon-shaped face. That elbow might even bash into Wynton's lip. Hard.

"Uh," Wynton grunted, checking for blood.

"Oh man, sorry. You all right?"

Wynton did not answer, only smiled, that chubby-cheeked best-boy-in-the-class smile, so down-home sincere, so full of you're-going-to-get-yours. It is a marvelous, disorienting Cheshire sort of smile. Like the twenty-one words Eskimos have for snow, it is a smile with multifarious definitions and intentions, including innocent. It can suck you in, make you forget exactly who you are up against. Like those scowly gym rats uptown a couple of weeks ago. Hip-hoppers all, they took one look at Wynton's somewhat stumpy body and scoffed, "Hey, Winston, where's your flute?" Maybe he had a couple of dollars to lose in a little, friendly contest of HORSE. Wynton just smiled and canned a dozen or so in a row. Before it was over those boys just shook their heads in genial surrender. That's the secret of Wynton's game. The way he does it, you don't even mind the ass-whipping.

"Yeah, man," Wynton said. His lip was okay.

This was a relief, because you don't want to be the guy who split Wynton Marsalis's kisser. Only the night before, in the claustrophobic kitchen-dressing room at the Village Vanguard, after playing three sets of (mostly) bop with Charles McPherson's quartet, hot on "Night in Tunisia," mournful on "Pork Pie Hat," Wynton had been talking about his lip, how sore it was. It happens to trumpet players, that puckered stress on the *obicularis oris*. During the thirties, Satchmo himself's own immortal chops suffered near permanent ruination from hitting those high C's every night. But throughout a history that includes the classic lips of Roy Eldridge, Sweets Edison, Clark Terry, Rex Stewart, Dizzy Gillespie, Clifford Brown, Miles Davis, Lester Bowie, and a hundred other bugle geniuses, never has so much been riding on singular embouchure.

That much was clear a couple days later, 100 feet above Columbus Circle, amid the swing of giant cranes and the hot blue blind of welding torches. They're building the new Twin Towers here, a pair of eighty-floor, 750-foot-tall spires, on the former site of Robert Moses's squatty old New York Coliseum. It is the biggest construction project in post–September 11 New York, a $1.7 billion complex that will include the new headquarters of AOL Time Warner, a five-star hotel, two hundred or so condos (with Trump-priced penthouses), and a vast, no doubt brutally upscale shopping mall. This is also the site of the new home of Jazz at Lincoln Center, Wynton Marsalis, Artistic Director. And today, Wynton, hard hat over close-cropped hair, has arrived along with other J@LC board members and officials to inspect the progress of their $130 million, 100,000-square-foot digs.

Wynton says American jazz is "the most abstract and sophisticated music anybody has ever heard, short of Bach." But the music of Mingus, Monk, and Charlie Parker has never seen anything like what's happening here on Columbus Circle. Columbus Full Circle you could call it, since it was here, where Eighth Avenue meets the park, that in 1910 a new music called ragtime made its New York debut at Reisenweber's café, a cavernous joint famous for $1.25 fried frog blue plate special.

Touted as "the world's first performing-arts facility built specifically for jazz," the new hall will have three separate performance spaces: a

1,100-seat, concert-style Rose Hall, named for the late, civic-minded Frederick P. Rose, who provided funds for the new planetarium at the American Museum of Natural History; the 600-seat, nightclub-style Allen Room; and a smaller "café" slated to accommodate 140 fans. Also in the plan are recording and rehearsal studios, plus a large jazz-education center. On square footage alone, you could fit twenty Village Vanguards in here, several Five Spots, Slugs and Minton Playhouses, the whole Cotton Club, and still have plenty of space for strung-out musicians to get high, not that any Wynton-fronted organization, however tradition-minded, would condone such unhealthy habits.

Wynton has long been thinking about a "permanent home" for the music he first played marching through the Vieux Carré streets with Danny Barker's Fairview Baptist Church Brass Band. The topic often came up back in the eighties, during the semi-legendary conversations-plotting sessions Wynton engaged in with his great friends and mentors (some say Svengali figures): the ever combative essayist Stanley Crouch and novelist-philosopher Albert Murray, a longtime confidant of Ralph Ellison and Duke Ellington, who called the dapper eighty-five-year-old Murray "the most unsquarest man in the world."

It was up in Murray's apartment on 132nd Street and Lenox, surrounded by "all these books, Faulkner, Hemingway, Malraux, most of which Stanley and Albert had actually read," Wynton recalls, "that I began to envision my life on a bigger scale than I previously thought possible. . . . I mean, you go to the bathroom and there's a photograph of the Army Air Corps, 1943. There's about two hundred uniformed officers, and Albert—the only black guy in the picture. . . . I knew a few things about music because my father was a musician. I'd grown up around jazz musicians. But I was just a kid, from New Orleans, with a New Orleans education, which is basically no education. This was something else altogether."

Amid much holding forth on the issues of free will in Thomas Mann and the majesty of Louis's solo on "Potato Head Blues," the conversation at Albert Murray's house always came back to the future of jazz, how this priceless heritage would survive the dark ages of ascendent pop idiocy and Sypro Gyra–style fusion. The need for the establishment of a jazz canon and a place where the music could be preserved through both repertory performance and instruction was paramount, everyone agreed.

Already involved with a Lincoln Center "Classical Jazz" series, Wynton was the logical point man. Armed with Crouch's social critique of how to play Establishment (read: white) organizations, that unbeatable smile and country-boy manner (even though Kenner, where he grew up, is a New Orleans suburb), Wynton offered an undeniable package. He was, after all, the ultimate crossover artist, arguably the best single jazz and classical trumpet player in the world, a most presentable and courtly young black man who had performed Haydn's Trumpet Concerto with the New Orleans Symphony at fourteen—someone to whom race and class barriers simply do not apply.

"That was what really amazed me," says one old-line Lincoln Center board member, "watching him play Purcell. . . . I said to myself, 'This is a once-in-a-lifetime individual.' If we ever wanted to do something with jazz, he had to be the one."

"Look," Wynton told the blue-blood board of Lincoln Center, his voice deep and smoky, the informality of his manner only adding moral authority, "I play classical and I play jazz and jazz is harder." There was no reason, Wynton said, no reason at all, that jazz, America's "greatest art form, a democratic triumph of order and beauty over chaos," shouldn't be accorded the same status as "European" Lincoln Center "constituents" like the Metropolitan Opera, the New York City Ballet, and the New York Philharmonic.

Smitten, the board agreed. However, it wasn't until 1998, when the decidedly un-hepcat mayor Rudy Giuliani idiosyncratically mandated that any plans submitted for the highly sought-after Coliseum site include a performance space for JLC, that Wynton set down, in the manner of Yahweh's deca screed from Sinai, "Ten Fundamentals of the House of Swing."

Written on cocktail napkins during a red-eye flight, "The Vision," as Wynton calls it, reads like what it was intended to be: "a metaphorical blueprint of a groove, to be articulated into design, and then made real."

Fundamental No. 1: "the entire facility is the House of Swing . . . we want all 100,000 square feet to dance and sing, to be syncopated and unpredictable, but not eccentric." Fundamental No. 5: "The two main performance spaces should represent two sides of the same thing, like night and day, or like a man and a woman." The rest, as they say, is commentary, that is, "The Rose Hall, representing "woman, or night—this is not Jazz at Lincoln Center's main hall, because like a family we play no favorites—should sound like Lester Young, Billie Holiday, Paul Desmond, and Miles Davis." The front, or "male," Allen Room "should have the feeling of a street parade . . . an ancient Greek theatre . . . there should be a question of where the band ends and the audience begins . . . the room should feel like Duke Ellington's Orchestra—sensuous, spicy, and able to accommodate all tempos."

The project's lead architect, the flamboyant Uruguayan Rafael Viñoly, who claims to be a former Tupamaro revolutionary and is mostly noted for designing massive convention centers, read Wynton's manifesto and was inspired. "The Fundamentals of Swing transcends every boundary," Viñoly says, "it is an architectural plan immediately translatable into the language of art and love. Wynton's Vision guided my hand in everything I did at JLC."

A copy of the "Fundamentals," accompanied by Viñoly's plans, now fills a bedroom wall in Wynton's homey and spacious riverview pad on Sixty-sixth Street, directly behind the Juilliard School he once attended as a seventeen-year-old trumpet prodigy. The apartment is just a few steps, past Balducci's, from the stage door of Alice Tully Hall, where Wynton has conducted the Lincoln Center Jazz Orchestra for the past decade. The move to Columbus Circle will mean a longer walk to work, but it will be worth it. "Sometimes I'll get up in the middle of the night and look at the plans," Wynton says. "It's like a dream, one I always knew would happen."

Truth be told, however, Wynton, hard hat on his head, but unhappy with heights and deep water, isn't thrilled be on the rickety catwalks of the rising House of Swing. Not that he'll ever let on, decked out in his Brooks Brothers casualwear. Being cool is part of being the star, the front man, the artistic director. Besides, Brooks Brothers is a corporate sponsor. This is no problem, since Wynton, who'd rather play backup for Kenny G than be caught dead in Phat Farm, is pretty much Brooks Brothers to begin with.

Hands on, he does all his own ironing, the board in the cedar closet of his bedroom, alongside twenty or so hats, each on its own hook. On the road, he sometimes irons the clothes of the guys in the band, too. "They bring them to me because they know I'll crease them right," Wynton says.

Clutching a naked girder as the late-fall wind whips through the open superstructure, Wynton says, "This is jazz steel." It is a phrase he likes, "because we're not after something that is going to disappear. We're building an institution, one that is going to endure." That's what people don't understand, Wynton says—the need for permanency. It is an issue, after all—this notion of an institutionalized House of Swing, especially a $130 million one crammed into the middle of the commercial colossus of the AOL Time Warner corporate headquarters.

"Institutions create institutional music, and that is not what jazz is about. This is a music where nothing is ever played the same way twice," says Howard Mandel, a writer who's president of the Jazz Journalists Association, echoing the often-heard objection against the supposed canonization of what is referred to as "the Marsalis-Crouch-Murray version" of America's music. It isn't that anyone doubts Marsalis's 100 percent dedication to the future of jazz (of the opinion that knowing the chord changes to "C Jam Blues" will absolutely save your soul, he's a tireless jazz educator, offering several dozen lectures and demonstrations each year). Problems arise with Wynton's alleged "neo-traditionalist," anti-avant-garde bias against everything he personally deems as "unswinging," that is, much of the past four decades. The fear is, while the legacies of Louis Armstrong and Duke Ellington will be forever celebrated on Columbus Circle, such post-Coltrane artists as Cecil Taylor, Don Cherry, Albert Ayler, and Sun Ra will be written out of the music's history.

Some just can't stand the imprimatur of the uptown big-money squares. For her part, Lorraine Gordon, who owns and operates the Vanguard, the club started by her husband Max sixty-six years ago, says, "I love Wynton; he's my favorite. But jazz in a shopping mall? What's that about?"

Even Ellis Marsalis, father of Wynton, Branford, Delfeayo, and Jason, reveals mixed feelings. Ellis, considered by some observers to be the "hippest" of the Marsalis clan, once drove for fifty hours straight from New

Orleans to Los Angeles to see Ornette Coleman. "I went with Alvin Batiste, my friend. We didn't stop, except for gas. We just wanted to hear Ornette and tell him thanks, because he was really doing something new." This is the same Ornette Coleman whose "harmolodic" approach has been found deficient in swingingness by the JLC brain trust, an aesthetic judgment that caused Ellis Marsalis to roll his eyes and shake his head. Standing in the crowded Vanguard dressing room, the elder Marsalis, a large, friendly man, casts a loving gaze at his famous son and says, "Jazz at Lincoln Center is a great thing. A lot of musicians are going to get work because of it. But Wynton's New York, you know, it's not my New York. My New York had clubs, little places to go, to relax and just play. This New York, it's kind of cosmetic. A really shiny surface. What's underneath, I don't know. But times change; you have to accept that."

Wynton, of course, has heard it all before. Bestride the construction site like a jazz Howard Roark, feet on the six-inch-thick rubber "isolation pads" that will muffle the rumble of the A train Billy Strayhorn said was the quickest way to Harlem, Wynton decries, "Who could be against this? . . . Who says jazz has to be played only in dark rooms filled with curls of cigarette smoke? Always on the margin. That outlaw thing. That's a romantic, limiting fantasy. This is the greatest music ever produced in this country, made by the greatest musicians. You think it doesn't deserve something first-class, like any other great art?"

Yet even now, with people talking about Marsalis as a New York cultural leader-commissar on the par of a Balanchine or Bernstein, there is another kind of permanency to think about: the tenuousness of life around here these days. Wynton was in L.A. during the WTC nightmare, getting ready to put on his most recent magnum opus, *All Rise*, at the Hollywood Bowl: "I saw it on television. The planes, over and over. All I could think about was how perishable everything was."

Indeed, our little tour of the future home of Jazz at Lincoln Center was held up for about half an hour that very morning. Bruce MacCombie, the JLC executive director, Laura Johnson, the general manager, and Jonathan Rose, the chairman of the building committee, were there. But Ted Ammon, chairman of the board, was not. It was strange, everyone said, because Ted, the investment banker–jazz fan who had contributed more than $2.5 million to JLC, was not the type to be late. It wasn't until the next morning that people heard Ammon was dead, murdered in his Hamptons home.

A week later, at a memorial service for Ammon at Alice Tully Hall attended by several representatives of the Suffolk County homicide squad, Wynton eulogized, "We want to know the particulars of death—it repulses us, it calls us, it fascinates us . . . but only the dead know the facts of death, and they never tell." Then, along with Wycliffe Gordon, Victor Goines, Walter Blanding Jr., and others from the LC Jazz Orchestra, Wynton broke into Jelly Roll Morton's "Oh, Didn't He Ramble"—"Didn't he ramble . . . Rambled all around, in and out of town . . . till the butcher cut him down"—a tune that has been played at New Orleans jazz funerals for a hundred years. They really ripped into it too, with Wynton, seemingly on the verge of tears, playing the happiest music he could muster, which, of course, is the N'awlins way. It was a priceless kind of thing, because even if Ammon's much-battled-over estate was worth $100 million, no amount of money could buy this: being sent off by Wynton Marsalis. Except the people at Alice Tully didn't quite get it, how to behave when a soul passes on. They sat there mute. Eventually Wynton had to say, "You know, you don't have to be so quiet."

A couple of hours later, Wynton, up in his apartment overlooking the Hudson playing chess with saxophonist Walter Blanding, remained puzzled. "To me," he said, "death is not morbid; it's people's reaction to it that's morbid . . . nothing lasts, that's a given, but that's exactly why you've got to keep on working." It was like on the final cut of the album *Last Date*, when Eric Dolphy, who would die less than a month later, says, "When you hear music, after it's over, it's gone in the air forever. You can never capture it again." It was like Charlie Parker dying at thirty-four. If you're a player, you take that as an inspiration to keep playing, harder than ever.

Impermanence only increases urgency, said Wynton, whose first extended work was *Griot New York*, a 1991 three-movement piece performed in collaboration with the Garth Fagan Dance company. "That summed up how I felt about New York," Wynton says. "In the middle, the city is destroyed. Then the lovers, the two dancers, build it back up again. Heal it. I really wanted it to have this feeling of myth, urban myth, ultimate danger and redemption. To me it is a heroic story."

The challenge is to battle disorder, things flying off into meaningless-ness. There has to be a center, says Wynton, paraphrasing Yeats, his fa-vorite poet. That's how it is in music, and buildings, too, Wynton said, especially "a temple" like the new JLC. Wynton addresses the issue in No. 8 among "The Fundamentals of the House of Swing." It says: "We must have an icon that serves as the symbol for the facility everywhere."

Certainly that icon will be the jazz temple's most spectacular design fea-ture, the fifty-foot glass wall facing Central Park South that will rise above the bandstand of the Allen Room. It will be something new to see in this beleaguered, beloved city. Soon a guy and his girl will be able to stroll through the park, ride west in a taxi or hansom cab, incline their eyes, and look at what Wynton has called "this gleaming jewel, a beacon of civilization and American expression . . . one more beautiful vision of New York."

"They will see Wynton," says architect Rafael Viñoly, who invented the idea of the glass wall after reading No. 8 of the "Fundamentals."

"Wynton in the window, blowing his horn."

Sitting on the ledge that surrounds the fountain in the middle of Lincoln Center, Wynton is contemplating what Albert Murray, in his book *The Hero and the Blues*, refers to as the epic "journey . . . the fundamental com-mitment" of the artist, a heroism "measured in terms of the . . . complexi-ties of the obstacles it overcomes." In a few hours, he'll be inside Alice Tully Hall, leading the Lincoln Center Jazz Orchestra, including Victor Goines, Wess Anderson, and Herlin Riley—musicians Marsalis has known most of his life—to play in a seventy-fifth-birthday-celebration concert for saxophonist Jimmy Heath. But now he is remembering when he first came to Sixty-sixth Street, in 1979, to try out for Juilliard.

"I was nervous. My teacher thought I could make it. But you never know. I just wanted to do good on my audition, get a good scholarship. I didn't want to stay in New Orleans, the shit I had grown up around. The segregation. I thought it would be better in the North. As I found out, New York was a segregated town, too, in a different way. I performed all my music from memory. I played the Haydn Trumpet Concerto. I played the Brandenburg, played Petrushka, overtures from Beethoven, Mahler's Fifth. The common repertoire, what you have to know if you play orchestral trumpet."

Wynton would be out of Juilliard by 1980, touring with Art Blakey's Jazz Messengers along with his brother Branford—a whole other kind of education.

"That was exciting," Wynton says, ticking off, with his usual total recall, the various apartments he lived in during those early, wild times when he first made his name. "I lived at 137th Street near Lenox, 108th between Broadway and West End, 99th and Broadway, 20th and Park, Bleecker and Broadway, in Brooklyn . . . I loved Harlem, I loved Brooklyn. Everywhere I lived, the City had something to offer. The musicians looked out for me. Art Blakey. John Lewis. Philly Joe Jones came and picked me up in his car. We'd pass a place and he'd say, 'Oh, that where this and that musician lives, oh, there's where to get the best suits, over there they got really good Italian sausages.' He wanted me to know these things, thought it might be useful to me . . . because I was here, I was going to stay, and I was going to carry it on."

One of the dumber, more patronizing misconceptions about Wynton is that he arrived in New York a malleable Mr. Natural, a Willie Mays–Joe Hardy tabula rasa of the brass section, to be molded by the neocon-ology of whatever mentor he encountered. The fact is, Wynton has always had a sense of his own destiny, from the time Al Hirt, the Bourbon Street tourist *macher* his father was playing with, gave him his first trumpet at six. He knew immediately that the trumpet was the instrument for him. "Trumpet playing is as old as dust, you know," Wynton says. "Joshua didn't knock down the walls of Jericho with a saxophone. A trumpeter announces himself, a trumpeter is a priest, a shaman. It gives you power."

We were talking about "Psalm 26," the cut that both opens and closes Wynton's 1988 disc *Uptown Ruler*. Looking through a Bible as we sat beside the Lincoln Center fountain, I wondered what so interested Wynton about this particular Psalm of David, which says, "I have not sat with vain persons, neither will I go with dissemblers, I have hated the congregation of evildoers; and will not sit with the wicked."

"Well it sure doesn't have anything to do with George W. Bush," Wynton exclaimed. Bush might seek to vanquish his own version of evil-doers, but Wynton didn't buy into this "us and them way of thinking. . . . I don't see why you shouldn't sit down with the supposed wicked. How else would you learn the ways of the wicked unless you sat with them?" But what really mattered to him about Psalm 26, Marsalis said, was the phrase "but as for me."

"But as for me, I walk in my integrity. Redeem me and be gracious to me. . . . My foot stands on level ground, in the great congregation," Wynton read aloud. "*But as for me* . . . like in all this magnificence, all creation, one individual voice could still be heard. That really jumped out at me."

That's why, Wynton says, "you've got to work on your legend," something the jazz man did most notoriously in his long-running feud with Miles Davis. Wynton (named for Miles's onetime piano player Wynton Kelly) had been viciously attacking Davis, claiming the lionized inventor of "the cool"—an early influence on Marsalis's own playing—was "tomming" by playing his *Bitches Brew*–style fusion. In retort, Miles said that Wynton was a "nice young man but confused" who should "mind his own fucking business."

"You're afraid of Miles," mocked Wynton's band members, betting him $100 each that he would not confront the famously irascible Davis when the two trumpeters played a festival in Vancouver, Canada. Taking the dare, Wynton jumped up onto stage right in the middle of Miles's show.

Wynton recalls: "Miles was playing the organ on a blues song, 'C.C. Rider,' when I got onstage. 'I've come to address the dumb shit you have said about me and my family,' I shouted. But Miles just kept playing. Like he didn't hear me. I had to say it again. 'I've come to address the dumb shit . . .' Finally Miles looks up and says, 'Come back tomorrow.' Then we got into it, him telling me to get the fuck off the stage. Then he picked up his horn and played. I guess he was trying to put me in my place, show me who was boss, but he played some sad shit. He had nothing left. That made me unhappy, to see a great player challenged like that and be without a response."

Not that Wynton regrets the incident: "No, man. Miles knew what was up. He knew the Oedipal deal, he'd done enough of it himself when he was young. Cutting the heart out of those guys he'd come up on. So I can't feel bad about what I did. Besides, *it was fun.*"

Other incidents, generally falling under the rubric of "the jazz wars of the nineties," have been less amusing. In 1993, reports leaked of an "artistic decision" by JLC to hire "an entire band of guys under the age of 30." Given the JLC credo about the continuity of the jazz message, firing people like altoist Jerry Dodgion, trombonist Art Baron, and baritone man Joe Temperly—who had played with Duke Ellington's band—was a strange, possibly illegal (and soon to be withdrawn) move that opened Marsalis up to accusations he was packing the band full of easily controllable crony-clones.

There have been charges of so-called reverse racism at JLC. In 1996, much was made of the fact that of all the musicians given "nights" at JLC, only one, Gerry Mulligan, who had already died at the time of the show, was white. What about to Bix Beiderbecke and Bill Evans? Didn't they deserve a night? "Blacks invented jazz, but no one owns it," complained Whitney Balliett in an oft-quoted *New Yorker* piece.

Marsalis was floored by the criticism: "I'm thinking to myself . . . *this is Lincoln Center and they're talking about no white people?*" To this day, Marsalis discounts the race issue, saying it was "all about resentment, about me using my power as artistic director, which is what I was hired to do." Today (when five of the fifteen LC Orchestra chairs are held by whites, including saxophonist Ted Nash, trumpeter Ryan Kisor, and the thankfully still-extant seventy-two-year-old Joe Temperly), Wynton insists, coyly, "I just want to have the best players who I feel good playing with."

This skirmishing has led to much intemperate commentary. New-waveist saxophonist David Murray slammed JLC's reliance on standards as "fuckin' macabre necrophilia or some shit." Pianist Keith Jarrett said Wynton was "jazzy the same way someone who drives a BMW is sporty." A particularly amusing critique of the Marsalis mystique appears in a Web page titled "Livingston Squat . . . a place devoted to mirth at the expense of Wynton Marsalis and Stanley Crouch." Here one finds the one-act play

Branford Tells Wynton, a recounting of the traumatic 1985 scene when Branford informed his earnest younger brother he would be leaving the Wynton Marsalis Quintet.

"That's cool, Steeplone," says Wynton (referred to as "Minton Bursi-tis"), understanding that a true jazzman must always seek to broaden his committment to the music. "Will you be going with some legendary vet-eran of the bebop tenor battles on Central Avenue in Los Angeles . . . or perhaps an underappreciated modern giant who cut his teeth during the fertile period of swinging sixties modernism?"

"Well, no," Branford replies. Actually, he says, he is going to play with Sting, describing the former Police singer as "a down cat," adding, "I can't be doing that historical shit *all* the time!"

Wynton wails: "Pop music! Pop music! *Oh, my brother! . . . my own brother!*"

Nowadays, Wynton claims he doesn't read what people write about him anymore. "There was a really bad article in the *Times*, and I wrote this long letter of rebuttal. I was wondering, should I send it? My son, Wynton Jr., said I had to send it. 'Daddy,' he said, 'if you don't, then they'll write it again.' After that, I couldn't take the bashing seriously anymore."

Besides, says Wynton, stretched out in his bedroom, he doesn't have time for jazz wars anymore. He's just gotten back from a month on the road with the LCJ Orchestra and another two weeks with his septet. "Playing, every night, playing." That's the easy part, he says, going from town to town, driving in the bus, playing ball, scheming a way to beat Walter Blanding in chess, spreading jazz love along the highways and byways. What's hard is "working for free . . . this nonprofit thing. When you're working for free, you're tired all the time."

Looking at the plans of the new building on the wall, Wynton says, "First, everyone was talking about $50 million. Then it was $74 million, $81 million. Then it's 115 . . . $115 million—heading toward 130! When I was growing up, if you got 130 pennies for jazz, you were doing good. Now we need $130 million. Can't be sitting around here, it has got to be gotten."

Chances are he will, since, along with the other things Wynton Marsalis can do really well, raising money is very definitely one of them.

Gordon J. Davis, founding chairman of JLC (and until his recent resignation Lincoln Center's president), testifies to Wynton's magic with "lead donors." "He's kind of the ultimate weapon," says Davis. "You open the door, and in walks Mozart. Fund-raising-wise, that can be a compelling argument."

It worked with Herb Allen, the legendarily secretive broker of such high-stakes media deals as the Disney-Capital Cities/ABC merger and Seagram's $5.7 billion purchase of MCA. A fraternity brother of Allen's at Williams back in the early sixties, Davis once managed to get Allen to write a $250 check for a campus civil-rights campaign. But he couldn't get anywhere with Allen on the jazz front until the financier had a little breakfast with Marsalis.

"Wynton came over and started talking, the way he does," Davis said. "As it turned out, Wynton and Herb had similar views on the corrosive nature of today's popular culture, how it undermines everything." Allen said he might speak to Steve Case, the AOL founder, who had also attended Williams and was often present at the Sun Valley confab Allen hosts annually for the likes of Bill Gates, Sumner Redstone, and Rupert Murdoch. Case was a jazz fan, Allen said. He might help.

After a few days, Allen called back, reports Davis. "My heart sank, because Herb said he hadn't gotten the money from Case. He didn't feel right about asking him. I was about to hang up when Allen says, 'So I'll give you the money myself.' Ten million bucks. He said it was meeting Wynton that did it. He believed in him."

The grand jazz patroness Baroness Pannonica de Koenigswarter may have sent her personal car to bring the junked-up Bird to the Stanhope Hotel on a near daily basis and put up Monk in her Weehawken estate, but Wynton's philanthropic reach is a whole other deal. Watching him work a room, as he did the other night at JLC's gala "Tribute to Tito Puente," pausing unhurriedly at every single $1,000-a-plate setting, is to see another bit of marvelous Marsalis class-defying technique. The knowing wink, the squeeze of the genius's hand upon the shoulder, the wordless Chaplinesque dance with the head and spreading cherub smile—you could call him Wynton Clinton, the way how he keeps the charm pumping.

Mostly he listens. It is a jazzman's gift, after all, listening to others. How else can you play? Talk to Wynton on the phone, and there will be a pause, a silence on the other end.

"You still there?" is the question. "Yeah," Marsalis says, "I'm *listening* to what you're saying." Oh, you say, surprised and pleased at the novelty of it all.

Still you wonder how long Wynton can stay iconic in the window of the jazz temple he's building over on Columbus Circle—and what might happen without him. "They've painted themselves into a corner at Lincoln Center, pushing Wynton so far out front," says one prominent jazz critic. "He's good, but he's not Louis Armstrong and Duke Ellington rolled up into one, the way they'd have you believe. Everyone knows, including Wynton, I bet, those long compositions like *All Rise* don't work. The way the programs are set up, you don't get Sonny Rollins, you get the Jazz at Lincoln Center Orchestra interpreting Sonny Rollins, like somehow that's better than the real thing. It is dangerous, I think, this cult of personality—Wynton and the Wyntonettes—and there's no turning back now."

Certainly, JLC is exceedingly Wynton-centric. Jonathan Rose, son of Frederick, says, "The whole idea of the facility is to make it welcoming and warm, the way Wynton is—for it to be a manifestation of Wynton's personality." Russell Johnson, the famous acoustician working on the new JLC, says, "It is rare a hall is built so clearly for one artist." Asked shortly before his death if JLC would be robbed of identity without Wynton, Ted Ammon said, "No one is indispensable. But to lose Wynton . . . that would leave a big hole, a very big hole."

Even Albert Murray, who has an opinion about everything, demurs when asked if Wynton's extra administrative duties might be hampering his playing. "That's my boy," Albert says. "Don't ask me to say anything about my boy."

Wynton, who says he's "a scrub, like everyone else," figures he can take the weight. Besides, he's too busy checking over this new translation of *The Iliad* and convincing me he is right about the popular culture (and I am wrong) to worry about his own mortality. It is part of a long-running conversation, the kind Wynton likes. I contend that if Sonny Rollins could make something great out of "Surrey with the Fringe on Top," shouldn't current musicians be able to improvise off today's pop songs. Wynton, who hates anything with even the hint of a backbeat, disagrees. He decrees this impossible because "all the pop songs they make now are so terrible you can't even mess with them."

Isn't there one he likes? Not one single tune?

"No," Wynton says. What about Nirvana's "Come As You Are"—that's got an interesting line. Wynton considers this, singing through Kurt Cobain's chord changes. "No, man," he says. "I'm looking to play the melody, and there ain't none."

So it goes. Wynton says the definitions of *hip* and *square* have never changed: the jazzmen remain eternally cool, everyone else is some bow-tie-wearing cornball. "That's the reason I can't get with the so-called avant-garde. All jazz is avant-garde. Sidney Bechet is still avant-garde. The squares are those fools on MTV, with gold teeth and the baggy prison pants, their asses hanging out. Minstrel-show shit. I won't let my kids watch it. 'But it's Jay-Z,' they say. I tell them, 'I don't care if it's F.U.-Z, you ain't watching.' Not when I'm around. Let them sneak their shit. That's what I had to do. My parents were strict. We always had to sneak our shit. If they're gonna watching that nonsense I better not know about it."

Then the phone rings, which it often does. You can always tell when it is a babe, especially one Wynton, who has never yet had to say he doesn't get around much anymore (and has never been married), doesn't exactly want to talk to. His voice gets low and his eyes roll about in their sockets. "I didn't say I didn't want you to call anymore. I said I didn't want you to call me thirty times a day," he says. When he hangs up, I say, "Don't make any entangling alliances."

"What?" he asks.

"Don't make any entangling alliances." I told him that's what George Washington advised his successors when he retired from the presidency.

"'Don't make any entangling alliances'"—Wynton repeats, writing it down in his looping handwriting on a napkin, which he shoves into his pocket. "Thanks," he says. "I'll remember that."

It is a nice day, so we walk across the Lincoln Center campus, as Wynton has been doing for more than twenty years. You forget how stitched into this community he is. He knows everyone, cops, maintenance guys, doormen. By Avery Fisher Hall, we run into Brandon Lee, whom Wynton introduces as "from Houston, one of the baddest motherfuckers on trumpet out here." Seventeen and rail-thin, Brandon attends the new jazz program at Juilliard. Largely because of Wynton and Victor Goines, who now heads the school, Brandon did not have to play Mahler or the Brandenburgs at his audition. He could choose from tunes like "Cherokee," "Round Midnight," "Con Alma," and "Willow Weep for Me."

Approaching Wynton's apartment house, we run into Beverly Sills, the former diva who now runs Lincoln Center. With a deft side step, Wynton slips ahead, opening the door for her. Rumors have been flying about that Sills was instrumental in pushing Wynton's friend Gordon Davis from his job as president, but the jazzman claims to want no part of the culture-industry politics that has recently beset Lincoln Center, calling it, perhaps disingenuously, "grown-up people's business." Kissing Sills on the cheek with a great flourish, he says, "She's always been great to me."

From the moment the elevator door opens on Wynton's floor, you can hear the music. Someone's almost always playing something at Wynton's, a horn or his grand piano. The sound beckons you forward, into this zone of sanity, this world where art lives. Why isn't *your* house like this? you wonder. Maybe Marsalis is a genius, maybe not, but this vibe might be his greatest achievement.

As usual, the pad is packed. Tony Parker, the gray-eyed cop from Detroit, is here. Ditto Mo the cook from New Orleans, dishing up mounds of gumbo and jambalaya. In the living room, where the LSU game is on the TV, Wynton has left notes for a composition he's been writing on top of the grand piano. "Emphasis on these elements," it says on a pad: "1. strength, 2. speed, 3. glamour, 4. pain, 5. heaven." A few minutes later,

Jumaane Smith, a Juilliard trumpet student, arrives with a tallish, cornrow-sporting thirteen-year-old.

"This is Steve," Jumaane says, introducing the kid, who's come down from the Bronx with his mother and sisters. It is a bit of a continuum, since Jumaane has been one of Wynton's protégés and Steve, a young trumpet player, is now under Jumaane's wing. Jumaane has been talking about the kid for several weeks, touting his moves to the basket as well as his horn tone.

"How good are you?" Wynton demands. "In basketball?"

Not bad, not bad at all, Steve answers, attempting modesty, looking Wynton in the eye, the way his mom told him to. He's got an outside shot, can also go to the hole.

"Why don't we go over to the court," Wynton says. "Beat me, I'll do two hundred push-ups. I beat you, you got to practice your horn two hours a day."

Steve thinks that will be fine, Wynton being such an old man and not that tall to boot. He takes the ball and bounces it between his legs.

An hour or so later, the boy returned. How'd he do? it was inquired.

"It was an ass-whipping," Steve remarked glumly. Then, brightening, he said, "So it looks like I got to practice two hours a day. That won't be so bad."

16

The Champ Behind the Counter

A few years ago, after doing a wholly desultory piece on the basketball player Stephon Marbury—the only time he looked me in the eye was when I told him my mother had graduated from his high school, Lincoln, in 1938. Marbury couldn't believe such a year existed—I took a vow never to write about another so-called "major sports" figure. Rendered unfailingly boring by an excess of corporate regimen, hubris, hangers-on, lack of education, etc., they just don't give you anything. "Minor" sports, like horse racing and boxing, popular before the leveling effect of television, are better. As a prizefighter the Syrian immigrant Mustafa Hamsho was more a linebacker than an elegant purveyor of the sweet science. But he got the job done. As with almost all fighters, with ample avenues to get out their aggressions, he's a heck of a nice guy. New York *magazine, 1999.*

In the Big City, you never know when you might walk into the corner store to buy a quart of milk and see a face from the distant, treasured past on the other side of the counter. This particular face, slightly battered but still handsome in a sleepy way, belonged to Mustafa Hamsho, now the owner and operator of the M & H Deli on Fourteenth Street in Brooklyn's Park Slope, but once the leading contender for the middleweight championship of the world.

"Mustafa, is that you?" Faded pictures hanging on the wall below the store's pressed tin ceiling showing the fighter, who is from Syria, in boxing gloves and a burnoose confirmed the ID.

From behind the phone card displays, Milky Ways, and Koranic quotations, a huge smile came across Mustafa's squarish countenance. "Mark! How are you?" he boomed. "Are you still working for the *Village Voice?*"

"How can you remember that?" I hadn't worked for the *Village Voice* for nearly twenty years, hadn't seen Mustafa for almost as long. It seemed the ensuing decades, along with the fact that Mustafa had been hit in the head often, and hard, by the likes of Marvelous Marvin Hagler, Wilfredo Benitez, Donnie LaLonde, and a host of others would preclude such mnemonic feats.

"No, no," said Mustafa, now forty-six, a dozen years past his last fight, chortled in his low-timbre but lively Arabic-inflected English. "I remember everything."

It being a beautiful spring day, Mustafa, with typical hospitality, drew two cups of coffee from his urn beside the Boar's Head sign, bid his nephew to man the Lotto machine, and set out a couple of folding chairs on the sidewalk. Ignoring his array of ringing cell phones and beepers, the erstwhile pugilist then filled me in on his highly particularized life and times. Or, what Mustafa, with offhand geniality, refers to as "my American thing."

Growing up with his brothers in the Syrian town of Lattika on the Mediterranean coast, Mustafa never imagined he'd make it in this country, much less come close to a world champion. His father, a sometime soldier who periodically fought against the Israelis, was a religious man who "wanted me to become a doctor," reported Mustafa, still looking formidable in his low-center-of-gravity way despite an extra twenty-five or so pounds. But after a friend arrived in Lattika with a few dog-eared pictures of Sugar Ray Robinson ("the most beautiful of all") and Joe Louis, Mustafa was smitten. When at sixteen, he defeated the twenty-eight-year-old Syrian middleweight champion, Mustafa began to think, "I might be good."

Seeking a "bigger world," Mustafa signed onto a Greek steamer that eventually pulled into a Red Hook pier for six months of drydock. In America for the first time, Hamsho was amazed and pleased to find the Atlantic Avenue Arabic community a short walk away from his disabled ship. It was at that time he began training at a couple of the local gyms. "I'd tell them I was sick and sneak off the boat to work out," he recalls. After a hazily remembered New Year's Eve in Brooklyn, Mustafa jumped ship permanently and took an apartment in Bay Ridge, where he still lives twenty-six years later.

The beginning of his fight career was inauspicious. He got nothing for his first fight, $75 for the second. Not being able to speak or read English, he signed a lifetime contract with a less than reputable (even for boxing) promoter who sought to change his name to a less Islamic Rocco Estafire. Soon, however, Hamsho fell in with a zany, if typically rapscallion array of New York fight crowd characters who would change his life.

"These people, they were crazy but what did I know? . . . I thought all Americans were crazy." Mustafa recollects with a bemused shake of his still bushy-haired head. There was Chuck Wepner, a.k.a. the Bayonne Bleeder, the model for Stallone's "Rocky" character, who had somehow managed to last fifteen rounds with Mustafa's great hero, Muhammad Ali. There were the two Als—Al Certo, of the millinery Certos of Secaucus, New Jersey, and Al Braverman, a crude-mouthed, pickle-nosed plug ugly with a secret passion for delicate porcelain dolls that he sold in his fussy antique shop located under an elevated platform of the Woodlawn-Jerome line of the IRT in the Bronx. Foremost of these denizens, however, was the floridly syntaxed, popeyed, and smash-nosed Irishman, Paddy Flood, who would not only become Mustafa's new manager but also his mentor and guide to the New World, if you want to call attending Yonkers Raceway to bet on trotters six nights a week guidance.

Well versed in the Barnumesque nuances of the sweet science, Paddy envisioned a massive Madison Square Garden showdown between Mustafa, whom he had dubbed the Syrian Buzzsaw, and Mike Rossman, who despite being brought up as the Italian Mike Dipiano, had taken his mother's maiden name and was campaigning as the Jewish Bomber.

It was in this context that I first encountered Mustafa, after climbing up the creaky stairs of the old sweatbox Gramercy Gym near Union Square, once home base for such luminaries as Floyd Patterson and Jose Torres. Paddy Flood sat in his accustomed spot, on the red vinyl couch by the window, drinking his usual cup of hypersweetened tea. The Hamsho-Rossman matchup would be "the biggest thing New York has ever seen!" Flood ballyhooed.

"*Arab vs. Jew! Jew vs. Arab!* We're gonna put a picture of a bomb on Mustafa's robe! Tick, tick, tick. Lock up your first born: *here comes the terrorist!* It'll be a sell-out! Every Jew in the City will come to boo him! They hate him! He hates them! He hates Jews!"

At this point the young Mustafa, dutifully working his southpaw jab upon the nearby heavy bag and scandalized by such talk, politely excused himself for interrupting. "But, Paddy, that's not so. . . . I don't hate Jews. *I like Jews.*"

Flood was apoplectic at this sabotage of his sales pitch. "No! No!" he boomed. "When you gonna learn? That's not what you're supposed to say!"

As it was, Mustafa never fought Rossman. He did, however, employing his inelegant but highly persistent attack, manage to beat almost every major middleweight in the late 1970s and early '80s. Colorfully monikered men like Bobby Boogaloo Watts, Bobby Czyz, and Willie "The Worm" Monroe fell before the Syrian Buzzsaw. The only one who stopped him was the nonpareil Hagler, probably the best fighter in the world at that time. After the fight it took sixty-one stitches to sew up Mustafa's face. "I look like a road map," he said at the time. Then, shortly before a second losing meeting with Hagler, Paddy Flood had a cerebral hemorrhage and died on the spot. Mustafa sobbed uncontrollably at the wake. "He was my best friend!" the fighter wailed.

"It was not the same after Flood. He talked about money all the time, but he never really cared about it. They said he lied, but he never lied to me. He loved me. I loved him," Mustafa says, sipping coffee in front of the M & H Deli. The store is only part of what Mustafa calls "my empire." In addition to owning the five-story building containing the deli with his partner and friend, Dr. Malik, a Pakistani internist, Mustafa also has the car service, Destinations Unlimited, around the corner and a Laundromat on Classon Avenue. Mustafa likes the Laundromat best because "it is just machines, dirty underwear and quarters, no people. . . . Sad to say, I have learned, you can't trust anybody." Mustafa says he gave all of his fight money to his family back in Syria, and now, with a wife and five kids in Bay Ridge (four between age five and nine), he has to work "night and day to keep up." He seems to be maintaining. It is no big thing to see Mustafa pull up in front of the M & H Deli in a black Mercedes, either the sedan or the sports model, designer sunglasses on, knit shirt with Plaza Hotel logo snug upon his barrel chest.

Noting that most of his former opponents have not shared this good fortune, Mustafa sighs. "Some hit me so hard I still have scars. I look in the mirror and I know Wilford Scypion did that to me. These men, they live in me. But some are not doing so well. It is sad. If you are a fighter, it is everything to you. When it is over, without education, there's nothing left, nothing to do. No one cares about you."

Mustafa has avoided this fate because "I know who I am and where I come from. . . . America is a great country, but you can get lost here. There is so much on TV, you can easily be confused. So I keep my culture. We speak Arabic in the house. I send my children to Al Noor Arabic school on Fourth Avenue. They teach respect for the family there. There is tradition. Public school is shit. The teachers fear the children, first time there's trouble, they call the police. In Islamic school, they call the parents. I don't care what the law says, family is more important."

Still an icon to those who turned up waving green flags as he fought in such less glamorous venues as the Jersey City Armory and the Villa Roma Resort of Callicoon, New York, Mustafa is a pillar of the Brooklyn Arabic community, a small business Don of sorts. He holds court in the tiny office behind the car service dispatch booth where of jugs of antifreeze and jumper cables compete for space with memorabilia like a replica of the trophy handed to the winner of the 1984 "Hamsho Pace" at the Meadowlands. "After I lose so much money maybe they think they owe me something," Mustafa says of the race named in his honor. Other items include photos of many good friends like Joe Frazier, NYPD nonpariel crime-buster Jack Maple, and a number of Saudi Arabian princes whom Mustafa, with some coyness, says he served in "a security capacity."

Today a fiftyish Palestinian man in form-fitting polyester shirt has arrived at Mustafa's office. After two decades in the Brooklyn coffee shop business, the man's most recent effort is failing and he is seeking the fighter's counsel. The rents on have skyrocketed, the Palestinian complains, he doesn't understand what the yuppies want. Mustafa listens patiently, hearing the man out. The restaurant business is difficult, he notes consolingly. "I had four different restaurants and never made money in any." After some talk comparing the dictatorial methods of Milosevic and Saddam, the man thanks Hamsho and leaves.

"He's a nice guy," Mustafa says. "But he's fucked in the head. Last year he comes to me with the same worries and I suggest a man who will invest in his shop. He takes the money and gambles it in Atlantic City. He never pays back my friend. Now he returns to me, same story as before. But there's nothing I can do for him. I send him to another investor and he goes again to Atlantic City, this time maybe he ends up with a knife in the neck. This is not the sort of business I wish to be involved with. After boxing, I like a quiet life."

Today is a big day for Mustafa because, finally, his boat, a twenty-five-foot fiberglass job he moors over by Marine Parkway, is going into the water. Mustafa can't wait to take his friend, one of the Saudi princes, out for a little spin around Sea Girt.

"I came here in the bottom of a ship," he says with sly smile. "Now I go as the captain of my own boat."

17

Mom Sells the House

This story got more letters, good ones that is, than any other piece in this book. Struck a chord, I guess. Or maybe it was that picture of me standing by my mom looking sheepish in my cap and gown because I showed up to graduation in shorts, an obvious sign of disrepect that earned me "a good klop" on the head. From New York *magazine, 1998.*

In the end, all Mom said was "Good-bye, house." She tossed the keys through the mail slot, got into her Subaru, drove down 190th Street to Underhill Avenue, turned the corner, and disappeared behind the Fensels' hedges. Forty-three years, and now the house on the corner of 190th Street and Fifty-third Avenue—*The House*—was officially sold. Gone, like that.

It reminded me of the night, two years earlier, when my father died in The House, the one I grew up in.

Years of kidney treatment, cardboard boxes full of dialysis equipment stacked in the hallway, and then one gloomy November evening he comes out of the shower and keels over from a heart attack. He managed to make it to my parents' room and lie down on the bed before dying. He looked so normal there, stretched out, seemingly ready to open one of the mystery books he took from the library a dozen at a time, skull and crossbones on the spine.

Except he was on the wrong side. The far side of the bed (the left) was his, but he hadn't made it there. He was lying on my mother's side. There were so many rituals in The House, and this was one of them: Mom slept on the right, Dad on the left.

The front doorbell rang, another breach. We always used the side door. Only the Jehovah's Witnesses came to the front. But the funeral parlor men didn't know that. Somber in their dark suits and peaked caps, they carried a stretcher and black leatherette zippered bag. Already late for what they called "another pickup," the men paced in the kitchen while my mother stayed in the bedroom staring at my father's body. She was sure she'd seen him move.

"Look," she said, pointing at his stomach. "He's breathing." I embraced her, trying to calm her down, be cool, be the man of the house. Then I saw him breathe.

Alive again, same as you or me. Soon he'd get up, open the drawer of his mahogany dresser, put on his Witty Bros. suit (the best Division Street had to offer), go off to teach NYC Bd. of Ed. shop class at Junior High 74 just as he had for the past twenty-five years. Then he'd be home again at about 3:20, put on paint-smeared dungarees and hat (a quiet eccentric, he favored woolen fezzes and Nepali skullcaps), and work in his basement on whatever moonlighting carpentry job he had lined up. At dinner he'd read the "school page" of the *World-Telegram & Sun* over a plate of pot roast or some other suitably overdone meat. This routine (in spring, add gardening) varied, but not much. There was something about The House, its Queens County rectangularism and boxy rooms, that narrowed the behavioral palette.

But he was still dead, still lying on the wrong side of the bed. It was "pretty common to imagine you see the loved one move," one of the funeral parlor guys said as they zipped their bag over my father's face and carried his body out the front door, the only time I ever remember him passing through that portal. As it turned out, one of the undertakers had gone to high school with me, thirty years before. We were both on the track team at Francis Lewis High School.

"Hey," he said, his face brightening as he recognized me. It was as if we'd just run into each other at a high school reunion."How you *doing,* man?"

"Not so good right now," I replied.

"Oh, yeah . . . well, maybe we can get together sometime," he said, carrying the bag containing my father's body toward the hearse waiting outside. Then they drove him down 190th Street, turned the corner, disappeared behind the Fensels' hedges, and were gone. Like that.

After that, The House's fate was sealed. As Mom, the master of utilitarian understatement, said, the place no longer "served its purpose."

"It was a reliable place to raise you and your sister," she summed up. And reliable (reliability being a key Mom meme) it was: strong and sturdy, a veritable Flushing fortress in red brick and gray siding. When that out-of-control Oldsmobile came tearing across the lawn and smashed into The House back in '58, did it crumble and fall? Not even a quiver. A couple of days later, I found the car's Rocket 88 insignia in the azalea bushes. My father nailed it to the basement wall. It was a Queens version of a moose head: an 88 bagged by The House.

I understand the existential positioning of this modest shingled dwelling in the vast sweep of the Jacobsonian immigrant saga. Built in 1949, purchased in 1954 from an acrimoniously divorcing couple for the then-staggering sum of $18,000, The House was the prize—compensation for the steerage, sweatshops, and years of dragging the coal bucket up five tenement flights. The House was what my father got for following General Patton into the Battle of the Bulge as a member of the Third Army. The House was what my parents and others like them had coming in this nation if they played by the rules, which for a fleeting, astounding moment were actually rigged in favor of people not very long out of the *shtetl*.

East of Gatsby's ash dumps, this part of Flushing was the "fresh-air zone," a municipal version of God's country ("G-d" to you). Once, when I was seven, a lady ran over a raccoon in the parking lot of the Bohack Supermarket on Forty-sixth Avenue; everyone crowded around the flattened animal, congratulating themselves for living in a place still touched by the wild.

"Still the country, in parts," someone marveled.

Here, on the frontier, we maintained the Queens version of a classless society. All of us—sons of Jews, Italians, Irish, and a couple of Poles—played million-inning thrillers with taped-up hardballs down in the vacant lots until the Parks Department built proper diamonds and wrecked everything. Our dads were firemen, cops, teachers. They all worked for the City, belonged to the appropriate union, made about the same amount of money. We didn't know anyone all that much richer than us. Back then .260 hitters made twenty thousand or less. It was another kind of playing field. We were little princes of the American Dream, snot-nosed scions of our parents' striving, piloting our bicycles through spacious, near-empty streets, scarfing pizza (extra mushrooms and hormones on mine, please) at fifteen cents a slice.

Like Babe Ruth built Yankee Stadium, my parents built The House for me. My suzerainty remained intact even after that night Dave Bell and I, blasted on Champale Malt Liquor (advertised on WWRL, it was a black man's drink), tried to sneak into The House at 3:00 A.M. "Ah-ha," my mother shouted, flipping on the kitchen light in ambush. Startled like cockroaches, we both immediately threw up, Dave Bell on my mother's fuzzy slippers. But no matter, you've got to grow up somewhere and The House was a better place than most. Indeed, that was the real social alchemy at work inside those ever-reliable walls—the fact that my parents, barely removed from the primordial precincts of the Lower East Side and Brooklyn, were able, in a single generation, to produce such a thoroughly self-referential, proto-hipster creature like myself.

I never believed she'd really sell the place. It was a story she often told: how, when she was a girl in the Depression, my grandparents moved almost every year. Back then, the Brighton Beach/Sheepshead Bay landlord class was so hard up they'd throw in a paint job with each new rental, so why do it yourself? Paint cost money; movers charged only ten dollars. Bargain or not, my mother hated this shiftlessness. She vowed her children would not be uprooted for the sake of free paint. The House would last forever, she thought. But now, with Dad gone, too many things evoked her outsized hebraic capacity for worry. The boiler, the rosebushes, water in the basement: in my parents' strict division of labor, there was so much *he* did. But it was more than that. The doughty democracy of the neighborhood had shifted to the next, inevitable notch: Now, more often than not, those little civil-servant-style houses on the block were occupied by widows, old ladies living alone.

Then again, this is a different Queens than the one where my mother and father chose to become Americans, a wholly Other place from the one where I grew up. In the middle sixties, in the waning years of my sojourn as an increasingly disgruntled outer-borough high school student, I'd return on the 7 train from some beatnik-in-training night in Manhattan and stand at the corner of Main Street and Roosevelt Avenue in Flushing. There, waiting for the Q-17 bus, which would take me deeper into what I regarded as the hopelessly provincial hinterlands, I'd look through the misty window of the Main Street Bar and Grille. On the steam table was a huge turkey with a giant fork jammed into its heavily browned breast. Men were at the bar, men about my father's age—Irish, Italians, Jews, the usual. They drank whiskey and watched *The Late, Late Show*. Even then, to the impressionable sixteen-year-old mind, it seemed like death.

Now the corner of Roosevelt and Main is a good deal livelier, and way more exotic. The bar is gone, replaced by places like the Flushing Noodle House, where a featured dish is "intestine and pig blood cake soup." Other landmarks of my youth, Alexander's department store and the RKO Keith's where I saw movies like Mr. *Sardonicus* and *Curse of Frankenstein* have been succeeded by establishments such as the Golden Monkey Pawnbrokers and the Korean Full-Gospel Evangelical Church. Down every street is a telescopic crush of neon Chinese ideograms hawking Taiwanese restaurants and sexual remedies. Billboards exhort travelers to sail down the Yangtze River. On the venerable Long Island Railroad Bridge hangs a sign advertising Asiana Airways: "Fly the youngest fleet to the old country." Somehow I don't think Bucharest, or Minsk, is one of those destinations.

I've always secretly believed that it was no mere coincidence that 1965, the year I left home to go to college, was also when Congress passed the Immigration and Naturalization Act, which threw the doors wide open and changed Queens forever. Now more than 125,000 Chinese and Koreans call Flushing home. A quarter of the city's newly arrived Latin

American population lives in Queens. Peruvians, Bolivians, Colombians, Nicaraguans—almost every country in the Caribbean and South America has a sizable representation. East Indians fill Jackson Heights. Once Jimmy Breslin, Queens' own Charles Dickens disguised as Archie Bunker, articulated the perfect nasal pitch of the borough's blue-collar white man. These days Breslin lives in Manhattan; much of his cop/fireman constituency has moved to Long Island or Florida; and if you go over to Elmhurst's Newtown High (a sleepy, Irish-dominated school when we played them in basketball during the middle sixties), you'll hear a hip-hop Babel of upward of forty different languages.

Thirty-five years after freezing on the corner of Roosevelt and Main, I am an eager tourist in the land of my upbringing. I love to get into the car and cruise the diversity hot spots, places like the intersection of Ninety-first Place and Corona Avenue, where within the space of a single block stand the Chinese Seventh-Day Adventist Church, Centro Civico Colombiano, Santería Niño de Atocha Botánica, Malaysian Curry House, Perla Ecuatoriana Restaurant, the Korean Health Center, and Elarayan Restaurante Chileano. Smack in the middle of this is Ana's hairdresser, where old Italian ladies, as if commanded by some recondite memory chip, still beehive their hair under conehead dryers. The Elmhurst Hospital emergency room is also good, especially on a Saturday night after a big soccer game piped from Bogotá. A more far-flung array of stabbing victims would be hard to find. Harried nurses call out the names of the evening's victims: "Gonzalez! . . . Patel! . . . Chu! . . . where the hell is Romanov's chart?"

These are a different crew from the immigrants my parents and grandparents came in with. My people, once they got on the boat—they weren't going back. It was a one-way ticket. America was their grail; they were here for the long haul. Now the world's smaller, it's sixty-nine cents a minute to talk to wherever at the *larga distancia* parlors on Roosevelt Avenue, and the new people aren't even called immigrants but "transnationals." You walk to Main Street, where the Hasidim are, and see that assimilation—becoming American—no longer seems the sole purpose of living in Queens. Maybe there are enough Americans. Indeed, sometimes, in the grip of postmodernist ennui, it seems to me as if these new people, by their very apartness—their refusal to buy the American deal lock, stock, and barrel—are the only fully fleshed-out humans around, the only ones with a palpable past, present, and potentially heroic future. They have rolled the dice with their lives; now the epic of New York belongs to them.

As for my mother, no one could ever accuse her of lacking a sense of adventure. Recently she went to Istanbul and preferred the Asian side. But she knows when things have come to an end. For months she walked the still quiet, verdant blocks around The House and felt out of place. "I'm lonely here," she said.

One fall day I was sitting at her kitchen table and heard the pounding. The realtor was outside hammering a FOR SALE sign into my father's lawn like a stake through the heart. Then they started to come, the prospective buyers. Local canard said someone Chinese would buy the place: a non-English-speaking man from Xi'an with a bad haircut, two daughters at the top of their class at Stuyvesant, and a suitcase full of cash, all of it up-front. But in this Queens you can never tell who might buy the house you grew up in. In the space of a fortnight, Syrians, Koreans, Chileans, and people from Bokhara and Thailand walked through the rooms my father painted and where he put up shelves. They sat on the sofa so long forbidden to me and my sister. It was a stirring ecumenical procession, a testament to the city's ever fecund, eternally replenishing genetic alloy. Soon The House would be the repository of an entirely different history, ringing with another sort of accent, the smells in the kitchen sharper, spicier. Soon the place, ever reliable, would serve someone else's purpose, only this time with a lot more TV stations than my sister and I ever got to watch.

My mother, she just wanted to sell. She's not the sentimental type. What no longer served a purpose had to go. In the end, Dominicans got the place. Nice people with a couple of kids and a travel agency business downtown, Mom said. Maybe she could have held out for another five or ten grand, with the market shooting up every day. But still, a 1,500 percent profit isn't too shabby, especially when all you want to do is get out.

"My heart is not broken," my mother announced at the closing.

Forty-three years ago, on the very first night I spent in my twelve-by-twelve-foot square room, Mom told me to bang on the floor if I got scared. Back on 174th Street, where we'd previously lived with my aunt and uncle, my room had been right next to my parents'. Here I was upstairs, by myself. But I never got scared. From the start I recognized the value of vertical separation. They were *down there* and I was *up here*. Ah, my room, that little incubator of me. What do you say about a place where you jacked off for the first time? Where you listened to Ali beat Liston on the radio? So much happened in my room, I thought, spending one last night up here, the movers due at seven the next morning.

The House was in boxes; my mother, never one to wait to the last moment, had started packing months before. I'd taken some things—my sixth-grade autograph book from P.S. 177 ("drop dead" is listed as my "favorite motto"), my Ted Kluszewski mitt, an old vinyl of *The Platters Greatest Hits*, the chair I sat in to do my homework. Mementos, souvenirs, nothing more. This seemed appropriate, since I'd always told myself that even though I'd grown up here, The House had never truly been mine. I was just passing through, marking time until my life started for real.

By midnight I was in the basement. It was straight down, like a plumb line, from my attic kingdom to that murky chamber of unresolved issues. Down there was what remained of my father's workshop. When I was a boy, this was the land of hulking steel machines upon which imposing sheets of plywood were made to scream in pain while being torn asunder. Now it was quiet. My mother had managed to sell the giant bandsaw and the huge metal lathe. Most of my father's hundreds of hand tools—he had dozens of files arrayed in varying increments of size and grade, at least fifty hammers and screwdrivers—had long since been given to friends and relatives. Their customized, meticulously labeled racks and holders were now empty.

The basement had always been an awkward place for me and him, not that we spent much time talking about it. I'd always assumed it to have been a source of mutual regret—that I hadn't inherited his marvelous skills, his reverence for the joining of two pieces of wood in a perfect right angle. It seemed like something a father and a son might do together, a gift to pass from one generation to the next in the old way. Now, however, on the last night of The House, with the machines gone or shut down, it was easy to believe that my father was relieved I'd shown no aptitude, that I was just another slovenly, uninterested teenager like the ones he taught all day long. In the stillness, I could feel him close, working away like some Queens hermetist in his fez, surrounded by his wonderfully precise toys, his files, planes, and grinding machines. Being a father now myself (as well as my father's son), I understood how Dad felt down here, his sanctum. With the ingressing ooze of life raging forth upstairs, it must have seemed like heaven.

That's when I started to pull that cabinet off the wall. It was one of the many built-in storage bins my father had attached to the paneling, each with several drawers bearing his familiar calligraphy (BRADS, ¼ INCH; BRADS, ⅓ INCH; BRADS, ½ INCH, etc). This was really what I wanted from The House, this symbol of his manic precision, a little bit of the peace he found down here. Except the thing resisted; I couldn't get it off the wall. I couldn't even figure out how and where he'd stuck it up there—the fastenings were invisible. It was something he'd always tried to teach me, how things might stick together without the gory slather of Elmer's, without the splintered bash of a dozen nails. This was the art of it, he said, to make things seem as if they'd always been there, as if they belonged. But then, like now, that sort of craft was beyond me. Anyway, I must have been making a bunch of noise, because soon my mother was descending the basement stairs.

There was an amusing retroness to the scene: Mom in her housecoat, demanding to know what I was doing, why I was making all that racket. She'd told the Dominicans those cabinets were "staying," and stay they would. I began arguing, saying that this cabinet meant a lot more to me than it could to anyone from Santo Domingo.

"You had your chance," she said with cold finality. She'd been trying to get me to take things from the basement for months, but I'd always been too busy.

"But Mom . . ." Reversion to former behavior is always lurking, even on the eve of your fiftieth birthday.

"He built those things for this place," my mother said. "They're not supposed to go anywhere else. So leave them."

Mom had pulled rank. There was nothing left to do but go upstairs, brush my teeth, and put out the light.

Six hours later, four Hell's Angels-style clad representatives of Movin' On (slogan: "The Company with the Clean Trucks") began carrying boxes out the long-shunned front door. It was more convenient, they said. By early afternoon the deed was done. "That," my mother said, "was that."

Now I visit my mom in her new apartment over on Seventy-fifth Avenue, near Bell Boulevard. Wanting to not move "too far" (no Florida for her), Mom found the place in a week. A totally nifty two-bedroom with a giant living room in a really nice development filled with "people to talk to," and close to her long-favored Key Food, the apartment "makes sense," Mom says, a little drunk on the novelty of it all. For Mom, to *hondle* is to live, and even as she misses my father terribly, there are all these new items to ruthlessly search out the best price on. At seventy-eight, she is finally living in a building that has an elevator. The view from the sixth-floor windows is fantastic. You overlook the old Vanderbilt Parkway, built as a private auto road by the old robber baron in 1908 so he could drive to his estate in Massapequa Park. Back in high school, my friends and I hung out on the overgrown parkway. It's where I first smoked pot, but Mom doesn't need to know about that.

After leaving Mom's place, as usual, I meander through the unending ethnikquilt that the borough of my birth has become. Driving past the Albanians and Afghanis on Hillside Avenue, I turn off to stop in at a candy store on Union Turnpike. My friends and I used to go to the place because the old man mixed his own Cokes and had a heavy thumb on the syrup. Now—the fountain long gone—it's owned by Sikhs. An old Russian, crucifix dangling on a key chain, is in there trying to buy cigarettes with food stamps. The Sikh won't allow it. "Why no? I pay tax!" the Russian screams in protest. This cracks up some Chinese kids who've been sneak-reading the comic books.

"I pay tax," they mock after the Russian has stomped off. Wise-asses. Like I said, now the epic of New York belongs to them.

In the end, I go by The House. It's been a couple of months now, and even if the grass looks a little patchy and my father would have have pruned the rosebushes, the place looks pretty much the same. But that won't last. Changes will be made. Which is fine, I think, silently watching from across the street, as the new people, all dressed up, come out the front door—as if they didn't know that, at The House, you always use the side.

18

The Boy Buys the Wrong Hat

When it comes to baseball, hate is a wholly acceptable family value. Written on the occasion of the "Subway Series." New York magazine, 2000.

The Yankee hater in me, sometimes dormant but never dead, stirred last summer at Modell's out by Caesar's Bay in Bensonhurst. I'd promised my ten-year-old son a new hat, and there on the wall was a veritable riot of sports merchandising. Logos as odd and alien as crop circles embellished snapbacks representing Devil Rays, Sharks, and Hokies. Through the glut, my son's eyes settled on a far more familiar emblem. There, a beacon among the ESPN trash jungle, stood the most famous trademark in all sports, maybe in all the world.

The N and the Y, like lovers so entwined, haughty, perfect. It was a fearsome icon, one that had been branded in my soul, stamped like a hot iron on my forehead, seared like a forever damning pair of letters on my back. My son, blood of my blood, DNA of my DNA, was about to purchase a Yankee hat.

This was a problem. For sometimes fashion is not just fashion and symbols are too evocative to be worn casually, by punk-rockers or little boys. Still, I'd promised. I'd get him a hat, any hat he wanted. As I drove home, the sight of this Yankee thing on my son's lovely, unsullied head struck me as a possibly ominous first salvo in a long-running Oedipal struggle. My son, the Yankee fan. It struck dread into the heart.

"I don't see what the big deal is," my son said, feeling the tension as we rolled up the Gowanus Expressway. "It's just a hat."

Just a hat. How to explain? How to make it clear that in our family tradition, it was not considered proper to cry when Gary Cooper gives that claptrap "luckiest man" speech in *The Pride of the Yankees*? That one need not feel awe while walking past Mickey Mantle's restaurant on Central Park South because, even with all that corny violin music about his knees and being the son of a coal miner, Mantle, soul of stolen youth or not, was still a Yankee? Like Serbia, like Hatfields and McCoys, there are ancient hatreds that transcend conventional irrationality. Wherever I am, whatever I'm doing, news of a Yankee loss makes my day.

But what choice is there? It is bred in the bone. Shot through the helixes. We do, after all, live in Brooklyn. Not counting Romania, Brooklyn is our ancestral home. A tug on the wheel of the ole Camry, a dodge of a few trolley tracks seeping up from beneath the tattered asphalt, and we'd be on Empire Boulevard and Bedford Avenue. Even now, the place remains a power vector, drawing you closer, even though all that remains are projects and the Ebbets Field Donut Shop, corn muffins $1.25. Holy Happy Felton!—even now it is like yesterday: how on May 12, 1956, date of my eighth birthday and year of the last Subway Series, I strolled with my grandfather down Franklin Avenue, to the legendary ballpark where Carl Erskine pitched a no-hitter against the Giants. "Some game, no hits," my father would later say.

It was an experience no eight-year-old forgets, especially as seen with Grandpa, the first generation of Jacobson Yankee haters, who spent his youth hauling overcoats through the Lower East Side and told me, in no uncertain terms, that the Yankees were the team of the bankers, every last one of them against meaningful social change and the workingman, from Jacob Ruppert on through DiMaggio, that flattop-headed Marine Hank Bauer, and the batboys, too.

Since Walter O'Malley really might be the third-worst person of the twentieth century behind Adolf Hitler and Joseph Stalin, it seems unfair to hate the Yanks all the more because the Dodgers left town in 1957. But that's when it clicked in for me. There they were: the all-powerful inevitable, like the phone company, the only game in town.

The Yankees: Take it or leave it. I just couldn't do it, couldn't root for a team that won the pennant fourteen out of my first seventeen years of life. Rooting for the Yankees was like declaring yourself to be a front-running prick, a defender of the status quo. Beyond this there was the fact that they played in the American League, always so Gentile in comparison with the funky National. There was the phrase *Yankee co-owners* (meaning Dan Topping and Del Webb, forerunners of indicted Nixon/Watergate contributor Steinbrenner). There was the much rumored passing-over of first baseman Vic Power because he caught the ball with one hand, which was so (jive) un-Yankee, not to mention the tacit reluctance to hire black players in general outside of Elston Howard, who, as Casey Stengel pointed out, couldn't even run. Beyond this were the pinstripes themselves, which, like Grandpa said, were so much more Wall Street than River Avenue.

Then came the Mets, the anti-Yankees, a team for their times. Instead of lockstep victory, the Mets offered Marvelous Marv Throneberry failing to touch first and second while hitting a triple, and Everyman Roger Craig throwing down his mitt after picking off a runner on consecutive throwovers only to have the first baseman, Ed Bouchee, drop the ball each time. The Mets were cosmic. What Yankee fan could possibly have found himself smashed on LSD in Berkeley, California, in 1969 as Ed Kranepool hit a homer to help beat the Orioles in the World Series, so giddy in the belief that it was all just one more fabulous hallucination?

This isn't to say that Yankee-hating has been a walk in the park. There have been moments of weakness, instances of doubt, dramas that cannot be denied. The Billy Martin story, from the Copa riot, to beating the crap out of the marshmallow salesman, to his lonely death on the highway, is epic. And who can discount Mike Kekich and Fritz Peterson swapping wives in the middle of the season? Mostly, though, you've got to hate them. Hate them even if Yogi and Phil ran a bowling alley off Route 3. Hate them even when they sucked and Horace Clarke led them in hitting with a .272 average.

Luckily, now there's Giuliani. In an era in which most Yanks (outside of Clemens—dig in, Rog, dig in) seem okay, the Yankee hater is thankful for Giuliani in his little shiny jacket, holding inane placards given him by the only adviser he actually trusts, Freddy the Fan. Even in his kinder, gentler mode, he's just so junior high. Still the prick hanging by the cyclone fence waiting to prey upon the weaknesses of the more sensitive, the less aggressive, the potential loser: hell's own perfect Yankee fan.

So that settles it. The Subway Series has finally returned to us after forty-four years, and the moral lines are firmly drawn—the Mets: good; the Yankees: bad.

Along with everyone else, my son Billy is psyched. Too bad B can't get his own Carl Erskine no-hit birthday party instead of the three-to-five slot at Funtime USA. But that's what happens when you're born on February 4 and mucky old baseball eats Latrell Sprewell's dust. Still, even if it will never be 1956 again, the current brace of games, waged by millionaires, dispassionate and not, offers a taste. Fodder for tales told too often twenty and thirty years hence. Also, it is an opportunity to do some yeoman Yankee-hating.

For Billy, the breakthrough came early this season. Someone gave us tickets, so I dutifully took him up to the so-called Big Ballpark. Bill couldn't figure why so many people were rooting for the Red Sox. At the Garden and Shea, no one cheered for the visitors. "They're not for the Red Sox; they're *against* the Yankees. It happens all the time," I told him, in all accuracy. He found something liberating in that, the idea that you didn't have to root, root, root for the home team, the subversive notion that you could be against the likely winner. Besides, the Yankees didn't need Billy to be their fan. They always won anyhow. They were the champs, just like back in 1956.

* * *

"If you're going to hate a team, it might as well be the Yankees," my son sagely told me this morning on the way to school. Just last night we found ourselves, two generations of Yankee haters, forced into hoping the Bombers beat the Oaklands, since their victory would assure the grail-like Subway Series. When the Yanks pushed across the winner, my son frowned as if he'd swallowed some bad but necessary medicine and went to bed without a word. A hard-core but wholly appropriate reaction.

Now, Mets hat firmly on his head, he was ready to enter the schoolyard. It wasn't going to be easy the next week or so. There were a lot of fifth-grade Yankee fans in there, annoying, smug, and loud, leaning against the cyclone fence, ready to pounce when their inevitable juggernaut began to roll. The Yanks will win, they always do. But Billy can handle it, secure in his love, secure in his hate.

19

The $2,000-an-Hour Woman: A Love Story

Needless to say I had to stay up past my bedtime to do this story. A report from after midnight in the Big City. From New York *magazine, 2005.*

Jason Itzler, the self-anointed world's greatest escort-agency owner, prepared to get down on his knees. When a man was about to ask for the hand of a woman in holy matrimony, especially the hand of the fabulous Natalia, America's No. 1 escort, he should get down on his knees.

This was how Jason, who has always considered himself nothing if not "ultraromantic," saw it. However, as he slid from his grade-school-style red plastic seat in preparation to kneel, the harsh voice of a female Corrections officer broke the mood, ringing throughout the dank visitor's room.

"Sit back down," said the large uniformed woman. "You know the rules."

Such are the obstacles to true love when one is incarcerated at Rikers Island, where Jason Itzler, thirty-eight and still boyishly handsome in his gray Department of Corrections jumpsuit, has resided since the cops shut down his megaposh NY Confidential agency in January.

There was also the matter of the ring. During the glorious summer and fall of 2004, when NY Confidential was grossing an average of $25,000 a night at its five-thousand-square-foot loft at 79 Worth Street, spitting distance from the municipal courts and Bloomberg's priggish City Hall, Jason would have purchased a diamond with enough carats to blow the eye loupe off a Forty-seventh Street Hasid.

That was when Itzler filled his days with errands like stopping by Soho Gem on West Broadway to drop $6,500 on little trinkets for Natalia and his other top escorts. This might be followed by a visit to Manolo Blahnik to buy a dozen pairs of $500 footwear. By evening, Itzler could be found at Cipriani, washing down plates of crushed lobster with yet another bottle of Johnnie Walker Blue label and making sure everyone got one of his signature titanium business cards engraved with NY Confidential's singular motto: ROCKET FUEL FOR WINNERS.

But now Jason was charged with various counts of criminal possession of a controlled substance, money laundering, and promoting prostitution. His arrest was part of a large effort by the NYPD and the D.A.'s office against New York's burgeoning Internet-based escort agencies. In three months, police had shut down American Beauties, Julie's, and the far-flung New York Elites, a concern the cops said was flying porn stars all over the country for dates. Reeling, pros were declaring the business "holocausted" as girls took down their Web sites and worried johns stayed home.

Many blamed Itzler for the heat. In a business where discretion is supposed to be key, Jason was more than a loose cannon. Loose A-bomb was more like it. He took out giant NY Confidential ads in mainstream magazines (the one you're holding included). In restaurants, he'd get loud and identify himself, Howard Stern style, as "the King of All Pimps."

Only days before, Itzler, attired in a $5,700 full-length fox coat from Jeffrey, bought himself a Mercedes S600. Now the car, along with much of the furniture at Jason's lair, including the $50,000 sound system on which he blared, 24/7, the music of his Rat Pack idol, Frank Sinatra, had been confiscated by the cops. His assets frozen, unable to make his $250,000 bail, Jason couldn't even buy a phone card, much less get Natalia a ring.

"Where am I going to get a ring in here?" Jason said to Natalia on the phone the other night. He suggested perhaps Natalia might get the ring herself and then slip it to him when she came to visit.

"That's good, Jason," returned Natalia. "I buy the ring, give it to you, you kiss it, give it back to me, and I pretend to be surprised."

"Something like that," Jason replied, sheepishly. "You know I love you."

That much seemed true. As Jason doesn't mind telling you, he has known many women since he lost his virginity not too long after his bar mitzvah at the Jewish Community Center of Fort Lee, doing the deed with the captain of the Tenafly High School cheerleader squad. Since then, Jason, slight and five foot nine, says he's slept with "over seven hundred women," a figure he admits pales before the twenty thousand women basketball star Wilt "the Stilt" Chamberlain claimed to have bedded. But, as Jason says, "you could say I am a little pickier than him."

Of these seven hundred women, Jason has been engaged to nine, two of whom he married. "It was really only one and a half," Itzler reports, saying that while living in Miami's South Beach he married "this hot Greek girl. She was gorgeous. The first thing I did was buy her this great boob job, which immediately transformed her from a tremendous A/B cup look to an out-of-sight C/D cup look. But her parents totally freaked out. So I got the marriage annulled."

This aside, not counting his sainted late mother, Jason says Natalia, twenty-five, about five foot three, and perhaps one hundred pounds soaking wet, reigns as the love of his life.

Without Natalia, she of the smoldering brown eyes that have excited who knows how many investment bankers, billionaire trust-fund babies, and NFL quarterbacks, Jason would never have been able to build NY Confidential into the icon of sub rosa superhotness it became. It was Natalia who got top dollar, as much as $2,000 an hour, with a two-hour minimum. In the history of Internet escorting, no one ever matched Natalia's ratings on TheEroticReview.com, the Zagat's of the escort-for-hire industry. On TER, "hobbyists," as those with the "hobby" of frequenting escorts are called—men with screen names like Clint Dickwood, Smelly Smegma, and William Jefferson Clinton—can write reviews of the "providers" they see, rating them on a scale of 1 to 10 for both "appearance" and "performance."

In 2004, Natalia recorded an unprecedented seventeen straight 10/10s. On the TER ratings scale, a 10 was defined as "one in a lifetime." Natalia was the Perfect 10, the queen of the escort world.

"Yo! *Pimp Juice*! . . . that her?"

It was Psycho, a large tattooed Dominican (*Psycho* was stenciled on his neck in Gothic lettering) who was referring to Jason by his jailhouse nickname. Itzler nodded. There was no need to gloat. Moments before, Jason scanned the grim visiting room. "Just making sure I've got the hottest chick in the room." Like it was any contest, Natalia sitting there, in her little calfskin jacket and leather miniskirt, thick auburn hair flowing over her narrow shoulders.

Besides, half of Rikers already knew about Jason and NY Confidential. They'd read, or heard about, the articles Itzler had piped to his pulp enablers at "Page Six," including how he could get "$250,000 an hour for Paris Hilton with a four-hour minimum."

But you couldn't believe everything you read in the New York *Post*, even at Rikers. Natalia's presence was proof. Proof that Jason, a little Jewish guy who still sported a nasty black eye from being beaten silly in his sleep by some skell inmate, wasn't full of shit when he told the homeys that he was the biggest pimp in the city, that he got all the best girls. How many other Rikers fools could get the Perfect 10 to visit them, at nine o'clock in the morning, too?

"Psycho . . . Natalia," Jason said. "Natalia . . . Psycho."

"Hey," Natalia said with an easy smile. She was, after all, a girl you could take anywhere. One minute she could be the slinkiest cat on the hot tin roof, wrapping her dancer's body (she was the teenage tap-dance champion of Canada in 1996) around a client's body in a hotel elevator. Then, when the door slid open, she'd look classic, like a wife even, on the arm of a Wall Street CEO or Asian electronics magnate. She was an actress, had played Shakespeare and Off Broadway both. Ever the ingénue, she'd been Juliet half a dozen times. Playing opposite Jason's however-out-of-luck Romeo was no sweat, even here, in jail.

Not that Natalia had exactly been looking forward to coming to Rikers this raw late-spring morning. Riding in the bus over the bridge from East

Elmhurst, freezing in her lace stockings as she sat beside a stocky black man in a Jerome Bettis jersey, she looked out the window at the looming prison and said, "Wal-Mart must have had a two-for-one on barbed wire."

It wasn't that she didn't miss Jason, or the heyday of when they lived together at 79 Worth Street, the harem stylings of which came to Itzler while getting his hair cut at the Casbah-themed Warren Tricomi Salon on Fifty-seventh Street. It was just that this marriage thing was flipping her out, especially after Jason called the tabloids to announce the ceremony would be held inside Rikers.

"Every little girl's dream, to get married at Rikers Island," Natalia said to Jason. "What are they going to get us, adjoining cells?"

But now, holding hands in the visiting room, surrounded by low-level convicts, just the sort of people who rarely appeared in either of their well-to-do childhoods or in the fantasy life of 79 Worth Street—neither of them, pimp or escort, could keep from crying.

"Are those happy tears or sad tears?" Jason asked.

"Just tears," answered Natalia.

"Crying because your boy is in jail?"

"That and . . . everything else."

It was a tender moment. Except then, as he always does, Jason began talking.

"Don't worry about this Rikers marriage," he said, back in schemer-boy genius mode. "This isn't the real marriage. . . . When I'm out we'll have the princess marriage . . . the white dress, everything. Your mom will be there. My dad . . . This is just the publicity marriage. You know: getting married at Rikers—it's so . . . rock star!"

Natalia looked up at Jason, makeup streaming from her face.

"It's great, isn't it?" Jason enthused. "A brilliant idea."

"Yeah," Natalia said wearily. "Great, *in theory*." Almost everything Jason Itzler said was great, in theory.

They call it the oldest profession, and maybe it is. The prostitute has always been part of the New York underworld. According to Timothy J.

Gilfoyle's *City of Eros,* in 1776, Lieutenant Isaac Bangs of the Continental army complained that half his troops were spending more time in lower-Manhattan houses of ill repute than fighting the British. In the nineteenth century, lower Broadway had become, in the words of Walt Whitman, a "noctivagous strumpetocracy," filled with "tawdry, foul-tongued and harsh-voiced harlots."

By the 1970s and 80's, the image of the New York prostitute encompassed both the call-girl minions of Sydney Biddle Barrows, the famous Mayflower Madam, and the hot-pants-clad hooker trying to keep warm beside a burning fifty-five-gallon drum outside the Bronx's Hunts Point Market. On Eighth Avenue's so-called Minnesota Strip were the runaways in the wan-eyed Jodie Foster-in-*Taxi Driver* mode. The nineties brought the "Natasha Trade," an influx of immigrant Russian girls and their ex-Soviet handlers who locked the women up in Brighton Beach apartments and drove them, fifteen at a time, in Ford Econoline vans to strip joints on Queens Boulevard.

The Internet would reconfigure all that. Today, with highly ad hoc estimates of the New York "sex worker" population hovering, depending on whom you ask, anywhere from five thousand to twenty-five thousand, horny men looking for a more convivial lunch hour don't have to cruise midtown bars or call a number scribbled on a piece of paper. All that's needed is a high-speed connection to any of the many "escort malls," such as the highly clickable CityVibe or Eros.

The typical site includes a photo or two, a sparse bio, a schedule of when the escort is available, and a price ("donation") list. There is also the standard disclaimer, detailing how any money exchanged "is simply for time only and companionship" and that anything else "is a matter of personal preference between two or more consenting adults." For, as everyone in the escort business is quick to say, selling "companionship" is not against the law.

The system is not without its bugs. The most common question: "Is she the girl in the picture?" Says a longtime booker, "About two-thirds of the time, when a guy calls up asking for a girl they've seen on the site, she doesn't work for us, quit six months ago, or we Photoshopped her picture from the Victoria's Secret catalogue.

"If they ask for Nicolette, I take out the three-by-five card with NICOLETTE written on top. It lists the contacts of girls who kind of look like the fake Nicolette. What blows my mind is the stupid bastards spend hours searching the sites looking for their superfantasy, are willing to shell out $700 an hour, and then when someone else knocks on the hotel-room door, they go, 'Oh, whatever.' They can still go back to Indianapolis, show the girl in the picture to their buddies, and say, 'See her? Like, *awesome, dude!*'"

It was this kind of slipshod, postmodern fakery that Jason Itzler says he started NY Confidential to wipe out. At NY Confidential, you always got the girl in the picture.

"That's because we were the best," says Itzler. "At NY Confidential, I told my girls that the pressure is on them because we have to provide the clients with the greatest single experience ever, a Kodak moment to treasure for the rest of their lives. Spreading happiness, positive energy, and love, that's what being the best means to me. Call me a dreamer, but that's the NY Confidential credo."

Such commentary is typical of Jason, who, in the spirit of all great salesmen, actually believes much of it.

Not yet forty, Jason Itzler has a story that is already a mini-epic of Jewish-American class longing, a psychosociosexual drama crammed with equal parts genius (occasionally vicious) *boychick* hustle, heartfelt neo-hippie idealism, and dead-set will to self-destruction. Born Jason Sylk, only son of the short-lived marriage between his revered mother, Ronnie Lubell, and his "sperm dad," Leonard Sylk, heir to the Sun Ray drugstore fortune built up by Harry Sylk, who once owned a piece of the Philadelphia Eagles, Jason spent his early years as one of very few Jewish kids on Philly's Waspy Main Line. If he'd stayed a Sylk, says Jason, "I would have been the greatest Richie Rich, because Lenny Sylk is the biggest thing in the Jewish community. He's got a trust that gives money to stuff like the ballet, a house with an eighteen-car garage, and a helicopter landing pad. Golda Meir used to stay with us when she was in town."

After his parents' divorce, Jason moved to New York with his mother, whom he describes as "the hottest mom in the world. She had this Mafia princess–Holly Golightly thing about her. Her vanity license plate was TIFF. My mother being beautiful made me into who I am today, because when you grow up around a beautiful woman, you always want to be surrounded by beautiful women."

Also a big influence was his mom's father, the semi-legendary Nathan Lubell, "the biggest bookmaker in the garment industry, a gangster wizard," says Jason. "He owned a lot of hat stores, a bunch of the amusement park in Coney Island, and was hooked up with Meyer Lansky in Las Vegas hotels. I used to love it when he took me to the Friars Club, where he was a king. Even as a kid, I could feel the action."

With his mom remarried, to Ron Itzler, then a lawyer in the firm of Fischbein, Badillo (as in Herman), Wagner, and Itzler, the family lived in the Jersey suburbs. Displaying his compulsive intelligence by setting the all-time record on the early-generation video game Scramble, Jason, "pretty much obsessed with sex from the start," wrote letters to *Mad* magazine suggesting they put out a flexi-record of "teenage girls having orgasms." Summers were spent in the Catskills, where as a cabana boy at the Concord Hotel he befriended people like Jason Binn, now the playboy publisher of the *Hamptons* and *Los Angeles Confidential* magazines, a name Itzler paid homage to with his NY Confidential.

Itzler remembers, "At the Concord, when Jason Binn said he was the son of a billionaire, and my stepfather told me, yeah, he was, I got light-headed."

In the late eighties, after getting through George Washington University, even though he was "mostly running wet-T-shirt contests," Itzler entered Nova Southeastern University, a bottom-tier law school in Fort Lauderdale, Florida, where he embarked on what he calls "my first great chapter" as "the twenty-two-year-old phone-sex king of South Beach." Advertising a "Free Live Call" (after which a $4.98-a-minute charge set in), Itzler's company was doing $600,000 a month, hitting a million and a half within a year.

"I had so much money," Jason recalls, "I bought an Aston Martin Virage, three hundred feet of oceanfront property. Like a moron, I spent half a million decorating a one-bedroom apartment."

Alas, it would all soon come tumbling down, owing to what Jason now calls a "kind of oversight," which left him owing $4.5 million at 36 percent interest. Forced to declare bankruptcy in 1997, he lost everything, including his visionary acquisition of one of the fledgling Internet's most valuable URLs: pussy.com.

The demise of Itzler's phone-sex company set a pattern that would be repeated in 2000 with his next big act, the SoHo Models fiasco. With typical overreach, Jason rented an eight-thousand-square-foot space at the corner of Canal and Broadway and declared himself the new Johnny Casablancas. Unfortunately for the young models hoping to find their faces on the cover of *Vogue*, the true business of SoHo Models was to supply Webcam porn. For a fee, the voyeur would type in "take off blouse . . . insert dildo." Squabbling among gray-market partners soon ensued. Within months, Jason found himself dangling over the side of the Canal Street building, held by the ankles by a guy named Mikey P.

Jason says he would have gotten through these setbacks more easily if his mother were still alive, but Ronnie Itzler died of cancer in 1994, "after which I went kind of a little nuts." Following the collapse of the phone-sex firm, he twice attempted suicide, once running himself through with a steak knife and on another occasion drinking "a milk shake" he claims contained "75 Valium, 75 Klonopin, and a couple bottles of Scotch." Much to his surprise, he survived both times.

Desperate for money after the SoHo Models disaster, Itzler decided his best option was to go to Amsterdam to buy four thousand tabs of Ecstasy. "In retrospect, it was a totally retarded idea," says Jason, who would leave Newark airport in handcuffs. He was sentenced to five years in the Jersey pen. The fact that his grandfather, whom he'd idolized as a gangster, stopped talking to him when he got locked up "was hard to take."

"Jail is terrible, really boring," says Jason. "But it does give you plenty of time to plan your next move."

On parole after serving seventeen months of his smuggling sentence, living in a funky third-floor walk-up in Hoboken per the terms of his release,

Jason started NY Confidential (he would remain on parole his entire pimp career) in late 2003. Business was spotty at first but picked up dramatically in early 2004, when Natalia walked into the company's place at Fifty-fourth Street and Sixth Avenue, an office previously occupied by the magician David Blaine.

"It was my birthday," Natalia remembers. "I'd just been cast as Ingrid Superstar in this play, *Andy & Edie*, written by soon-to-be famous sex criminal, Peter Braunstein. "I wanted to be Edie," Natalia relates, "but Misha Sedgwick, Edie's niece, also wanted it, so forget that. I was eating in a restaurant with Peter Beard, the photographer. I was a kind of party girl for a while. I met Peter one night, and we hit it off. He said I should meet this guy Jason."

Beard, a nocturnal bon vivant known for his "discovery" of exotic models like Iman, and who had been associated with Jason during the SoHo Models episode, warned Natalia off Itzler's new venture. Eventually, however, Natalia decided to give Jason a call. "Being an escort never crossed my mind. It wasn't something girls like me did. I was an actress. From a very nice home. But I was involved in an abusive relationship, with this Wall Street guy," she says. "In the beginning, all I wanted was enough money to move out."

Jason says, "When Natalia came over with Peter, I said, Wow, she's so hot. She has one of the all-time great tushes. But there was this other girl there, too. Samantha. When she took off her shirt, she had these amazing breasts. So it was Natalia's butt against Samantha's boobies. I went with the tits. But when Natalia came back from making a movie, she moved in with us. Samantha could tell I was kind of more into Natalia. So we became boyfriend and girlfriend."

At the time, Jason's top girl was Cheryl, a striking blond ballroom dancer from Seattle who says she got into the business to buy her own horse. "I did NY Confidential's first date," Cheryl recalls. "I had on my little black dress and was shaking like a leaf. Jason was nervous, too. He said, 'Just go up there and take your clothes off.' I told him, 'No, you've got to make it romantic. Special.'"

It was Cheryl who came up with the mantra Jason would later instruct all the NY Confidential girls to repeat, "three times," before entering a hotel room to see a client: *"This is my boyfriend of six months, the man I love, I haven't seen him for three weeks. . . . This is my boyfriend of six months, the man I love."*

"That's the essence of the true GFE, the Girlfriend Experience," says Jason. As opposed to the traditional "no kissing on the mouth" style, the GFE offers a warmer, fuzzier time. For Jason, who says he never hired anyone who'd worked as an escort before, the GFE concept was an epiphany. "Men see escorts because they want to feel happier. Yet most walk away feeling worse than they did before. They feel dirty, full of self-hatred. Buyer's remorse big-time. GFE is about true passion, something genuine. A facsimile of love. I told guys this was a quick vacation, an investment in the future. When they got back to their desks, they'd tear the market a new asshole, make back the money they spent at NY Confidential in an hour.

"What we're selling is rocket fuel, *rocket fuel for winners*."

Jason decided Natalia would become his great creation, the Ultimate GFE. It mattered little that Natalia, for all her French-Scottish sultriness, might strike some as a tad on the skinny side. Brown-eyed, dark-haired, olive-skinned, not to mention lactose-intolerant, she didn't fit the usual description of a big ticket in an industry filled with PSE (Porn-Star Experience) babes with store-bought bazangas out to here. Jason took this as a challenge. If he was into Natalia, he'd make sure everyone else was, too. It was a simple matter of harnessing the available technology.

The main vehicle was the aforementioned TheEroticReview.com, "the *Consumer Reports* of the escort industry," according to the site's founder and owner, the L.A.-based Dave Elms, a.k.a. Dave@TER. "The most important thing was to break Natalia out big," Jason says. "To get the ball rolling with a number of fabulous reviews, I sent her to some friends, to sort of grease the wheel. I knew those 10/10s would keep coming, because no man wants to admit he got less. They're brainwashed that way."

If any hobbyist had the temerity to hand out a paltry 8/8, or even a 9/10, he would be contacted. "Don't break my girl's streak, this is history in the making," Jason cajoled, offering to throw in a couple hours of free time to get the customer to do a little recalculating. If that didn't work, good reviews could be ensured by the $5,000 everyone working at NY Confidential (except Jason) swears was FedExed to Dave@TER on the fifteenth of every month. Dave, who says he "would not argue with that" when asked if he is the single most important person in the escort business, vehemently denies any payoffs, from NY Confidential or anyone else.

With her 10/10s piling up, Natalia's hourly rate jumped from $800 to $1,200 with a two-hour minimum. (The split: 45 percent for the escort, 45 percent for the agency, 10 percent for the booker.) If clients haggled, they would be told to call back when they were "more successful." Jason says, "I always ask prospective clients to give me strong points about themselves, where they went to school, if they're good-looking. It established rapport but also put them on the defensive, let them know that *I was interviewing them,* to see if they were good enough to go out with our girls."

Jason's hyping sometimes was faintly embarrassing. "Jason would be saying, 'Natalia is the greatest escort in the history of the world, as good as Cleopatra or Joan of Arc,' " says Natalia, "and I'd be like, '*Jason!* Joan of Arc was not an escort, she was a religious martyr.' Then he'd be saying I was the greatest escort since Mary Magdalene."

But all the hype in the world (an Asian toy manufacturer wanted to mass-produce Barbie-style Natalia dolls, complete with tiny lingerie) wouldn't have helped if Natalia, who never imagined she'd wind up staying in "every expensive hotel in New York," hadn't turned out to be a natural.

"I'm a little moneymaking machine, that's what I am," she says as she takes a languorous drag of her Marlboro while stretching out on her apartment couch in a shiny pink satin corset, Marlene Dietrich style. Then she cracks up, because "you know, the whole thing is so ridiculous sometimes."

People wonder what it is about Natalia that made her the Perfect 10. "From the start, you know this is going to be fun," says one client. "It is like having sex in a tree house." Says another, "Nat isn't this all-knowing geisha thing. But in a way, it's deeper, because she gets to a place inside where you used to be free." And another: "When you're with her, there's none of that feeling that 'this is costing as much as a first-class ticket to

London and the chick is in the bathroom half the time and couldn't care less.' From the first minute Natalia comes in and bats those brown eyes you know this is a nonstop this-is-all-about-you experience."

Suffice it to say, it's in the pheromones. According to Natalia, she's always gotten along with men. "Jason understood who I was," she says. "Yes, he sold the shit out of me, but he sold me as myself, someone anyone can be comfortable with, someone who really likes sex. Because the truth is, I do. I loved my job, totally."

It is another old story, along with the heart of gold, that many "providers" actually like what they do. But even if she professes to be "horrified" by stories about sexual trafficking and "sickened" by nightmarish exploitation of the street prostitute, Natalia says, "At the level NY Confidential was at, the guys I was meeting, I would have gone out with 80 percent of them anyway. People have so many misconceptions, preconceptions, about my life. Last year, I got a call to play an escort in a Broadway play. But the part was so dark, so icky, I said no. It didn't fit my experience at all."

You never knew who might be behind the hotel door. Once, she was summoned to a guy's room, told only that he was a famous, Super Bowl athlete. "I'm not a big sports fan, but I recognized him, the quarterback. He turned out to be very laid-back. He mostly wanted to make me happy. In the middle, he looks up and says, 'Well, you know me, I'm more of a giver than a receiver.' "

What no one could have predicted, least of all Natalia, was how driven she would be. "I knew she was talented," Jason says. "But once she started going, she was unstoppable, like the Terminator."

A glance at Natalia's booking sheets raises an eyebrow. Annotated with Jason's exhortatory commentary ("Awesome guy!—$5,200, wants to be a regular!" "Big Wall Street guy!" "Software king." "Hedge fund heavy! Says he will give investment lessons!"), the records of Natalia's bookings through June and July of 2004 reveal a workload exceeding 250 hours, or nearly a normal nine-to-five, at an average of $1,000 per hour, not counting little presents like fancy $350 underwear from La Perla.

"Victoria's Secret is all right," Natalia says. "But you know you have a good client when you get La Perla."

Some weeks were particularly frenetic. From July 29 to August 1, she had a four-day date in the Florida Keys for which Itzler charged $29,000. The very next day was a four-hour appointment. August 3 was filled with a ten-hour appointment and another two-hour job. August 4, three hours. August 5, a three-hour followed by another four-hour. August 6, two hours. August 7, one four-hour job and a two-hour. August 8, she was off. But the 9th was another ten-hour day, followed by a pair of two-hour jobs on August 10.

"It was like a dream," Natalia says. "I never got tired."

Asked if the work affected her relationship with Itzler, Natalia says, "Sometimes he'd say, 'Everyone gets a chance to spend time with you except me.' I'd say, 'You're the one booking me.' " As for Jason, he says, "If she ever did it with anyone for free, it would have broken my heart."

Moving from Fifty-fourth Street following a nasty fallout with partner Bruce Glasser (each party claimed the other had taken out a contract on his life), Itzler ran NY Confidential out of his parolee apartment in Hoboken. One visitor describes the scene: "The place was full of naked women and underwear. It was a rain forest of underwear. In the middle on the couch is Jason with all these telephones, one in either ear, the other one ringing on the coffee table."

Seventy-nine Worth Street, with its twenty-foot ceilings and mezzanine balconies, where Jason and Natalia would move to in the summer of 2004, was a whole other thing. "Right away, we knew this was it," says Natalia. "The loft felt like home." As per usual, Jason would take much of the cost of the lease from Natalia's bookings—money she would never receive. But money was never an issue with Natalia. If Cheryl, Jason's first superstar, experienced "a rush of power when the guy handed me the envelope," for Natalia, collecting the "donation," while essential, had a faintly unseemly feel.

"Maybe it sounds crazy," she says, "but I never felt I was in it for the money."

For Jason, the loft was an opportunity to make real his most cherished theories of existence. "To me, the higher percentage of your life you are happy, the more successful you are," says Jason, who came upon his philosophy while reading Ayn Rand. "I was really into the 'Who is John Galt?' *Atlas Shrugged* thing. I thought I could save the world if I could bring together the truly elite people, the most beautiful women with the most perfect bodies, best faces, and intelligence, and the elite men, the captains of industry, lawyers, and senators. This would bring about the most happiness, to the best people, who most deserved to be happy."

Years before, Jason wrote out the precepts of what he called "The Happiness Movement." Assuming his findings to be big news, Itzler packed up the manifesto, a copy of his half-finished autobiography, and a naked centerfold picture of Elisa Bridges, his girlfriend at the time, and mailed it to Bob Woodward. "I stuck it in this $3,000 Bottega Veneta briefcase so he'd notice it. He said I was a nut job and to leave him alone. I was so bummed I told him to keep the stupid briefcase."

On Worth Street, however, Jason (who says "the best thing about bipolarity is how much you accomplish in the manic phase") saw the chance to manifest his ideal. One of his first acts was to approach painter Hulbert Waldroup. Waldroup, a self-proclaimed "artist with attitude" who has been collected by Whoopi Goldberg and once appeared on the cover of *Newsday* along with his epic graffiti memorial to Amadou Diallo, was selling his work on the West Broadway sidewalk. "You're the greatest painter I've ever seen," Jason said. When Waldroup heard Itzler wanted to commission a ten-foot-by-ten-foot canvas of a "hot-looking" woman, he said the picture would never get in the door. No problem, Itzler said, Waldroup could do the painting inside the loft.

Waldroup soon had a job working the phones. "It was like I went in there and never came out," says Waldroup, now on Rikers Island, where he resides a couple of buildings away from Jason.

Seventy-nine Worth Street became a well-oiled machine, with various calendars posted on the wall to keep track of appointments. The current day's schedule was denoted on a separate chart called "the action board." But what mattered most to Jason was "the vibe . . . the vibe of the NY Confidential brand" (there was franchising talk about a Philadelphia Confidential and a Vegas Confidential). To describe what he was going for, Jason quotes from a favorite book, *The Art of Seduction,* a creepily fascinating tome of social Machiavellianism, by Robert Greene.

Discussing "seductive place and time," Greene notes that "certain kinds of visual stimuli signal that you are not in the real world. Avoid images that have depth, which might provoke thought, or guilt. . . . The more artificial, the better . . . Luxury—the sense that money has been spent or even wasted—adds to the feeling that the real world of duty and morality has been banished. Call it the brothel effect."

Accentuated by the fog machine at 79 Worth Street, people seemed to come out of the shadows, float by, be gone again. "It was full of these familiar faces . . . like a soap-opera star, a politician you might have seen on NY1, a guy whose photo's in the *Times* financial pages," says one regular. In addition to Sinatra, music was supplied by the building's super, a concert pianist in his native Russia, who appeared in a tuxedo to play on a rented Baldwin grand piano.

"It was like having my own clubhouse," says Jason now, relishing the evenings he presided as esteemed host and pleasure master. He remembers discussing what he called a "crisis in Judaism" with a top official of a leading Jewish-American lobby group. Jewish women were often thought of as dowdy, Jason said. If the American Jew was ever going to rise above the prejudice of the *goyishe* mainstream, creativity would be needed. A start would be to get Madonna, the Kabbalist, to become the head of Hadassah. The official said he'd look into it.

Seventy-nine Worth Street was supposed to be Jason and Natalia's home, where they would live happily ever after. They had their own bedroom, off-limits to everyone else. "We were actually trying to live a seminormal life, carry on a real relationship," says Natalia. "Jason felt abandoned after his mother died; my father left when I was very young. We sort of completed each other."

Natalia wrote her mom that she'd moved into a beautiful new place with a highly successful businessman. Her mom, a sweet cookie-baking lady leery of her daughter's life in New York, wrote back that she'd like to come down to visit. Natalia was going to put her off, but Jason insisted. Looking around the loft at the naked women, Natalia asked, "How am I going to have my mom come *here?*" Jason said he would close the place, and take the loss, for the time Natalia's mom was in town. Family was the most important thing, he said.

"Well," Natalia says, "Jason never closed the loft. My mom and I stayed in a little apartment uptown. Jason was supposed to come by to meet her, but it started getting late. Then the doorbell rings at 2 A.M. It's Jason, in his knee-length coat with these two nineteen-year-old girls. I'm totally flipping out: *Like, what the fuck are you doing?* He looked like the pimp from Superfly. My mom is saying, '*This is him?*' But then Jason sits down and starts telling my mom I'm a great young actress and my career is going to take off, how living in New York is so terrific for me. He charmed her, completely. She left saying, 'Well, your boyfriend is kind of weird. But he's very, very nice.'

"It was always like that."

Few expected 79 Worth Street to last very long. There were too many, as Natalia puts it, "variables."

For Jason, the main difficulty in running New York's hottest escort agency while on parole was the curfew. Even though his lawyer on the Jersey Ecstasy case, Paul Bergrin, was eventually able to extend Jason's lights-out time to 3 A.M., he still had to leave his Worth Street happiness house to sleep in his apartment in Hoboken.

"Everyone's partying, having the best time in the world, and the Town Car is outside to take me back to goddamn New Jersey."

"It was a big strain," says Natalia. "I finally get home from my appointments. All I want to do is sleep in my own bed, and Jason is screaming about how we've got to go back to Hoboken. He hated to be alone out there. We had horrible fights. One night, I jumped out of the car right at the mouth of the Holland Tunnel and ran away. Broke my heel on a cobblestone."

The parole situation led to other traumas. Court-mandated drug tests caused Jason to alter his intake. Always "on the Cheech-and-Chong side of things," Itzler couldn't smoke pot, which turned up on piss tests. Instead, Jason, who never touched coke and often launched into Jimmy Swaggart–like speeches about the evils of the drug, dipped into his personal stash of ketamine, or Special K, the slightly unpredictable anesthetic developed for use by veterinarians. "They didn't test for it," Jason says by way of explanation. He was also drinking a $200 bottle of Johnnie Walker Blue every day. Natalia's drug use cut into her Perfect 10 appearance. One night, she cracked her head into the six-foot-tall statue of an Indian fertility goddess Jason had purchased for their room. Knocked cold, she had to go to the emergency room.

Still, the business charged on. It takes a singular pimp to think it is a good idea to stage a reality-TV show at his place of business, but Jason Itzler is that kind of guy. "It was incredible," says independent producer Ron Sperling, who shot the film *Inside New York Confidential*. "Big-shot lawyers and Wall Street bankers flipped when they saw the cameras. Jason told them the movie was no problem. That it was *a good thing*. If they didn't want to be in it, they should just walk behind the camera. That's Jason. He can't shut up about anything. If he was a billionaire and no one knew about it, it wouldn't be anything to him."

Despite misgivings about legalities, VH1 expressed interest in *Inside New York Confidential*. A meeting was set up. Arriving late, Jason swept into the TV office with several girls. Along for the ride was a young Belgian tourist whom Itzler had encountered only moments before on West Broadway. "You're beautiful," Jason told the young woman. "But your clothes look like shit." Itzler bought her $2,500 worth of threads in about ten minutes, convincing her she would be great in his TV show.

"He asked for a million dollars an episode," says a VH1 exec. "We told him that was insane money, so he got mad and left."

Jason's manic spending increased. One afternoon, splashing on Creed Gold Bottle cologne ($175 per bottle) as "kind of a nervous tic," he bought twenty-six antique crystal chandeliers at $3,000 apiece. "We had so much furniture, there was nowhere to walk. I used to jump over the stuff for exercise," says Natalia. "We had this room upstairs we called the Peter Beard Room. Peter likes to sit on the floor, so we got these beautiful Moroccan pillows. One day, I come home, and there's a Playboy pinball machine there, with Hugh Hefner's face on it. Then I knew there was no point saying anything."

Jason's class insecurities also cropped up. One night, upstairs at Cipriani's, Itzler went over to where Lizzie Grubman was sitting with Paris Hilton. He asked Grubman about representing NY Confidential. Grubman, whom Jason regarded as just another Great Neck girl with a rich dad under the glitz, supposedly sneered, "I don't do pimps." Returning to his table, Jason said, "I hate that bitch. She runs over sixteen people and thinks she's better than me."

Jason's utopian house of happiness turned into a stage for an ongoing paranoid soap opera. Feeling his grip slipping, Itzler begged his former fiancée Mona to help with the day-to-day running of the place. Mona, who had helped organize things in the earliest days of NY Confidential, ran a tight ship. But there were complications. It had been only eight months since Mona had been Jason's girlfriend, living with him in Hoboken. They broke up, leading to an enormous screaming match during which Mona called the police, claiming Itzler attacked her. Jason disputed this, allowing he "might have squeezed her hand too hard, trying to get my keys back." Mona would drop the charges, but not before Itzler spent some time under house arrest.

Jason says, "Maybe I'm just soft, because after Mona wrote the judge a tear-stained letter how I never beat her up and how she loved me, I forgave her." With Jason's parole problems increasingly keeping him in Hoboken, Mona soon filled the power vacuum at 79 Worth Street. Her key ally would be Clark Krimer, a.k.a. Clark Kent or Superman, a muscle-bound young banker Itzler met at a nearby bank and hired to manage the agency's credit-card accounts, making sure the statements of those using NY Confidential services appeared to be spending their $1,200 at fictitious firms like "Gotham Steak." Clark and Mona soon became an item, consolidating their power.

The Clark-and-Mona regime upset "the vibe" of 79 Worth Street, turning it into, in the words of one working girl, "just another whorehouse." First to feel the fallout was Natalia. As queen of the castle, Natalia always dismissed the jealousies of the other escorts as "stupid girl stuff." This was different. She says, "Mona was a psycho-bitch. She hated me, and now she was running the place." When clients called, instead of Jason's rapturous invocations of Natalia's charms, Mona said, "I've got this other girl, she's six-one, a rower on an Ivy League college scull team. She's cheaper than Natalia and way better." Natalia's bookings fell off.

This brought up another issue: where was Natalia's money? In her however short-lived career as the Perfect 10, she'd amassed bookings worth more than a million dollars, most of which Itzler claimed to have plowed back into the business. "We used to laugh about it, how I was making all this cash and he was giving me an allowance, like I'm a kid," Natalia said. With Mona in charge, however, she was having trouble getting any money at all. "Clark and Mona, they just wouldn't write me a check," Natalia said.

One November afternoon, Natalia arrived at the loft to find Mona standing in front of the door to her room—*her room!*—demanding she turn over her keys to the loft. "This is where I live. My home," Natalia screamed. Eventually, however, Natalia decided to move out.

People began telling Jason he'd better cool things out. A few weeks before, in a downtown restaurant, he'd met half a dozen second-grade school teachers vacationing from Minneapolis and brought them by the loft "just to show them how we do it in the big city." This was also around the time that ominous-looking vans began parking across Worth Street. The guys inside could only be one of two things: cops or gangsters bent on rip-off and/or extortion. In such a climate it was suggested the least Jason could do was make sure the front door stayed locked, something he was loathe to do, as not in keeping with his "happiness" mystique.

"What do I have to hide?" Jason scoffed. "I'm not doing anything illegal."

Much of this colossal self-delusion was based on the contract Jason, utilizing his best Nova U. legalese, worked up between himself and the NY Confidential escorts. The document, signed by all the girls, stated they were "specifically forbidden" to have sex with the clients. Itzler showed the contract to Mel Sachs, the floridly attired defender of Sante Kimes, Mike Tyson, and, more recently, the pint-size exhibitionist-rapper Lil' Kim, whom Sachs somehow lawyered into an unheard-of (since reduced) thirty-year sentence for perjury. Sachs made a couple of adjustments and said Jason's contract was "brilliant," just what Itzler wanted to hear.

"I'm bulletproof. Rich people don't go to jail," Jason proclaimed. He was certain that if anything came up, Sachs and Bergrin, a former army major, could handle it. "Mel's my personal Winston Churchill, and Paul's the tough Marine general," Jason rhapsodized, either unaware or not caring that Bergrin is currently under federal investigation for his alleged part in the death of a police informer slated to testify against one of his drug-dealer clients.

"Mel became my best friend," says Jason, always impressed by a man in a fancy suit. "He was always in my place. We all loved Mel." Asked about these visits, Sachs, after much uneasy deliberation, said, "Well, Jason is a personable guy. I liked talking to him. It was an interesting place, full of fascinating conversation. A lot of business people, financial people, professional people."

Amid this gathering train wreck, one incident in November 2004 stands out as the beginning of the end. That evening, accompanied by a mutual friend, two mobsters, members of the Genovese family, according to Jason, stopped by the loft.

"I never did any business with them, not their kind of business. I just thought it might open a new line of high-priced clients," says Jason, who bought a $3,500 Dior suit for the occasion, with a matching one for his bodyguard, a former Secret Service agent. The meeting had barely begun when a girl named Genevieve burst through the door. A tall blonde, she was returning from her first NY Confidential date, reputedly stoned out of her mind, and was demanding to be paid immediately. Told to wait, Genevieve started yelling, threatening to call the police to adjudicate the matter.

"What's wrong with that girl?" one of the mobsters asked. Itzler asked the bodyguard to quiet Genevieve down. But as the bodyguard approached, Genevieve pulled a can of pepper spray from her handbag and blinded him. With the bodyguard writhing on the floor, Genevieve locked herself in a room and called 911. A dozen cops and an engine company of firemen arrived.

There was some debate about whether to open the door, but the mobsters said, "It's the cops. You got to let them in."

"I'm looking at the security-camera monitors," remembers one witness. "In one is the cops, another the gangsters, the third the screaming girl, the fourth the Secret Service guy rubbing his eyes. That's when I thought, I'd take a vacation from this place."

The encounter would end relatively harmlessly. "It looked like one of the cops recognized one of the gangsters," says the witness. "They started talking, everyone exchanged business cards, and left."

After that, the cops started coming to the loft almost every day. "They'd knock on the door, come in, look around, and leave," remembers Hulbert Waldroup. Almost always, they took a stack of Jason's distinctive metal ROCKET FUEL FOR WINNERS business cards. The card had become something of a collector's item at headquarters, one cop says. "Everyone wanted one." Rumor has it that one ended up on Mayor Bloomberg's desk, to the mayor's amusement.

What really finished NY Confidential were the typically cocky/cracked quotes Jason gave a *New York Post* reporter to the effect that he had nothing to fear from the NYPD. "The cops don't bother me," Jason said. "The cops are with me. They're on my side." After that, says a vice squad detective, "it was like he was daring us."

When the big bust inevitably came down on January 7, 2005, the loft was nearly empty. Krimer and Waldroup were at an art gallery when someone's cell phone rang. The caller said no one was picking up at NY Confidential. That was a bad sign, Waldroup said.

Frantically, Krimer and Waldroup attempted to connect to the Webcam security system Itzler had installed so he could watch the activities at 79 Worth Street from his Hoboken apartment. The cam was available from any wired-up computer. But no one could remember the password. "Fuck!" screamed Krimer. Eventually the connection was made.

"The place is being raided, and we're watching it on the Internet," says Waldroup. "The cops were like ants, over everything, taking all the files, ledgers, computers. On the couch were these people I'd worked with for months, in handcuffs. It was very weird."

Jason wouldn't find out about the bust until sometime later. "I was shopping for rugs with Ed Feldman, who is kind of a legend in the fashion business," Jason says. It was Feldman who, years before, had given the young

Jason Itzler a copy of Budd Schulberg's all-time delineation of the Hebrew hustler, *What Makes Sammy Run?*

"Read it," Feldman said. "It's you."

Jason says, "I immediately checked into the Gansevoort Hotel and began partying. Had a couple of girls come over because I figured I wouldn't be doing that for a while. When the cops came, I thought, 'Well, at least I'm wearing my $2,800 rabbit-fur-lined sweater from Jeffrey's, because who wants to look like a guy in a sweatshirt when they lead you away?' All I remember thinking was how I thought NY Confidential would last for twenty-five years."

Almost six months later, Jason is still in jail. In the beginning, he was confident that his lawyers, Sachs and Bergrin, after all that money and all those free drinks, would bail him out. That did not happen. With none of his regulars, the trust-fund babies and famous artists Itzler considered his friends, rushing to his aid, Jason wound up in front of Judge Budd Goodman at the 100 Centre Street courthouse, penniless and lawyerless, tearfully asking to defend himself, a request that was denied.

"Ask me if I feel like a sap," Jason says.

Down deep, he always knew that when all was said and done, after everyone had had their fun, he'd be the one to pay for it. With the Bush administration coming down heavy on sexual trafficking—the religious right's top human-rights issue—Robert Morgenthau's office is not of a mind to offer deals to loudmouthed brothel owners, not this election year. As a "predicate" felon from his ill-considered Ecstasy import scheme, Itzler's facing a four-and-a-half-to-nine-year sentence. Even if he beats that, there is the matter of his busted parole in New Jersey. Sitting in Rikers, playing poker for commissary food, once again Jason has a lot of time on his hands.

One of the things to think about is what happened to all the money that was made at NY Confidential. A common theory, one Itzler advanced in a recent *Post* story, is that Clark Krimer, who may or may not be cooperating with the D.A., took it all.

"He stole $400,000," Jason says. "He should be in jail. If anyone laundered money, it's him." Asked if it was possible that he, Jason, had managed to spend a good portion of the missing money, Itzler scoffs, saying, "Who could spend all that?"

When it comes down to it, however, Jason says he doesn't want to think about Krimer or the fact that Waldroup remains in jail even if he only answered the phones. "I'm staying optimistic," Jason says, free of bitterness. "It is like I told the girls, if you smile a fake smile, keep smiling it because a fake smile can become a real smile."

"The problem with NY Confidential was it didn't go far enough," Jason says now. "If you really want to put together the elite people, the best-looking women and the coolest guys, you can't stop with a couple of hours. It has to be a lifetime commitment." Jason has consulted his prison rabbi, who presided over the recent Passover ceremony during which Itzler got to sit with recently arrested madam Julie Moya (of Julie's) during the asking of the Four Questions. The rabbi told Jason that as a Jewish pimp who sold women to Jewish men, he was liable for the crime of *kedesha*. The rabbi did not, however, think this transgression necessarily prevented Jason from becoming a *shadchan*, or a traditional matchmaker.

"I'm thinking about the future, the next generations," Jason says from his un-air-conditioned prison dorm. "I think I have a chance to do something good before I die. Who knows, the answer to the question 'Who is John Galt?' could be 'Jason.'"

As for Natalia, she is "keeping a low profile." Last week, she went to see Jason again. Thankfully he didn't talk too much about getting married inside the prison. Mostly they talked about the strange times they'd been through and how, even if it turned out the way it did, somehow it was worth it.

"I was a young actress who came to New York like a lot of young actresses, and I wound up with the role of a lifetime. I was the Perfect 10. I totally was. It wasn't the rabbit hole I expected to tumble down, but Jason and I . . . we were happy . . . for a time, really happy."

Since she received hardly any of her booking money and is pretty broke these days, people ask Natalia if she's planning on coming back to "work." The other night, a well-known provider, who said she used to hate Natalia when she was getting those 10/10s, offered to "pimp her out."

"That would be a feather in my cap," said the escort. "To be the one who brought back the famous Natalia."

"No, thanks," said Natalia, which is what she tells her old clients who call from time to time. "I say I'm retired, in repose. They say, 'Come on, let me buy you a drink. I'll be good.' I tell them, 'Look, we had fun and I love you. But that is over.' Mostly, they understand. Some are willing to stay friends, some can't wait to get off the phone. They've got other numbers in their book."

That doesn't mean a girl has to stay home at night. New York, after all, is a big place, full of opportunity. In a way, things have gone back to the way they were before she met Jason. "Wiser, but not necessarily sadder," Natalia says. Tonight she's going downtown. It is always good to look good, so Natalia goes through what was a familiar ritual back in the days when she was the Perfect 10—getting her nails done at the Koreans' on Twenty-ninth Street, combing out her wavy hair. For old times' sake, she's got on what she used to call her "money dress," a short satin pink number with gray jersey inserts, with the shoes to match. About ten, she's ready. She goes out into the street, lifts her arm, gets into a cab, and disappears into the night.

Afterword

I like to keep up with people I write about, the ones that are still talking to me. That's most of them, because truth be told, I try to find the good in my subjects, no matter how difficult that may be to locate. As for the bad stuff, that will ooze out on its own. This said, I regret to report that George Schultz, and, alas, my mother, have passed away in recent years. Marta Bravo's cigar storefront has closed. Ditto Mustafa Hamsho's deli. Dover garage is long gone. Father Sudac has returned to Croatia. Nicky Louie apparently lives on, last seen in Toronto. Patty Huston was never, ever apprehended. Natalia, the Perfect 10, spent a month on Riker's Island and is now back in her Montreal hometown. Jason Itzler remains in jail, currently in the state of New Jersey, which did not appreciate him running a whorehouse while on parole. But that's how it is in the Big City: here today, gone tomorrow. You should see the corner of Fourteenth Street and Third Avenue now; the whole block is NYU dormitories.

As for Frank Lucas, he called me just the other day. Now seventy-seven years old, more or less permanently in a wheelchair, but still sounding like Satan, Frank wanted to complain that the *American Gangster* movie people were running him ragged, dragging him around for "some publicity shit." He had to talk to some radio people and some "other motherfuckers from the TV." The whole thing had him pooped out, Frank whined, adding that if this is what it took to make him big again, maybe it wasn't going to be worth it. What he wanted—because Frank Lucas is not the sort of guy who calls you just to say hello—was that I should come with him on his next PR junket.

"You should come with me. Give me someone to talk to," Frank said. It would be like old times, when I used to drive over to Newark three times a week to write down the old gangster's life story. It was the least I could do, Frank said. "Because it was you that got me into this shit to begin with."

I could have argued that point, but what would have been the use? So I said, sure. If Lucas wanted someone to talk to, I could listen. I told him to call me anytime. He had my number.